Nazis and Fascists in Europe, 1918-1945

Nazis and Fascists in Europe, 1918-1945

Edited with an Introduction by
John Weiss

✇ a New York Times Book

Quadrangle Books
CHICAGO

Contents

Nazis and Fascists in Europe, 1918-1945

Introduction

THE HISTORICAL RECORD of fascism numbs the imagination. The Nazis shot, gassed, or buried alive some six million Jews. Three or four million other passive or potential opponents of the regime were slaughtered. Perhaps as many as two million prisoners of war were shot or starved to death. Entire populations of hundreds of villages in eastern Europe were destroyed by fire or bullet, often down to the last woman and child. Hundreds of thousands of ordinary civilians were enslaved, tortured, and otherwise abused to further the economic aims of the Third Reich. World War II, a direct consequence of fascist imperialism and militarism, took the lives of seventeen million soldiers in Europe and Russia alone. One out of every ten Russians alive in 1941, it has been estimated, died at the hands of the Germans and their allies during the war.

Pity for the victims, disgust and indignation for the murderers—these are appropriate responses to the massacre of innocents. But no one is capable of responding emotionally to slaughter on this gigantic scale. Paradoxically, the only adequate response must be cold, analytical, and intellectual. One must study the recent European past in order to understand what fascism is, how it comes to

*For convenience and unless otherwise noted, I have used the collective terms "fascist" and "fascism" to include both Italian Fascists and German Nazis.

power, and, once in power, why it is so destructive.* In spite of its demonic character, fascism must be analyzed like any other political movement as the product of normal political and social conflicts. In that knowledge lies the only sure defense against a recurrence of fascism.

These are the relevant questions: Who were the fascists? From what social groups were they recruited? What did they want? Who voted for them? Who financed them? Who gave them access to influential political leaders? Why did fascism succeed in Italy and Germany but not elsewhere? Finally, and most important, which nonfascist social groups and classes supported Mussolini and Hitler, and why did they do so? For those who hope to prevent another wave of fascism or fascist-like movements, this last question is crucial.

Fascism arose after World War I in central, eastern, and southern Europe as an ultra-conservative counter-challenge to the threat from the left which followed the turmoil of the war. Thus, in 1919, Mussolini sent his Fascists into the streets and countryside of Italy to do battle with striking workers, peasants agitating for land, and liberals, democrats, socialists, and communists who sought social reform. Mussolini's "shock troops" were composed of those most often attracted to the ranks of the militant radical right: ex-army officers, sons of the upper and lower middle classes, and unemployed marginal workers from small businesses or the lower civil service. Ultra-patriotic, militaristic, and hyper-nationalistic, Mussolini's streetfighters broke up the meetings and cracked the skulls of pacifists, internationalists, socialists, and those ethnic minorities (Slavic or German) who denounced war and scorned the alleged "imperial destiny of Rome" to conquer and rule southern Europe and the Balkans.

Hitler's Nazis were the most successful of many ultra-patriotic, radical right, and paramilitary groups which sprung up to defend traditional Germany from the rise of the left and the consequences of a lost war. Soldiers still in uniform and led by their former officers fought fierce battles in the east to defend Germany's borders against what they called the menace of Slavic and Russian barbarism and bolshevism. In Germany proper, they fought against radical workers, peasants, pacifists, and, of course, democrats, so-cialists, and communists. In every year of the Weimar Republic, right-wing extremists assassinated hundreds of leftists, and, for that matter, moderate liberal supporters of the government. Thus, between the wars, Italy and Germany presented the first examples of a new and unusual phenomenon—powerful radical, revolution-ary, and at the same time ultra-conservative movements.

Neither Mussolini nor Hitler had enough followers to seize pow-er without the votes, funds, and influence of nonfascist but tradi-tionally conservative classes in Italy and Germany. In spite of their violent and revolutionary idealism, neither leader came to power through street battles alone, nor simply on the shoulders of his immediate party membership. Both learned through bitter expe-rience that they must have the support of large masses of ordinary citizens as well as influential groups of powerful and established social elites. Mussolini and Hitler were able to defeat rival radical-right leaders in the competition for power because, like normal politicians, they were willing to adjust their programs and activ-ities so as to attract the votes and influence necessary to gain office legally.

Mussolini recognized his need for a broad social base in 1919 when he was crushed in a bid for a seat in the Chamber of Dep-uties by his Socialist rival—180,000 votes to 4,064! Until then, the Fascist party program contained much designed to appeal to discontented workers and leftists as well as to established con-servative groups. But regardless of fascist theorizing, the prole-tariat of Europe could see the anti-worker activities of fascism. As for traditional conservatives, they remained friendly but distrustful of the revolutionary anti-capitalist rhetoric which accompanied early fascist denunciations of the left. Traditional conservatives were not yet frightened enough by social reformers to desert their usual political friends—those who defended property, status, wealth, and social order.

From 1919 to 1923 Mussolini worked to make himself in word and deed unambiguously a man of the right. He decisively repu-diated his own socialist past. He purged his party of those who really believed that fascism ought to work for the benefit of the working classes. He led his legions to closer identity with traditional Italian conservatism, and worked to blunt the influence of those fascist idealists who would not be satisfied until the older Italian ruling elites were replaced by faithful party members. Thus, Mussolini ended his early ideological attacks on monarchists, the church, and industry. Increasingly, large landowners found fascist toughs at their disposal for terrorizing radical peasant groups who were attempting to end the exploitation of the Italian rural worker by land seizure, boycott, and arson. Industrialists used Mussolini's legions to break the rising wave of postwar strikes and factory seizures. Small property owners—the shopkeepers, salespeople, and white-collar workers of the lower middle class—the groups most directly threatened by trade-union activities, filled the ranks of the *fascisti* and gave them their votes.

Democratic liberalism was still, after all, a recent innovation in the political life of central, eastern, and southern Europe. The older conservative classes despised and feared what in western Europe had become the accepted way of resolving political differences and social conflicts, and these groups still had great social power in Italy and Germany. Thus, Mussolini's call for "sacred violence," military discipline, and authoritarian direction in the service of patriotic, conservative, and militant nationalism, met with the neutrality or benevolence of Italy's established leadership groups. As the left grew stronger, traditional conservatives sensed a need for strong and radical measures for self-protection. On October 27, 1922, the Fascists were able to march on Rome, unopposed, partially armed, aided by the police and army, and in general welcomed by the propertied middle, upper middle, and aristocratic classes of Italy. Mussolini proclaimed both his need for the support of the army and the "productive bourgeoisie," and his desire to provide a "true government" for the "better part of the nation," that part "which does not go to the left . . . but moves to the right—toward order, hierarchy, discipline."

In November 1923, Hitler attempted his own "March on Rome" in the streets of Munich. Accompanied by General Ludendorff who had commanded the German field army in the last years of World War I, Hitler led a group of Storm Troopers in a revolutionary *coup*. The police and the army were not ready to support such revolutionary radicalism, even if it was from the right, and fourteen Nazis were shot dead on the spot. Ludendorff, the very symbol of the old German order was, however, allowed to go free. Hitler spent a few months comfortably imprisoned in a fortress writing *Mein Kampf*. Only left-wing traitors or assassins received rough treatment at the hands of the conservative and anti-democratic German judiciary.

Hitler, like Mussolini, understood the political meaning of his first failure: he must gain allies among the nonfascist conservatives of Germany. In *Mein Kampf* he declared himself willing to play "the dirty game of liberal politics." Casting aside his revolutionary purism, he proceeded to compromise and negotiate for votes and leverage beyond the narrow circle of the militant party faithful. During the next ten years, Hitler demonstrated his usefulness to the older and more respectable upholders of German conservative traditionalism: Junker military officers, aristocratic landowners, upper civil servants, and the corporate businessmen of German heavy industry. At the same time, he collected increasingly large numbers of voters from the German lower middle classes.

Sheer political skill alone cannot create the social base necessary to give a movement power. The loss of World War I, the chaos of the inflation of the twenties, and the Great Depression of the thirties provided the kind of desperation and deprivation upon which extremist politics—left or right—feeds. The largest category of voters for Hitler were self-employed small businessmen. Throughout Europe (and the United States) the small traders have always been receptive to the appeals of the radical right. As property owners they tend to identify in aspirations with upper-class wealth, property, and "respectability." At the same time their marginal incomes deprive them of the security of real wealth and make them highly vulnerable to the demands of labor unions and the superior competitive power of big business. Inflation destroyed German currency in 1923, and thus destroyed the savings and pensions of the lower middle class. The Great Depression brought the collapse of their markets. Debt, bankruptcy, and the ultimate threat—reduction to the status of a blue-collar worker—drove the

German middle classes to despair and intensified their search for a strong leader to defend their tenuous hold on property and self-respect.

The German middle classes were the very model of the famed "achieving ethic" of the western European middle classes. By self-discipline, hard work, savings, and deferred consumption, they had always believed they could make their way to the top. Now their vision of social reality was mortally threatened. The Nazis offered the force needed to smash the left along with subsidies and economic regulation to protect the property and competitive position of the little man. The Nazis stood for traditional Germany, not the liberalism and bolshevism of the left. Only those who have been completely frustrated, with all their values, work, and training ruined by uncontrollable events, can afford easy moralizing about the support this class gave to Hitler. The radical right gains power because of genuine social grievances, and if one hopes to block their access to power, one must attempt to ameliorate those grievances.

Fascist ideology, accordingly, represented in modern guise some older values of conservative thought. Wherever large-scale capitalism had spread in nineteenth-century Europe, it had been feared and resisted by the small shopkeepers, artisans, and guildsmen of the old order. Freewheeling competitive capitalism threatened the ancient and regulated order of village and guild. Markets, prices, wages, and the quality of the products had been governed by an intricate network of rights, privileges, customs, and laws in the pre-industrial order. The unlimited financial resources of liberal capitalism, the technology of steam and power, and the total disregard for traditional limits on economic aggrandizement, made liberal capitalism seem a revolutionary threat to central and eastern Europe. From the beginning of the nineteenth century, German theorists and revolutionary activists had attacked by word and deed what they referred to as the "un-German," "un-Christian," alien, and "Jewish" spirit and practice of unregulated free enterprise. They appealed for the restoration of the old "organic" and "Teutonic" order of the rural village, the stolid peasant, the skilled and modest craftsman, and the stability and predictability of a regulated economic system. Long before Hitler, during times of economic depression, local demagogues and upper-class conservative politicians had attempted to thwart the liberalization of German society by encouraging radical right, nationalistic, and anti-semitic movements in rural Germany. Hitler was but the latest and most successful of a long line of potential rightist demagogues.

Hitler's major political task was to maintain his grip on his small-business following, yet not alienate the corporate wealth and landed support he needed in the hectic campaigning of the early thirties. To achieve this uneasy alliance, he diverted the anti-corporate sentiments of German small-business groups into anti-semitism and hyper-nationalism. Thus his famous distinction between solid "creative" Nordic industrial capitalism (Krupp and Co.) and "parasitical and Jewish" destructive international finance capitalism. The latter were held responsible for Germany's economic ills, not the loyal German industrialists of the mighty Ruhr. Hitler also blamed economic distress on the reparations clauses of the Versailles Treaty and the French attempts to enforce those clauses. Those liberals and democrats who argued that Germany support the Weimar Republic were held guilty as traitors collaborating with the armies of Germany's enemies. In total, the ultra-conservative program seemed to make sense to the embattled small-propertied classes of Germany: ultra-nationalism, military regeneration, anti-semitism, and violence against the traitors of the Weimar Republic became the counter to the left's call for progressive social reforms.

The second major category of Nazi voters came from the various white-collar workers: civil servants, public officials, salespeople, office workers, and clerical personnel. White-collar associations and unions had always been conservative and ultra-patriotic, and they had always identified their status with that of the ruling elites. Traditionally, duty to Prince, Kaiser, and nobleman, combined with contempt for complaints from below, had been embedded in the behavior patterns of Europe's most efficient and least democratic civil service. Here too the move to the radical right resulted from the rise of democratic liberalism and socialism, and from the disastrous effects of economic chaos on salaries, pensions, and savings. A vote for the Nazis was not a change in ideology, since the conservative parties supported by the white-collar classes generally shared the Nazis' ultra-conservatism. To vote for the Nazis meant to vote for the party which, by street violence, had demonstrated an iron will in defense of ultra-conservatism against Weimar liberalism and socialism. For the lower-middle-class conservative, unlike his well-off colleague in the upper class, supporting the radical right is essential for his survival because the "little man's" position always seems more precarious. (This may be seen in the United States where the wealthy Southern conservative may vote for a Goldwater or a Nixon, but the "redneck" will want Wallace.)

The smaller the town, the larger the proportion of Nazi votes. This reflected native ultra-conservativism as well as the appeal of Nazi ideology. Rural Germany and the stable ways of village and peasant life were praised, the big city was feared and scorned. In central and eastern Europe, industrial urbanism was to the old classes an alien order, threatening the ancient environment of village, guild, peasant, and lord. Was not the city the home of radical workers, rootless intellectuals, "Jewish" internationalists, and the Bolshevik menace? Was not the city the center of moral decay, contempt for the achievement ethic of the lower middle class, scorn for stolid peasant and village ways, and loose sexual morality? Radical-right movements (including those in America) have always gained support from that generation of small towners who first come into contact with big-city ways. For example, Hitler and his followers feared and hated Vienna. It was the very symbol of all that threatened the traditional values of what was held to be the Nordic, Aryan past. Radical, cosmopolitan, and immoral, Vienna to the radical right was an offensive mixture of Jewish intellectuals, Slavic "subhumans," traitorous liberals, socialists, and Bolsheviks, as well as the parasitical exploiters of the virtuous countryside. Too degenerate to maintain its rightful historical role, Austria could not even maintain its eastern Empire. Hitler would correct all this.

In central and eastern Europe, Jews were overrepresented in those professions and callings closely associated with the modern, urban, and liberal sectors of changing traditional societies. Kept by law and discrimination from landowning, skilled trades, and guilds, Jews found their opportunities in commerce, education, and the professions. They were not assimilated, if by that one means a random diffusion through all trades, occupations, and classes. They were, of course, absent from the traditional order of peasant and noble, and were also kept out of the officer class of the army and the ranks of the upper civil service. As Bismarck once put it, no Jew should be a high public official in a Christian state. Hence, anti-semitism was more than simply racism or scapegoat-finding; it was a conservative "backlash" against those sectors of the society which seemed to present the greatest threat to the old order and the old ways.

As with black anti-semitism today, it is easy for the unsophisticated to confuse symptom with cause and to strike at the wrong target. The local Jewish money-lender, cattle dealer, or mortgage holder was hated and feared by peasants who had been made desperate by increasing indebtedness. Yet the cause of peasant misery was hardly the marginal Jewish speculator, who was himself part of an exploitive economic system utterly dominated by Nordic (and usually anti-semitic) Berlin bankers and Rhineland industrialists. Again, Hitler's violent anti-semitism and ultra-nationalism served to protect conservative interests by diverting lower-middle-class revolutionary frustrations away from the ruling elites and toward the alleged conspirators of Zion. This was the political usefulness of Hitler's seemingly irrational appeal to upper-class conservatives: the ills of the social system they had created and the war they had lost could be blamed on an alleged international conspiracy of Jewish financiers and Jewish Bolsheviks. Ever since Metternich blamed the French Revolution on a handful of Masons, such theories have enabled conservatives to overlook the defects in their own social order and condemn leftist criticism as conspiratorial subversion.

Lower-middle-class votes gave Hitler mass support in the early thirties. Upper-class conservatives opened his road to the chancellorship. From the start, both Hitler and Mussolini kept their movements open to the "respectable" classes, even though this made them suspect in the eyes of some of their more revolutionary followers. Nevertheless, in party congresses and on the floor of the Reichstag, Hitler made sure that his Nazis did not support legislation directed against traditional conservative interests. Nazis did not vote for attempts to expropriate Junker estates to aid the land-less rural workers. As Mussolini once explained to an overzealous left-fascist, "We cannot expropriate the property of landlords. We are Fascists, not Socialists." Both Mussolini and Hitler understood the need for the support of landed and industrial wealth, army officers, high state officials, and aristocratic elites. Such men, in turn, needed assurances that fascism was not, like liberalism, a revolutionary movement directed against them.

World War I polarized the potentially revolutionary confronta-tion between right and left in Germany and Italy. Until 1918, and in spite of universal suffrage, Germany had been ruled by a co-alition of Junker landowners, army leaders, high state officials, and co-opted industrialists. Indeed, Germany was the first power-ful industrial nation dominated by pre-liberal elites and attitudes. While other European states moved in liberal-democratic direc-tions, the Junker aristocracy maintained its hold on Germany. In part this was due to the most famous son of the Prussian Junker class, Otto von Bismarck, who united Germany by defeating its two ancient foes, Austria and France, using the greatest creation of the Prussian spirit, the Prussian army. In France and England, national unity and glory were associated with revolutions against monarchical absolutism—either in the victory of the British Parlia-ment in 1688, or in the radical republicanism of the French Rev-olution of 1789. German nationalism, however, was irrevocably associated with aristocracy, hierarchy, discipline, and militarism. And since Prussia itself had been carved out by the sword at the cost of Slavdom, Prussian domination of Germany also meant a general German assumption of superiority over the Slavic masses of eastern Europe and Russia, and the moral and historical right of Germans to rule the east. In Germany, more than in other European states, attitudes favorable to the radical right had im-mense power and social prestige right up to World War I.

Liberalism first came to Germany as a reaction to the bayonets of Napoleon's armies. Groups of reformers from various parts of Germany mounted a resistance movement against the French and tried to end serfdom, increase self-government, gain constitutions limiting the powers of German princes, and open the Prussian bureaucracy and army to talent regardless of birth and class. Both the resistance movement and the reforms failed; the liberals never achieved German unity—that came from German conservatives, not liberals. Thus the German conservatives of the nineteenth century had avoided the liberal transformation of Germany. One leading Junker, writing for his class in 1811, held that such "new-fangled theories" would turn Prussia over to the Jews, "the enemies of every state," who through their financial power would replace "our old and honorable Brandenburg-Prussia with a Jewish state."

The defeat of Germany in World War I brought with it the next attempted, and much feared, liberal reformation of Germany. Since 1910 the Social Democrats, theoretically Marxist and revolutionary but in practice democratic and left-liberal, had been the largest single political party in the Reichstag. For the first time, because of allied command, the Reichstag had real power, and now those who would govern Germany must win the approval of a majority of the masses. At first the socialists held the majority. Overnight and by force of allied arms, all that German conservatism had feared seemed to have triumphed.

The implications were obvious to embattled former ruling elites. Junker landowners would lose their favored treatment because socialists demanded land reform and an end to the tax privileges granted large landowners. Peasant radicalism and resettlement programs would now be encouraged by the central government. German industrialists would have to learn to live with the bargaining power of organized labor, for the Social Democratic party was the left wing of the German trade union movement. Higher wages, work stoppages, strikes, and perhaps even the nationalization of key industries seemed to be in store for Germany's industrial aristocracy. German industrialists were overjoyed at the chance to blame the depression on the Versailles Treaty. (In the West, of course, capitalism itself was blamed, to the benefit of the left.) As for the German army, if the Weimar Republic lasted, Germany might maintain the terms of the Versailles Treaty which had reduced the army to a mere 100,000 men. The German officer class would lose its political influence. The German territory, German colonies, and German nationals removed from Germany by the Versailles Treaty would be forever lost if the army remained weak.

To add to conservative fears, from 1928 to 1932 the Communist share of the German electorate rose from 10 to 17 per cent; and the Social Democrats, though declining, still held 20 per cent of the vote. But the Conservative party (DNVP) declined from 14 to 8 per cent, and the conservative middle-class parties practically disappeared during those same years. In such a situation, no one should be surprised that German conservatives began an underground war against the Weimar Republic. As Hitler's votes rose from 2 per cent in 1928 to 33 per cent in 1932, it is also no surprise that, however reluctantly, most German conservatives came to see Hitler as their only deterrent to the rise of the left. As Germany's most important political general, Kurt von Schleicher, put it in 1932, "If the Nazis did not exist, we should have to invent them."

There has been much dispute about the role of German business in the Nazis' rise to power. The facts seem to be as follows: Until 1929 Hitler had not attracted the votes necessary to persuade a significant number of upper-class conservatives that his movement had a chance to overthrow the Weimar Republic legally, without the risk of Allied intervention. Until then, German business interests saw no reason to aid the Nazis, though Hitler always had the sporadic support of the southern German small-business interests. When Hitler's votes leaped from 2 per cent to 18 per cent in 1930, and the conservative share of votes in both upper- and middle-class parties was cut by 50 per cent, some German businessmen and corporation heads began to channel significant funds to Hitler. By 1932 Hitler had important but not overwhelming financial support from highly influential business interests in banking, steel, coal, and the all-important press and film industries. He had little or no support from the international- and liberal-minded export-import firms and large retail and wholesale traders. Heavy industry, however, was predominantly pro-Nazi, especially after early 1932 when Hitler personally assured its representatives that the Nazis were defenders of private property, regardless of what the term "socialism" in "National Socialism" might seem to imply. Hjalmer Schacht, president of the mighty Reichsbank, Fritz Thyssen, head of the third largest industrial empire in Germany, and Hugenberg, head of the Conservative party, a co-director of Krupp, and ruler of a vast press and film network, saw to it that Hitler gained funds and access to business leaders in the crucial and hectic election years of the early thirties. In return, the Nazis adopted a program which advocated heavy industry as a cure for the depression: public spending on arms production, government support for collapsing markets, heavy cutbacks of already meager social welfare programs, and a firm line against trade-union demands. In Italy, heavy industry had supported fascist-like movements even before World War I.

The peculiarities of the Weimar constitution allowed President Hindenburg, former commander-in-chief of the German Army, to rule by emergency decree, which he did as the depression worsened. Before Hitler was appointed Chancellor by Hindenburg, the aging symbol of Germany's Prussian past tried to rule with traditional conservatives—Bruening, von Papen, and General Schleicher. None of these gentlemen could gain a majority in Parliament. A parliamentary majority could be found only by moving to the radical left or the radical right. When General Schleicher attempted to form a coalition with the Social Democrats to create such a parliamentary majority, Junker oligarchs and business leaders persuaded Hindenburg that Hitler was the only choice. Reluctantly, Hindenburg appointed Hitler Chancellor in January 1933. The German Army remained suspicious until June of 1934, when Hitler had those Nazis shot who insisted that the next step was revolution against the established ruling elites. In return, German Army officers allowed Hitler to take full power by combining the office of Chancellor and President upon Hindenburg's death in August 1934. In an unprecedented and fatal move, the German Army swore an oath of personal allegiance not to Germany but to Hitler.

The general conclusion one can make from the rise to power of Mussolini and Hitler seems to be this: The radical right has its best chance in societies where older but still powerful elites see their values and interests eroded by rapid and modernizing social change, change which generates a massive liberal and left threat to "old ways." When this happens conservatives, ultra-conservatives, and reactionaries of differing ideologies and classes tend to unite and to strike back "by any means necessary." Hitler won in Germany because he appeared to be the last viable political alternative for both the upper-class establishment and the radicalized and desperate lower middle class. In the end, both groups suffered from his rule. Few outside the immediate party hierarchy wanted the full range of destruction that Hitler visited upon Germany and the world. This does not lessen the responsibility of those conservatives who gave him the means to gain power. It simply means that Nazi supporters need not be seen as demonic villains willing to go to inhuman extremes to cling to the remnants of their power and prestige.

In power, fascism was totalitarian, not merely despotic. Both Mussolini and Hitler attempted to reshape society in order to remove for all time the threat from the left. In traditional despotisms (for example, Franco's Spain) this is not necessary. Where the left is weak and disorganized, and where industrial development has not produced massive liberal challenges to the old order, landowners, church, army, and business can rule with the casual violence and sporadic terror of a Franco. But fascism comes to power, as noted, in societies polarized between powerful or potentially powerful forces of right and left. Hence Mussolini and Hitler found their rule in peril if they did not change the structure of society and transform social experience itself so as to dominate and prevent a revival of liberalism and leftism.

Both Mussolini and Hitler not only destroyed trade unions and liquidated their leadership, they also created new "labor fronts" which were in reality fascist-controlled paramilitary propaganda organizations. The purpose of such "labor fronts" was not to bargain for increased workers' benefits but to locate and end worker discontent by propaganda or terror.

Where conservatism was already strong, the Fascist and Nazi purges were relatively unnecessary and correspondingly weak. The German civil service was purged of only about one member in ten (except in Prussia where, because of the previous influence of liberalism and socialism, almost 30 per cent had to be purged). While workers' coops, clubs, and publications were smashed, employers', landowners', and industrialists' associations not only survived but had great influence on both regimes. Army leadership, of course, remained more or less as it had been under Weimar, right up to the first year of World War II.

The most dreaded and unique institution created by the Nazis was the S.S. of Heinrich Himmler—the ultimate defender of the pure Nazi spirit. The S.S. ran death camps, supervised slave labor and extermination programs in the occupied territories, and destroyed potential opposition within the Third Reich by terror, torture, and murder. Yet even the S.S. did not draw exclusively on the militant and new party faithful from below but attracted many members of the old conservative social elites. Indeed, the S.S. had an abnormally high percentage—when compared with the general population distribution—of upper-class and aristocratic families represented in its top leadership. It is not surprising that many fascists grumbled about the way Hitler and Mussolini had sold out to the "old gang."

Two potent sources of potential liberal and left opposition, however, did have to be purged and transformed: the mass communications media and public education. Traditional despots censor the news media; fascists take it over and dictate its contents. Public education was purged, and the beneficial rule of the one-party state and its ideology became the content for all nontechnical courses. Militarism, imperialism, and a crude Social Darwinism (history as nothing more than a pitiless death struggle between races for living space) became the precepts which every schoolboy was to know. In Germany, the alleged racial inferiority and degeneracy of Jews and Slavs was taught. In Italy, where anti-semitism had little force, the blacks of Africa were seen as the subhuman objects of potential Italian rule. Altruism, humanitarianism, internationalism, and pacifism were looked upon as oppressive remnants of a Judeo-Christian attempt to emasculate the heroic spirit of a violent and life-enhancing warrior elite.

Fascist nations, in short, do not merely outlaw disapproval; they manufacture approval. Both Germany and Italy, for example, set up controlled and state directed leisure-time organizations. They did not want the individual to draw his standards from private, spontaneous, or class experiences. To prevent such experiences meant the control of culture. Subjective art, i.e., post-impression-istic and expressionist art, was outlawed in Germany. Art since Cezanne was held to be the product of diseased imaginations—"degenerate, foreign, Negroid, Jewish, cosmopolitan, and Bolshe-vik." Art in both Reichs was to reflect the rural, military, and ultra-conservative traditions of the Aryans and the Romans. Vi-olence and sacrifice in the service of the nation were to be the norms for social behavior and culture. Fascist art and sculpture thus became a dreary yet awesome succession of steely-eyed, gre-nade-tossing soldiers, thick-bodied peasants, and torch and weap-on bearers marching with grim determination, dynamic sweep, and tensed muscles into the Nordic or Roman imperial future. Fascist architecture, similarly, was bleak, monumental, and unadorned. The human scale of ordinary life was dwarfed by thick marching columns, outsize blocks and walls, military symbols, eternal flames, and convenient balconies poised high for leaders to hurl down the verbal symbols of violence and command to the shouting masses below.

In Italy, terror was moderate compared to the horrors of Nazi Germany. In both nations, however, the function of terror was to forestall potential resistance and prepare the warrior elite for its future role as the rulers of Europe, Russia, and Africa. In 1933 the first concentration camp was opened—though extermination programs did not begin until 1938. Those held to be genetically, racially, and ideologically unfit to join the ruling elite were the victims. Among them can be counted such groups as the mentally ill, criminal offenders, congenitally diseased, retarded children, Slavic "subhumans," Weimar supporters, socialists, communists, gypsies, and Jehovah's Witnesses, as well as Jews. In the end, perhaps a total of ten million persons were exterminated, some seven million in the camps alone.

Slaughter on such a vast scale, the equivalent of all the battle deaths of World War I, can hardly be the act of a mere handful of demented party leaders. It had to be a massive social act of great complexity. Those who helped were not only the triggermen; bureaucrats, physicians, transport experts, lawyers, building con-tractors, industrial firms, foreign office officials, army officers, and ordinary citizens were also involved. Furthermore, those directly responsible, the Himmlers, Eichmans, Bormanns, Streichers, and others, were not technically or clinically insane. That fact is the terrible truth about normal human potential we will have to accept. To the murderers and their accomplices, their act was one of social hygiene in the service of a higher morality. They never thought of themselves as criminal, and most of those who survive and live in Germany today seem not to suffer from excessive pangs of conscience.

The social policies of the radical right in power should not be misunderstood because of the term "National Socialism." In the conservative European intellectual tradition, the term socialism did not mean the redistribution of property and income in favor of the workers. It meant the sacrifice of private interests and material gain in the higher service of the state. Workers under National Socialism (or Italian Fascism) were asked to increase their productivity without an increase in wages, so as to contribute to the power of the nation for its imperial destiny. Fascist Labor Front leaders, accordingly, were not selected from the ranks of the workers, but from the anti-union street fighters of the early days of fascism. It is hardly surprising that real wages and the workers' percentage of the national income fell under Nazi and Fascist rule.

In Italy, the old conservative idea of the "corporate state" was used to defend the notion that the state should discipline both capital and labor in the interests of economic growth and just distribution. In both nations, however, business leadership was forced into line only when it resisted plans for rearmament. Under the Nazis, the profit rate rose. As Robert Ley, head of the Labor Front, put it cynically in 1935 to an assembly of industrialists: "When the worker knows that the employer is a comrade, one can demand anything of him." Fascist or Nazi expenditures for leisure time and social welfare never compensated for labor's losses. Proletarian participation in these activities was far behind that of the lower middle classes, and the sums involved were minimal. Ideological statements about the alleged social benefits and neutral stance of the two regimes *vis-à-vis* capital and labor must be measured against actual policies.

Hitler's most notable achievement for the German workers

nonetheless should not be ignored. When Hitler gained power, nearly seven million Germans were unemployed. By 1937 the unemployed numbered fewer than one million. No liberal Western state had anything close to comparable success. Hitler could provide work because he suppressed the left and prepared for war. Lower wages, early retirement, lowered pensions, and anti-inflation measures could all be used at the expense of the workers. Many found jobs in the booming war industries, work provided in part by public funds and the forced reinvestment of profits. Many were enrolled in the paramilitary labor service, working for subsistence wages on public projects, highways, and railroads. Army recruitment placed many unemployed. Conquest and the exploitation of conquered territories were to be the "final solution" to the problems of the depression.

Rural landless labor was disciplined under Mussolini and Hitler to the benefit of the great landed proprietors who had aided their rise to power. The middle-class landowning peasant, a heavy Nazi voter, was idealized by the Nazis and favored by Nazi policies. Here was "the life source of the Nordic race," to use a famous Nazi slogan. Ultra-conservative fear of and contempt for the radical city, and love for the ancient order of village, peasant, and lord, made its presence felt in Nazi legislation. Price and market controls aided the small farmer, and peasant holdings were made hereditary by law, in line with the theory of the "organic state."

In the Nazis' view of the future, eastern Europe and Russia were to be without cities, the native population was to be exterminated or enslaved, and sturdy Nordic peasant warriors were to make the land their own. War was to resolve the need for productive land and employment without disturbing the possessions of established large landowners. It was not enough for Mussolini to drain marshes in Italy; he would need Ethiopia and imperialistic resettlement programs. The Slavs and Africans were to pay the costs of preserving the old elites, for otherwise land could come only from established German or Italian landowners. That was the essential meaning of incessant fascist cries for "living space." In Germany until the war, the larger the landowner the more he benefited from Nazi rule. In spite of everything, the small farmer was little better off than he had been under Weimar.

Small businessmen had been the backbone of Nazi support before the war. Yet they suffered the most of all Nazi supporters. The Nazis had taken up their angry cries against the trusts and monopolies of big capitalism. By 1930–1932, Hitler had begun to desert his lower-middle-class right-radicals as he searched for big business support. Once in power, he turned the German economy over to many of Germany's leading industrialists, as Mussolini had done before him. Hitler suppressed his small-business following, and forbade idle theorizing about the sanctity of a small-business order with its populist radicalism. After all, a nation of small property owners could not fight a modern war. Again, the "Aryanization" or seizure of Jewish-owned property, and the fruits of future conquests would have to resolve the needs of the German lower middle classes. Death, in short, was to be the final solution to the social discontents that brought fascism to power.

Big business nevertheless did have to follow government controls, and those who resisted them were disciplined or removed from power. Nazi controls were directed toward preparation for war, the one social policy to which the Nazis were utterly devoted. Nazi law encouraged the formation of large firms. Profits and property remained in the hands of private owners, but means were found to redirect surplus wealth to arms production and army recruitment. The sacrifices of business were more than compensated for by the destruction of trade unionism and the left. German business would exploit the European and Slavic empire. Indeed, the rewards for Germany would be such that in the end even the German worker would find nothing to complain about.

Fascism cannot be understood if it is viewed as a revolution. It was a counterrevolution. Its purpose was to prevent the liberalization and radicalization of Italy and Germany. Property and income distribution and the traditional class structure remained roughly the same under fascist rule. What changes there were favored the old elites or certain segments of the party membership. The newness of the New Order is to be found in its destruction of the left and its drive to war.

Those of us who live in the nuclear age ought to note this well:

fascism needs war. As Mussolini put it, "He who has steel has bread." Otherwise the social order must be transformed in those leftist and progressive ways which alleviate the economic crises that bring radicalism, left or right, to power. While the results of social welfare in England, France, and the United States were feeble and unimpressive, they nevertheless thoroughly frightened the harried establishments of eastern, central, and southern Europe. As for Hitler and Mussolini, the Great Depression would eventually ruin them too if they did not resolve the very social discontents that had brought them to power. Yet they could not move to the left and stay in power. War, conquest, and exploitation became the only way to avoid discontent without a betrayal of all they stood for and had supported in the past.

Hitler summarized his ideology in the familiar terms of vulgar Social Darwinism: "The first rule of life is to defend yourself." The use of force to correct social ills is a familiar ultra-conservative policy, whether it be to restore law and order in the streets or "contain" international communism. As for Germany, conquest would reverse the Versailles Treaty, revive the German Army, enrich business, provide the aristocratic landlords with a new social basis, maintain the viability of Teutonic discipline, militarism, and alleged genetic superiority, satisfy the workers and peasants, and, finally, destroy European Jewry and the very heart of world bolshevism.

Hitler wanted war and prepared for it, but he did not believe it necessary to reorganize totally the German economy. He did not expect France and England to resist his invasion of eastern Europe. Should they do so, he thought the German Army would make short work of them. He was correct. When he attacked the French and British armies in the spring of 1940, the French surrendered and the British fled the continent in a few short weeks. The German Army, in order to avoid a stalemate as in World War I, had developed the tactics of swift attack with armored tank advances, unencumbered by infantry and not tied down by long waits for supplies. In fact, Hitler believed, shortages of supplies and productive facilities could be relieved by conquest. The peaceful takeover of Austria and Czechoslovakia, for example, added some three million tons to Germany's annual steel production. Hitler's fatal error, but one he shared with the vast majority of Western political experts, was to underrate the capacity of Russia to resist German onslaughts. After the battle of Stalingrad, Hitler started to reshape the German economy from top to bottom. It was too late, but not by much. Had Hitler conquered Russia, it is hard to believe that the West could ever have successfully invaded the continent.

In spite of all this, Hitler had hoped to be better prepared for war than he actually was by the fall of 1939. The radical right in power may find it easy to smash the left, but difficult to discipline their own economic aristocrats. Thus, Hjalmer Schacht, who had done so much to win business to Hitler's side, continually thwarted Nazi plans of directed economic growth and heavy controls over corporate industry needed to prepare for war. Through Schacht, important business and financial circles objected to heavy expenditures for rearmament (excepting the firms which received the orders), they feared deficit financing, and they resisted all attempts to tax wealth. (In Italy, one of Mussolini's economic directors complained that Italian business circles seemed to think fascism was nothing more than a policy of high profits and low wages.) Hitler's war plans for the rapid expansion of the steel and ore industries had to be shelved. Traditional business conservatives insisted upon their need for traditional, conservative policies. Too much industrial expansion would drive their prices down, the money market might be artificially expanded through deficit financing, and the costs of expansion would be prohibitive and unrewarding. It is to the credit of German business leaders that they did not see that Hitler really intended to conquer Europe and Russia. Frustrated and angry, Hitler removed Schacht from power in 1936 and put Goering at the head of his four-year plan for war. He warned business leaders, as he was later to warn his cautious generals: either they would subordinate themselves to Nazi war plans or they would be replaced. Nevertheless, Hitler never completely succeeded in disciplining his own conservative constituency until Germany faced defeat.

There were, however, some important economic preparations for the war during the middle and late thirties. Forced investment, subsidies, and import-export controls were used to divert portions of the German economy toward war production. Raw-material production and stockpiling were increased, synthetics were invented, and food production—vitally necessary even for a short war—was drastically increased by price and market manipulation. Credit was extended to vital industries so that they might expand. By 1939 munitions production had soared. The work force, unlike management, could be controlled, disciplined, and underpaid, though only moderate numbers were shifted to direct war production, except for the all-important metals industries. As government budgets rose rapidly after 1933, the German Army received ever higher proportions of it, some 75 per cent by 1938.

The literature about the causes of World War II has been obsessed with the notion that a firm stand by the West some time before the invasion of Poland in September 1939 would have stopped Hitler and avoided a four-year war. But Hitler needed war if he was to stay in power, just as he wanted war by ideology and passionate belief. Finally, war was necessary if he was to resolve the domestic tensions that had ended the Weimar Republic. In view of all this, it seems that military action by the West before September 1939 could at best have brought on the war more quickly, or postponed it for a few years.

Given the assumptions upon which international diplomacy is based, it seems wrong to expect that the West would have taken any armed action before Hitler demonstrated, by invading Poland, that he was after much more than simply the return of all German nationals to the Reich. When Hitler violated the Versailles Treaty, he did so with the general approval of much of enlightened international opinion. The treaty *was* unjust and humiliating. The League of Nations *was* a failure. Unfortunately, French conservative governments had insisted on enforcing the Versailles Treaty in order to keep Germany weak. (In the opinion of the average German, this worked untold harm on the Weimar Republic. Thus is it always with the reasoning of "hawks." Oppression rarely breeds submission, and usually encourages its opposite.) When Hitler remilitarized the Rhineland in 1936, he was doing no more than what every nation does with its own territory. When Hitler invaded Austria in 1938, he was still just bringing Germans into the Reich, and with substantial Austrian approval. Finally, when

England and France agreed to allow Hitler to invade the Czech Sudetenland at Munich in 1938, it could still be maintained that Germans were being united with Germans in line with the widespread liberal ideology of the right to national self-determination. None of this was just in any moral sense; all of it after the Rhineland ought to have been resisted, but international diplomacy and international public opinion was not then and is not now responsive to such moral persuasion.

The truth is that Western leaders could stop Hitler in Europe only if they were willing to ally themselves with the USSR. Eastern Europeans did not wish to have the sort of "protection" Stalin could offer; Western conservative governments were hardly anxious to unite with what to them at the time seemed to be the greater menace. England and France did move after Poland was invaded, but even then no nation but Russia was strong enough to stop Hitler, and Stalin had already agreed, in effect, not to do so by signing the Nazi-Soviet Pact in 1939. In spite of the declaration of war, there was no real conflict in western Europe until Hitler attacked in the spring of 1940. The French and British feared a renewal of the dreadful bleeding of World War I, and hoped that an economic blockade and the bombing of civilians might end the war with little effort. If such a policy ever works, it is difficult to imagine it working with fascists!

From all that has gone before, it ought to be obvious that Hitler's final and absolutely unavoidable goal was the total destruction of the USSR. The war against France and England was a mere prelude. It has been said that Hitler would have won had he not invaded Russia in June 1941. True, but Hitler had to conquer Russia, and he knew it from the start. This was no ordinary conflict between states. Hitler's domestic policies and his power in Germany would stand or fall on the results of his war in the East. As Hitler once told his generals, this was a war to the death between ideologies and races. Had Germany won the war, tens of millions of Russians and eastern Europeans would have been exterminated. The remnants would have become a vast labor reserve, nomadic peoples with no communal life, no national identity, deprived by the S.S. of the psychological and social means of resistance. Indeed, extermination and resettlement pro-

grams began with the invasion. General von Manstein, not of the
S.S. but of the regular German Army be it noted, put it thus:
"The Jewish-Bolshevik conspiracy must be crushed forever."

The study of the past must be of some use to the human spirit
or we can hardly justify spending our energy and effort on re-
viewing it. The study of fascism in Europe, however painful, is
more than just a study of a transient, unique, and ugly phase of
the past. Unfortunately, it is a study of attitudes and acts which,
given the necessary conditions, can thrive in many different societies undergoing rapid change. Fascism in the particularly horrible
German form may never occur again. But the use of force by
threatened groups is bound to continue into the future. Every
radical-right group has within itself some fascist potential. It is
not enough to declaim against ultra-conservatism, or to declare
one's moral purity. We ought to learn from the past to recognize
the coming danger from its earliest symptoms. And we should
learn to use social controls to make sure that no class or group
must bear the largest cost of social change. Only in this way can
totalitarianism, right or left, be stopped.

Part 1

THE RISE OF FASCISM

IT SEEMS DIFFICULT enough even now to understand fascism. How could the most able journalists be expected to understand it at the time it occurred? In fact, many of the writers for *The New York Times* in the thirties seem to have understood the essential reasons for the rise of fascism better than many academic scholars after World War II.

Hindsight makes the reasons for this seem clear. It was only near the end of the war itself that the full horror of Nazi activities were revealed. The death camps, extermination programs, and destruction of whole populations in eastern Europe and the Soviet Union seem to have shocked even the most careful scholars into the belief that such horror could not be explained by usual methods of political or social analysis. Furthermore, Western scholars had come to accept the notion that historical change encouraged the growth of liberalism, democracy, and humanitarianism. Fascism seemed to be a unique outbreak of the barbaric forces of the irrational. Thus one group of scholars argued that the rise of the Nazis must be due to some dark and terrible defect in the German character, while others argued that only a handful of violent madmen could have been responsible.

By now we are used to the notion that social change generates a tendency among ultra-conservative groups to move to the radical right. Furthermore, the variety of radical-right models makes it unnecessary to measure all such movements against the Nazi party or to regard such movements as totally dissimilar if they do not conform in all details to that most extreme of extremist movements.

Thus we can gain much from articles that first appeared in the thirties. Before the full terror of Nazism in practice was revealed, journalists and scholars analyzed the rise of the Nazis and Fascists within the accepted historical categories: class and group conflicts within changing societies with highly complex class and status structures. All observers understood what Hitler was, of course: ultra-conservative, anti-semitic, and hyper-nationalistic. But they could not know then how far he would go once he gained power. They recognized his close relationship to nonfascist conservatives of the upper and lower classes. Indeed, they shared an illusion with many German conservatives, that Hitler in power would be easily controlled by the old social elites. There was, in fact, no real way of predicting whether Hitler would be like Mussolini or push to new and unimaginable extremes of terror. William C. White, in an article for *The New York Times* (not included here) tells us that even Ernst Thaelmann, head of the German Communist party, did "not fear the results if Hitler should take power by force." Liberals and traditional conservatives made many similar statements. Those who scornfully regard such attitudes as naïve ought to reconsider. We have not yet done enough, especially those of us who are historians, in illuminating future trends and explaining them to a general audience.

When Mussolini Led the March on Rome

by C. J. S. Sprigge

WHEN MUSSOLINI BECAME Prime Minister of Italy fifteen years ago last week few people of the outside world—except those who had attended international Socialist congresses before the war—had heard of him. Even in Rome not many knew him by sight or had more than a vague knowledge of his previous career.

Scarcely any one could account connectedly for the fact that this agitator-journalist who only six months earlier, at the Genoa conference, had tried vainly to interview David Lloyd George had suddenly himself become a Prime Minister. Was he at the head of affairs by right of successful insurrection or had he been called to office according to constitutional rules? Mussolini himself, in his first speech to Parliament, said he left such questions to "melancholy fanatics of super-constitutionalism."

What foreign correspondents had wired their papers was something like this: On Oct. 24, at Naples, Mussolini had harangued a great gathering of followers from all over Italy and uttered these words: "It is now a matter of days, perhaps hours. Either they shall give us the government or we shall capture it with a swoop on Rome. I tell you, I assure you, I swear to you that the orders, if necessary, will come." His followers had applauded with shouts: "Rome or death!"

For the next four days high politicians at Rome discussed how these Fascists who talked so loud but were also strong in the grip they held on certain cities of Northern and Central Italy could be given some participation in nominal powers and thus be held responsible for the exercise of their real but hitherto irresponsible power. The Fascists, meanwhile, concentrated some dozens of thousands of men in Central Italy, with headquarters in Perugia.

The government was presided over by a cheerful old gentleman named Luigi Facta but, pushed by Giovanni Amendola, a junior Minister of intrepid character, it proclaimed a state of siege on Oct. 28. A few hours later it withdrew that order. On the twenty-ninth Mussolini received a telegram from the King inviting him to come to the capital to discuss forming a government. Next day he arrived and the day after that the Fascists marched into Rome.

Mussolini was thus appointed Prime Minister by the King but evidently the King had not chosen him because he had the confidence of Parliament. Parliament was not even in session and its party leaders had not withdrawn their confidence from Facta. Had the King violated the Constitution in refusing to work with the Facta Government and summoning a new Prime Minister who could not have got half of the Chamber's Deputies to back his candidature? Perhaps he had. But then in May, 1915, he had already gone so far as to refuse the resignation of a Minister (Salandra) whom a majority of the Deputies had publicly repudiated. On that occasion huge crowds surging through the streets of Rome, demanding the gallows for the man whom Parliament wanted, had impressed the King, and one of the leaders of those crowds had been Mussolini. One breach of the Constitution had taken Italy into the World War and now another was going to wind up postwar confusion.

Amid such stir of passion and hope, who cared much about the Constitution? Not the man in the street, who wanted Mussolini to assume responsibility for the government. For two years the Fascists and the old labor parties had been at civil war with each other—not on a grand scale nor everywhere, nor all the time; but often one read that ambushed Communists had somewhere shot a Blackshirt or two, whereupon Blackshirts in trucks had raided a small town, captured the Town Hall, beaten up the Mayor or the schoolmaster or the trade union secretary and burned the municipal library. By late 1922 these plots and reprisals were fewer than they had been in 1921. The Fascists were lording it over large parts of Italy with the connivance of the local army authorities and despite helpless or hypocritical protests by civil authorities. In August the old labor parties called a general strike in an attempt to help or force the government to shake off this usurpation. The Fascists broke the strike and ravaged the country anew. By the end of October the man in the street in Rome—no zealous custodian of high principles—was all for letting Mussolini try his hand at governing, since he would not be governed.

Mussolini arrived in Rome by train from Milan, waving an olive branch from the window. But while he went to see the King in frock coat, top hat and white spats, he asserted at the same time the rights of conquest. He occupied Rome with troops—young men who had shouted in Naples, "Rome or death!"

When Mussolini and his friends gave their followers this pass-word they were speaking, as any Italian schoolboy knew, words uttered half a century earlier by Garibaldi. Now, Garibaldi had learned his Roman rhetoric from Mazzini. Mazzini, who inflamed so many Italians to sacrifice themselves to make a free and independent Italy, told them that Providence had assigned them the task of extirpating effete Papalism and planting in its place the new Roman civilization that was to radiate love and brotherhood round the world.

Outraged that any one should think of "uniting" Italy without Rome, he called incessantly for a march on the city of the Popes. Many keen partisans of Italian unity were utterly opposed to this, remaining devoted sons of the Roman Church and wishing to leave the Sacred City to its anointed master. Cavour, the great practical politician, wanted Rome for Italy, but all in good time, and without a fight: he thought Mazzini's declamations were just heady rhetoric. Garibaldi, at first a Mazzinian, then came to terms with Cavour, but swung back to Mazzini's views. For the first ten years of the Kingdom of Italy Rome remained in the hands of Pius IX and a French garrison while Garibaldi and Mazzini conspired and agitated for a march on Rome. Both had defied the Italian Government, and become outlaws, by the time Victor Emmanuel at last marched in and took possession.

To march on Rome, then, means to any one who has been to school in Italy something more than to capture a city, even the most famous city in the country—whoever marches on Rome cannot but claim (such is still the echo of the phrases of Mazzini and Garibaldi, or was still in 1922) to be setting up an authority to propagate from the Eternal City a new and brilliant ideal.

Mussolini's march on Rome in 1922 was less of a military assault, more of a holiday excursion than even Victor Emmanuel's in 1870. Throughout the march the trains came in and out of the city laden with tourists and ordinary ticket holders, at worst with a few hours' delay. The marchers themselves in great part arrived by railway at the suburban resorts where they were concentrated for a final converging pedestrian advance through the center of the town, entering at the Porta del Popolo, crossing the vast expanse of the Piazza del Popolo, legging it up the straight and narrow Corso, chief highway of ancient and modern Rome, to the ice-white edifice, with its glittering gilt appurtenances, built in front of the Capitol to commemorate 1870.

What we saw in Rome, then, was a parade of youths sure of the garlands and kisses given to heroes, without any fear of having to fight for them. We who were lodged comfortably in Central Rome suffered no more by the march than that the restaurant offered a simplified menu, having to feed some dozens of the boys, and that from noon to dusk the parade was marching across Rome, cutting our line of communications with the theatres.

Some of the black-shirted marchers, exhibiting ugly but primitive weapons at their waist (and from waist down they wore a fantastic variety of breeches, leggings, trousers, spats, whatnots with equally odd headgear), looked capable of administering bodily harm. Yet most were gay, smiling, cockawhoop lads, whom chieftains on bicycles, horseback, or in small cars, tried to marshal into order, together with some hearty and hefty looking females, and some squads who wore not black but blue shirts. (These were the Nationalists, who were soon cajoled or cudgeled into more uniformity.) We heard these holiday-making history-makers singing on far into the night—but then we were well removed from some less elegant Roman quarters which hung out red flags and received castor oil or contusions, and a bullet or two, for their pains.

Such was the march on Rome—a carnival-like procession of youths, with some more staid middle-aged and even elderly people among them, filing through the narrow streets under the bunting, with the cheering crowd on either side. During two days' pause in various places in the Roman hills the Blackshirts had had time to recuperate under the bright, warm Autumn skies from the fatigue of one or two broken nights in crowded railway cars or trucks. Those who had stayed in their own towns sometimes had been harder worked, having to take their turn at capturing public buildings from bewildered sentries.

The fighting which won Rome for Mussolini had been done weeks or months before, not in or near Rome but at Parma, Ferrara, Cremona and towns in Central Italy, where "Reds" had given way to Blackshirts in a long campaign of daily and nightly mutual ambushing and massacre. In that civil war those for whom wealthy, respectable and powerful friends provided almost the equipment of an army could not fail to triumph in time over their scantily furnished rivals.

Neither then nor later did Rome see more of that struggle than a few skirmishes in working-class suburbs, one or two raids on political premises, a few beatings and—less than two years after— a kidnapping that ended in death for a revered popular leader and almost in counter-insurrection. Indeed, many Romans who watched the Fascists file up the Corso knew little more than foreign spectators of the bloody scenes in which some marchers had participated in places whence they had marched—or taken the train. They knew of some forcible doings with castor oil and were ready to dismiss them as youthful exuberance so long as the youths would keep their daggers, bludgeons and revolvers well tucked in their belts all the way through Rome and out again. Save for a biff or two, this was what they did.

Very wisely, Mussolini at once packed these youthful thousands, who are now staid men in their prime, back to places where they need not keep on such good behavior for the benefit of diplomats and newspaper men. He at once gained thereby the favor of those who wanted a peaceful background for the Winter's social events.

For the Italy of 1919 to 1922 had not been a soothing stage for the performance of an elegant social routine. Among memories of those years, here are some that rise to the surface of one observer's mind. He was then very young, had no stake of fortune in the country to worry over, and watched what happened with curiosity, yet with an affection for the handsome, intelligent people he had fallen among.

A tall young officer in a crack regiment, monocled, whirling his blue cloak round his shoulders, is remembered announcing to a little group of English and French youths, "We are going to have a new form of society in Italy. We shall be Socialists very soon now." (Autumn, 1919.) This young officer came from a landowning family in Central Italy; not long after he was among the most whole-hearted adorers of the man who "saved Italy from bolshevism."

Just off the main square of Florence several men rush forward, seize a horse by the bit, empty some astounded tourists (English or American?) out of the carriage and throw a bleeding man into it; a whip-crack and away full speed. Then shots from somewhere, a frightened crowd running back into side streets (August, 1920).

The Turin-Rome express ambles at a few miles an hour somewhere near Pisa and stops at a wayside station where a pretty tobacconist sparkles and smiles at railwaymen and passengers. A lawyer in the train looks anxiously at his watch, pulls out a 50-lire note and walks up with it to the engine; the train gets on a fine speed and reaches Rome only an hour or two late (October, 1920). . . .

In the enormous Ministry of Finance a Neapolitan employe introduces the young Englishman whom he has met in a cheap hotel; all the employes in the room, all the afternoon, chatter with the Englishman. "The government pays half a day's wage; we shall not work a full day for that." (Spring, 1921.) . . . .

The waiters frantically run round, collecting the money from such customers as have not bolted from the tables the very moment the electric current was without warning switched off throughout the town. This time the authorities are prepared. Great military searchlights sweep up and down the Via Nazionale to insure safe passage (any evening, perhaps, 1920–21). . . .

Such are the stray memories of one who, having lived in Rome in those years, is now asked whether Mussolini, with the march on Rome, saved Italy from "bolshevism." No doubt whatever but that after Mussolini's accession one could order one's life with less allowance for such untoward happenings.

Yet long before Mussolini put in a serious claim to national leadership authority was regaining its grasp. On Nov. 11, 1920, second anniversary of the victorious end of the World War, the King and the Prime Minister proceed with military pomp to the gilt-festooned ice-white "Altar of the Fatherland" and commemorate the victory. Old Giolitti, who did not want the war, is Premier; he has arranged this pageant, and people smile at his slyness; he is ready enough (they remark) to unfurl the flag and rattle the saber if the people can be better shepherded that way than another. Now Nitti, in 1919, had kept the military as far as possible from observation, and would risk no display to commemorate the war.

A dweller in Rome in 1920 and 1921 suffered discomforts and annoyances perhaps, but seldom ran into any show of violence on the part of either of revolutionaries or of their opponents. A dweller in Naples or Palermo could live as tranquilly perhaps in 1921 as in 1911—on the opaque surface of a concealed underworld.

Those in the Valley of the Po "where the destinies of Italy are decided" were living much more dangerously: squatters at times appropriated land from which no organ of the State would stir to expel them; scowling peasants would frighten the well-born lady as she got into her car; and stones might follow the scowls.

At one moment, indeed, in Autumn, 1920, the workmen of many factories in Northern Italy had "occupied" the factories, in a stand-up rather than a sit-down fashion, since they attempted to continue production as long as they had raw materials. Mussolini bade these strikers godspeed. But from 1920 to 1922 the employers found the trade unions ever more ready to negotiate for concrete and detailed advantages, ever less disposed to bring their men out on strike for political ends, except as a counteraction to the Fascists' "punitive expeditions" against whatever political groups, Socialist, Catholic, or otherwise, might be blocking their attempts to usurp the functions of the State. Such a great industrialist as Agnelli, of the Fiat works, was able to negotiate politely and effectively with the Socialist spokesmen of his teams.

But across this well-enough attested industrial pacification there cut the turbulence of growing legions of ex-soldiers without jobs, young farmers at loggerheads with their farm hands, bloodthirsty revolutionaries who saw that the Socialists wanted no bloody revolution, but wanted still to play a part: rhetoricians and poets who wanted a new Italy because they found the existing one rather slow and shabby—and holding all these together, the reddest of the pre-war Reds, the same Mussolini who ten years earlier had expelled men from the Socialist party for shaking hands with the King and organized vast strikes to prevent Italy from winning the Libyan War.

Mussolini's men and youths wanted an Italian Republic and a more royalist kingdom, a fair deal for the workers and more authority for employers, free import of foreign goods and more protection for home industries, the Mediterranean for the Mediterraneans, and a close alliance with England. Mussolini did not mind what they wanted as long as they followed him in his march to power.

The Blackshirts marched on Rome a day or two before the fourth anniversary of the victorious armistice. Mussolini has merged the anniversaries into a festal season, and since 1924, when rival factions in the procession fired on each other, the annual pageants have been remarkable only as a spectacle.

But the Blackshirts of 1937 march through a Rome which Mussolini has meanwhile embellished and adorned, sweeping away whole quarters of the town, demolishing, revealing and reconstructing.

Simultaneously in every great urban center in Italy the Blackshirts hold vast parades. And who, male or female, escapes being officially a Blackshirt today? In nearly every such center they stand amid the monuments of a huge State expenditure on embellishment and clearance.

Milan has a colossal new railway station; Turin a central artery arcaded in marble; Naples a great esplanade; Bari a grandiose port frontage; Palermo a monstrous postoffice. And between such pairs as Milan and Turin, Pisa and Florence, Rome and Naples, the Fascist Government has built broad straight highways reserved for swift automobile traffic. New tunnels have meanwhile greatly shortened the railway journey from Rome to Naples, and from Florence to Bologna, two of the most crowded sections of the system.

The traveler who pokes around Italy away from such great centers will not find such new splendor altogether evenly spread; the slums of Sicily could never have been ignobler than today.

For the outward glamour of new marble and the inward glamour of self-recognition as wielders of an imperial power the luckier Italians have paid by consenting to eat and drink less select products, and to wear less select clothing; to work longer and harder, and to forgo somewhat the pleasures of contemplation and conversation over a coffee and a Tuscan cigar. The unluckier have paid for it by a more painful tightening of the belt. And those few men and women who need, for their happiness, to be speaking out their mind in conversation, literature, or the spontaneous oratory of the natural leader of men, pay for it in the loss of occasions for self-expression—though many drawing rooms and taverns, and maybe factories, give opportunities for talk that foreigners seldom hear.

And how many teachers and journalists must not only check their tongues but choose daily between writing in praise of what they would blame, or in detraction of what they admire, or, if they will not, having a family without sustenance on their hands? But any one who sees a streetful of Italians may guess that millions are content with a sense of being bigger people in the world, and unaware of paying for this new grandeur; they attribute anything they suffer rather to Mr. Eden than to any one nearer home. (The raucous campaign against President Wilson when he withstood the Italian claim to Fiume in 1919 was a first exercise in an art of abusing "Anglo-Saxon" politicians that has now been greatly improved upon.)

Yes, the Mussolini who was an unknown man outside Italy in 1922 is now one of the world's chief figures; he rules his country with unshaken and apparently unshakable authority; but other minds are at work in Italy, and will one day continue his experiment in a direction he himself cannot guess.

Germany Turns from Junkerism

by Emil Ludwig

ALTHOUGH THE JUNKER spirit in Germany is not broken, Junkerism has greatly declined in influence and cannot be revived as a system. The Junkers can no longer utilize their sole virtue, military bravery, and in the course of time the occasions for its employment will grow even fewer. As the protectors of Germany's kings, they resembled those statues placed in front of medieval cathedrals. These monuments are fine to look at so long as they stand proudly on their pedestals as defenders of the great edifice which in turn protects them. But let them be thrown down from their pedestals, or let the edifice behind them fall, and they lose all their significance.

Only as individuals, not as a system, can the Junkers hope to regain their influence. Formerly, since they alone held the highest offices, the great national policies were in their hands. Now that the democracy has come they can protect even their own interests only indirectly by means of their influence in the rural districts.

This class, that once governed the nation, has become a class fighting for its very existence. For two centuries it ruled against the spirit of the age and now the spirit of the age has at last turned on it. That is the meaning of the German revolution, as all the leading minds of Germany agree. No important writer, poet or thinker is to be found on the side of reaction. It is impossible that the Junkers could return to decisive power in an age when all the Presidents, dictators and leading statesmen of the world have risen from the ranks.

Yet there are survivals of the Junker spirit in Germany today in these forms—respect for authority, obedience and physical strength. For 200 years all authority in Prussia sprang from the noble class and the people today carry over this conception of government. A bourgeois could scarcely be elected President of the republic; Hindenburg's authority is due to his character and not to his noble rank, but without his rank his prestige would be less.

The sense of obedience is so strong in the German people and has been cultivated for so long that without authority they feel themselves unprotected. "If everybody were equal," a Munich waiter said to me one day, "whom then should I obey?"

Again, the Junker spirit is still evident in the respect shown for arms. The armed organizations of the three great political parties compete in smartness and seek to enlist former officers as commanders. Among the political leaders of the Nazis one finds about a dozen Junkers and a number of princes; and among the members, some of whom are speakers, are also three sons of the former Kaiser.

But it would be a mistake to regard the Hitler movement as a recrudescence of the Junker spirit. The Junker spirit was hereditary, exclusive, aristocratic; the Hitler spirit derives from the individual and his achievements without regard to his origin and so it has not the aristocratic shortcomings and would not be so deplorable if it were not so unintelligent.

Among the Nazis are thousands of youngsters who want to play soldier, to seek adventure, to sit around camp fires—romantic youths who would rather fight in the medieval manner than work in the modern way. The old Junkers, on the other hand, were neither romantic nor adventurous, but were sustained by the sense of power peculiar to a ruling class accustomed to dominate their inferiors and to serve their king.

When, during the war, the world indicted Prussian Junkerism, it did not do so without justification; for the Junker spirit had had its day and had become something of an anachronism. This is not to say that the Junker class had not served the State in earlier times or that it might not, after considerable transformation, have done so again. But it had too long enjoyed exclusive and uncontrolled power and had stubbornly refused to give way to modern forces—much like the owner of a gas works who would attempt to prevent the installation of electric lights in the twentieth century.

This Prussian evangelical Junker, this squire and farmer, this colonist living upon what was, for the most part, rather poor and unfertile soil, must not be confused with the richer, more tolerant and more cultivated Catholic nobleman of Western and Southern Germany, who represents a type that has been favored by wealth, good fortune and history; and even among the Prussian Junkers the more prosperous landed nobility of Silesia is a class apart. But the world has classified the German nobleman, in so far as he was a squire and an officer, along with the Junker and so condemned him.

Since one cannot understand the change which has come over this class without taking account of its former character and status, let us recall the statements of one of the most modern of Junkers, the Baron von Rheinbaden, who has recently made an excellent critical analysis of the shortcomings of his own class.

"The nobility [in the nineteenth century] was entirely dependent upon the favor of its sovereign," he writes. "Its self-consciousness was no longer an expression of a feeling of pride in itself, but a reflection of the lustre of the court. It prided itself upon absolute loyalty; hence the dogma that whatever policy the king advanced must be accepted blindly as the right one. If a member of this class had dared, whatever his motive, to oppose the policy or the acts of his prince, he would have been shoved aside by the ruler and proscribed by his fellow-noblemen. This 200-year-old system so effectively discouraged thought and initiative that a nobleman hardly dared be seen with an opposition newspaper in his hand and branded all opponents as unpatriotic and contemptible without so much as giving them a hearing."

This analysis by a Junker of the spirit of his fathers explains, he thinks, "the incapacity for independent political thought or independent courageous action" in the late crisis.

Since the German Junker, in contradistinction to the English, remained dependent and loyal to the sovereign, he could develop courage and bravery, but was less distinguished for thought and judgment; consequently he was well suited to be an army officer, though lacking all the qualities necessary for political leadership. Relying naturally upon this class, unconditionally devoted and also trained to military leadership, the kings entrusted to it likewise the direction of politics and administration and thus maintained the form of State typical of an earlier century while the nations of the West chose their leaders from all classes.

Thus it happened that the German Junkers remained a princely class rather than a national aristocracy, obedient and reverential toward their princes, haughty and arrogant toward the people, calling themselves "the jewel of the nation" and never noticing that nearly all of the intellectual and creative activities, nearly all science and art, sprang from other social groups, mostly in opposition to the Junkers.

From their estates, where for centuries they had been well educated (but principally in physique and manners), they came to the casinos and castles, displayed their ability to command a regiment and sometimes to administer a Prussian district or a province, but seldom showed themselves capable of filling a Ministerial post or of directing foreign policy, which determined war and peace and the fate of the State. In July, 1914, all important posts in the government and the army were occupied by nobles.

The great exception to the rule, Prince Bismarck, was bitterly opposed by his fellow-nobles. Moreover, nearly all the noblemen who distinguished themselves as statesmen or in other capacities were the sons of middle-class mothers (Bismarck, Caprivi, Bülow, Moltke, Hindenburg). Thus they sprang from physically sound ancestors; and it would seem that intelligence, which has not otherwise particularly distinguished this class, also came from the bourgeois stock.

Kaiser Wilhelm I bestowed titles of nobility very rarely, but Wilhelm II handed them out quite lavishly and created a new "money nobility" having the same status as that which derived from feudal times. This he did by means of the "Fideikommiss," or entailed family estate, which could not be sold or divided. Finally nobility became literally purchasable. Between 1900 and 1913 Wilhelm II established 223 of these entailed estates, often accompanied by titles of nobility, and at the same time gave to the Junkers so many of the most important offices in the State that not only were nearly all the Generals and corps commanders noblemen, but—in spite of their general lack of perspicuity and knowledge of world affairs—titled persons occupied the principal foreign posts as well.

The entailed estate insured the Junker against poverty. He lived well and cut a shining figure without having to work on his land; and even if he became bankrupt he must somehow be assured an income "suitable to his station." So the Junker often left his lands in charge of superintendents, who were frequently incompetent or dishonest, and he lived in luxury in Berlin among his comrades and fellow-noblemen while his farms deteriorated. In 1912 some 40 to 52 per cent of all the large Junker estates were not even occupied, much less managed, by their owners. Many made no effort to transform forest into arable or pasture land and a few enthusiastic huntsmen (as Professor Aereboe records) bought up whole villages and turned the land into forests merely because some of the villagers had poached.

After the World War this class suddenly lost its position and influence when the system which had nurtured it collapsed. The Junkers did their duty during the war as officers. I cannot agree with certain democrats who try to show from documents that the guard regiments drawn from the feudal nobility spared themselves in the conflict. This may have happened in an exceptional case, but in general the nobility in the World War, as in earlier times, defended their privileges with their blood.

When the German Army collapsed, the Junkers' lack of ideas and independence left them in complete mental and moral confusion at the decisive moment in which they might otherwise have come to the defense of their rulers. The king ruled by the grace of God, and to serve him was, to them, an article of faith; so when the king went the Junkers found themselves in the tragic situation of a believer who suddenly becomes convinced that there is no God.

"The nobility," wrote one member of that class, "was neither cold nor warm; it had neither the resolution to stand by the monarch and defend his sworn rights, nor the courage to assert itself as the aristocracy of the country and to plunge in and take its part in the decisions and work of reconstruction. Instead it silently stepped aside, later showing its disappointment and wrath."

When the Constitution of the new republic abolished all the privileges of nobility, it introduced by a single paragraph the most important innovation in Germany in a thousand years. The "Fideikommisse," or entailed estates, were to come to an end and titles of nobility were to be permitted only as part of the name.

Meanwhile the nobles were divided as to what attitude to adopt. Hindenburg, whose family had been landed Junkers and officers since 1280, came over to the new order after a few years and took the oath to the black, red and gold republican flag. Ludendorff, whose ancestors had been Pomeranian landlords for 300 years, wrote not long ago: "Herr Paul von Hindenburg, by the rules of the old army, has forfeited the right to wear and be buried in the field-gray uniform of the old army." The Stahlhelm, the reactionary organization of former combatants, a year ago held a prolonged discussion as to whether it should allow von Hindenburg to remain an honorary member; and a son of the former Kaiser declaimed against the President in a public speech, saying that his "senile misunderstanding of the German powers of resistance" had caused him to "bow to the Reds and to call upon the German people to hold their tongues."

In November, 1918, during the revolution, there came to see me a Saxon Junker whom I knew to have been extremely advanced during the war and inclined to accept Wilson's peace program.

"And now," said I somewhat naïvely, "has not the moment arrived for some Junkers to abandon their titles?"

He looked at me with astonishment and replied: "On the contrary, from now on I intend to seal my letters with my coat of arms."

The first thing the Junkers discovered was that they had suddenly become poor. Having lost their public posts and being forced to return to their lands, they realized, especially after the inflation —that is, from 1924 on—that they had overestimated the value of their properties by some 30 to 50 per cent, that they had been cultivated in a quite inefficient and old-fashioned manner, and that the world market and world prices had completely changed.

Having neither the initiative nor the experience to adapt themselves to the crisis, and no longer enjoying the special favor of the State or their privileges or their former self-confidence, they lost within a few years both the social and the material props of their existence. Had not these lands been for centuries the source of an income by which they had lived fulsomely, sending their sons into guard regiments and marrying their daughters to neighboring squires? Must the ancient property now suddenly become a business which one had to understand and even to work at one's self? This was their greatest problem.

In these circumstances they were obliged to change their manner of living. The brilliance of their position, their privileges, the consciousness of being the uppermost class, had passed with their material prosperity. About 30 per cent of the Junkers remained upon their estates, 10 per cent became officers of the Reichswehr, and about 5 per cent went into diplomacy or other branches of the civil service. The others had to find entirely new careers. About 30 per cent went into banks and trade and, by virtue of being personable and having distinguished names and good manners, they became agents for manufacturers, motor car dealers, steamship lines, &c. About 25 per cent remained unemployed, although thousands of these received military pensions. A number of former staff officers, who had long ago been selected for their capability, now sit as aristocratic directors of industrial corporations.

In the government itself the privileges of the Junker are diminished, but not altogether at an end. Although there is at present only one nobleman in the government, the important diplomatic posts abroad are largely in Junker hands: of the nine Ambassadors appointed by the new republic only two are commoners; seven are noblemen—several of them very able. The selection of these representatives is a much more prudent one, now that the whims and prejudices of class rule have been done away with. Among the commanders of the sixteen military districts, ten are Junkers.

The Junker is most useful in the Reichswehr, which seeks to preserve the spirit of the old army. Of the 9,000 officers of the imperial army, 15 per cent are in the Reichswehr. There is a danger, however, that the Junkers may introduce the ancient caste spirit into the new democratic professional army. Not long ago a retired General of aristocratic antecedents who had served in the Reichswehr several years spoke publicly "against the Jewish republic" and for the old régime. Thereupon the energetic new chief of the Reichswehr, Baron von Hammerstern, denounced the political activities of officers even after they had left the service, and made this significant observation: "This may give the impression that officers serve the State only for their material advantage and that they conceal their real opinions while in the service."

The difficulty of the Junker in the Reichswehr arises from his natural distrust of the republic and the necessity of taking an oath to follow a flag whose appearance signified the end of his ancient class privileges. In the morning he goes through target practice under the black, red and gold flag of the republic and in the evening he reads in the Junker newspaper, the Deutsches Adelsblatt, such declarations as this: "We repudiate unreservedly the republic and the democracy which it has proclaimed and shall continue to fight by all permissible means for a monarchy independent of the will of the masses."

From this dilemma come many contradictions. Had they not been obliged by the bankruptcy of their estates to earn a living— that is, to profit by their training, which was primarily military —no Junker would serve under the new flag. The few who have modernized their opinions are disdained and socially boycotted by the majority of their fellows.

In the cities the Junkers have lost most of their influence in that the officer, who under the monarchy had pre-eminent social standing, has today in the Reichswehr a reduced significance: the modest uniform allotted to him is proof of it. The semi-uniform displayed in the streets by the youths belonging to the "storm detachments" of the political parties is a hundred times more popular than the legitimate uniform of the Reichswehr, for the latter represents only the remnants of a once brilliant army. No one is interested in the appearance of this remnant, although its behavior in a crisis might decide the future of the republic. Indeed, I may add that the Reichswehr's action would most probably be on behalf of the republic and against any reactionary uprising.

In rural districts, however, the Junker influence is almost as important now as it was before the revolution. Western Germany has always been more independent than Eastern; for centuries the Elbe has divided the country into two cultural regions, of which the western inclined toward the ideas of democratic countries to the west. There the peasant looked upon the Junker as his enemy, and in Holstein he even now celebrates the anniversary of the day when his ancestors slaughtered the Danish nobles. Catholic influences have strengthened this attitude. Therefore, here in the new Prussian provinces, where Junkerism has never properly established itself, there was less to change in 1918.

East of the Elbe, however, in Old Prussia, kings and nobles were inclined toward the traditions of their neighbor, Russia. The system of hereditary submission which forbade the peasant to sell or even leave his land had induced an attitude of mind so slavish that even now, a century after the end of this system, these traditions are still influential.

When the peasant turned homeward from the trenches, he hoped that the republic would distribute the enormous landed property of the nobles as was being done by the neighboring Russians, Czechs, Poles, &c. Millions voted Socialist with that end in view. When the German land reform, owing to a disagreement on principle between the two Socialist factions, failed to take place, the bitterly disappointed peasant fell back upon the old system. He blames the new form of government, instead of the lost war, for the increased taxation. He joined again with the Junkers to vote against reparations and heavy taxes and so reinforced the Junker's position.

Today the German Junkers control the "Landbund," in which the 99 per cent of peasant members support—at least in Old Prussia—the moral and political power of the 1 per cent Junker element, although the hereditary chief magistrate of each village is now replaced by an electoral official. The Junker, who owns 7,500 acres or more, holds a dominating position over the peasants of his district who have in all perhaps 2,500 acres. For that reason the free peasant, in greeting the squire, calls him even today "Gnädiger Herr." For even now he is dependent at all times on the squire's favor. When he needs the doctor brought from the town, or rents a bit of meadowland, or wishes to gather wood or leaves in the forest—which generally belongs to the Junker and is reserved by him for hunting—he can do so only by favor of the squire. This favor he can only keep by voting against the democratic régime.

Only recently, when a petition for the overthrow by referendum of the Socialist Prussian Government was brought forward, many Junkers issued a public warning in the press and on hoardings that any peasant or artisan who did not sign it could look elsewhere for customers and patronage. The result was an increase of many thousands of signatures over the previous poll.

This association of rural Junkers furthermore controls the election of the Chamber of Agriculture, which has a decisive influence on tariff policies. A third source of the Junker's power lies in his possession of the advowson, or church patronage, which gives him the right to appoint the minister. In Prussia, which is predominantly Protestant, this country parson is a monarchist and warns his peasant congregation from the pulpit against the republic which, he believes, will not last.

He likewise takes care to inform the squire if any of his flock expresses democratic sentiments, and thus keeps the people in check. The Catholic priest, on the other hand, is invariably a republican, and so is the schoolmaster, generally speaking.

A fourth source of the Junker's power is to be found in the organizations to which, under former officers who are Junkers, millions of former soldiers belong. A fifth lies in the Junkers' management of the committees for land settlement. Agricultural laborers and younger sons of peasants to whom the government is granting allotments of public land, receive the expropriated land from these committees. It is allotted at the expense of those who have ventured to vote democratically.

With proper education and knowledge the younger sons in these rural districts could probably distinguish themselves in business and science, as do those of the English nobility. Instead, thousands of Junkers are living today on their brothers' estates, and, since they have nothing to do but hunt, they go in for political agitation.

Naturally the number of middle-class marriages has increased. Whereas formerly in these castles the admissibility of a marriage was decided by "the sixteen ancestors" and marriage with a girl from an undistinguished family would be forgiven at best only after many years, nowadays every Junker considers it a piece of luck if he can marry his children into the rich middle class. The slogan of race purity is more than ever in the air in Germany, but nevertheless the different social classes are intermixing as never before.

It is possible that Junkerism may revive in new forms and that the severe lesson which it has had may save it from decadence. The weakness of the Junker's ambiguous position cannot be better described than in the words of that Junker, von Rheinbaden: "The present time is a test for the nobility. It must show whether, alone and by its own strength, it is still capable of assuming moral leadership along new paths, or whether two centuries of princely service have robbed it of the aristocratic attributes which every nobleman must look for in himself. Otherwise the impression will be that the demand for restoration of the monarchy merely conceals incapacity to assume, without the protection of a king, the place in the State to which the nobility lays claim."

Prussianism Returns in a New Guise

by Harold Callender

THE UPHEAVAL WHICH has taken place in Germany is often referred to by enthusiasts as a national renaissance. In a sense it is.
For it marks a rebirth of Prussianism, though in a somewhat
altered form. The new Prussianism, like the old, is thoroughly
militaristic, extravagantly Pan-German, bitterly anti-liberal and
anti-democratic. It manifests, like its precursor, a sublime faith
in force and a mystical veneration of the State as the embodiment
of force, a thirst for greater power and more territory, a rankling
envy of other nations, a militant and aggrieved nationalism pre-
occupied with its own dreams and consequently given to grotesque
misjudgment of foreign events and opinion.

To these familiar characteristics of the traditional Prussianism
the new Prussianism has added others: a revolutionary and dictatorial technique borrowed from Italy; a vague, half-formulated
socialism which represents a revolt against big business and industrial civilization; a racial myth which ministers to the German
sense of national inferiority and inequality by supplying the conviction that the Germans, in spite of their political mistakes and
their defeat, are nevertheless a great and superior race.

As its tincture of socialism and its pseudo-anthropology indi-

From the *New York Times Magazine,* May 14, 1933, copyright © 1933,
1961 by The New York Times Company.

cates, the new Prussianism is a popularized soap-box version of the old. The original Prussianism, which flowered upon the rugged plains of the eastern marches and thence slowly pushed westward to the Rhine, was imposed by kings and a martial nobility upon a people who, after brief periods of resistance, eventually came to accept it. The new Prussianism had to make its way in a time when kings were gone and discredited and the prestige of the nobility had undergone a notable slump. It had to overcome a republic which, while essentially alien to German traditions, had accomplished a monumental work of national reconstruction after the greatest of German disasters and hence had won strong support among liberals, Catholics and the working class. It had to work up and maintain a revolutionary mood, to enlist on its side all possible varieties of political and social discontent, to incite the non-Catholic and non-Socialist masses to an uprising against the existing State, to pitch its propaganda in an ultra-popular key.

Consequently, the new Prussianism is no creation of a Junker-aristocratic caste reinforced by its professors and intellectuals. It is a mass movement of the middle class—a class impoverished, embittered and deprived of its equilibrium by the inflation which, like all its woes, it has been adroitly taught to attribute to the Treaty of Versailles. It is a movement almost bereft of intellectuals and without a clear program. It is based upon emotion and owes its success to skillful agitation and showmanship rather than to definite ideas. Though it annexed a few stray princes and counts, it had to carry on until the very eve of its triumph without the help of the Junker squirearchy which formed the mainstay of the old Prussianism.

Finally, however, the small party of the monarchistic Nationalists, following the familiar political principle, "If you can't beat 'em, join 'em," reluctantly sided with Herr Hitler. They did not like his socialism, but they assumed, as some leading industrialists who supported him had previously done, that it need not be taken seriously save as a vote-getting device. They hoped to guide and use Hitler. Thus the old and the new Prussianism became somewhat incompatible allies.

But if the Nazis' socialism served merely for campaign purposes, almost as much may be said of the alliance with the Nationalists, for ever since the election the Nationalists have been receding into the background while the Nazis' power and control of patronage have grown. It is the petit-bourgeois Prussianism of Hitler, not the country-gentlemanly Prussianism of the Junkers, that has extended its dominion over Germany.

The new Prussianism is notably lacking in pedigrees. It is not to the manor born. It reflects the farm and the small store and office rather than the manor house or the palace. Its Bismarck is no offspring of the landed nobility, trained in the university of a military academy; he is not even a Prussian; he is the son of a small official in a little Austrian village; he has had little academic training and writes and speaks most unscholarly German—which is not a political disadvantage in the leader of a mass movement. Its encyclopedists—its "brain trust"—are the Rosenbergs, Goebbels, Wageners, Fricks and Feders, whose language is more fervent than illuminating, who talk of a pure German race as though it were not well known that the population of Northern Germany from Memel to the Elbe (the stronghold of Prussianism) is largely Slavic in ancestry.

In his essay, "Preussentum und Sozialismus," Oswald Spengler lucidly defines the principles that animated the old Prussianism. Contrasting individualism with socialism in its broadest sense, he cites Great Britain as an example of the individualist State in which freedom is the aim, Prussia as the Socialist State in which service is of first importance.

> To serve [he says] is the old Prussian principle, related to the old Spanish, which united a people in its struggle against the heathen (in East Prussia). No "I," but rather a "we," a sense of community in which the individual is merged. There is no question of the individual, who must sacrifice himself to the commonalty. Not each for himself, but all for all; an inner freedom of a larger kind, the freedom in obedience which marks the best examples of Prussian discipline. The Prussian Army, the Prussian civil service, Bebel's socialism—all are products of this disciplinary idea.

The Englishman and the American, according to Spengler, strive for individual wealth, while the ideal of the old Prussianism was "socialism in its most fundamental sense; will to power, struggle for the happiness, not of the individual, but of the community." "The English nation is based," he says, "upon the division between rich and poor; the Prussian, upon the distinction between command and obedience."

The classic model of a social organization based upon command and obedience is, of course, the army. Hence Prussia developed as a military State; not only did she advance and expand by use of her army, but the very principles of her social life were, as Spengler shows, military. The military ideal was also the political ideal. After the short and highly successful wars against Denmark, Austria and France in the 1860s and 1870s, militarism seemed a decidedly profitable affair, and the general staff was almost idolized.

Pan-Germanism and anti-liberalism were natural and logical consequences of the Prussian philosophy and the Prussian State. Its "will to power" and its quest of "happiness, not of the individual but of the community," inevitably led it to undertake to unite the Germans under Prussian rule and so to form a powerful empire. In a community organized on the principle of command and obedience, where the individual's one duty is to sacrifice himself to the State, there is obviously no room for liberalism with its emphasis upon individual liberty and its suspicion of the State.

This, then, was the old Prussianism, imposed from above by a ruling class, which dominated Germany until 1918—signally failing in its last few years to provide that which was held to be its supreme justification.

Many detached observers thought that, after its final performance, the Germans would decide they had had enough of Prussianism in any form. Some did so decide. Thousands had come to that conclusion as early as 1848, and had fled to America in consequence. Others lost their illusions after the defeat. (Their feelings are vividly depicted in Herr Remarque's books, "All Quiet on the Western Front" and "The Road Back.")

But there were many, even among those who fought at the front, who attributed Germany's downfall not to military defeat but to disloyalty at home. In a romantic country much given to myths there sprang up the myth of the "stab in the back." Although the

German commanders had acknowledged defeat in the field and the government had asked for an armistice long before the revolution began at Kiel, many Germans convinced themselves that the reason the war was lost was that Socialists and pacifists revolted against the Kaiser. This was, in Hitler's words, "the crime of 1918." Thus the defeat and the penalties which grew out of it were not ascribed to Prussianism and its empire, but to the Socialists and to the republic which arose upon the ruins of the monarchy. To the rest of the world the events of 1918 may signify that Prussianism led Germany to catastrophe; to millions of Germans they signify that Prussianism, which had made Germany great, was foully betrayed by German renegades.

Consequently, it was possible, after a dozen years of incessant propaganda, for a new Prussianism to arise, breathing righteous indignation at the "crime of 1918" and determined to avenge it by overthrowing and punishing the "Marxists" and pacifists who, according to the myth, were responsible for Germany's humiliation. It was possible for Prussianism to be reborn in the form of a mass movement, equipped with the same old creed, but with an added touch of socialism (which, as Spengler says, is eminently Prussian in principle) and a soap-box anthropology providing pseudo-scientific reassurance of the essential superiority of the Germans in spite of their defeat. This new Prussianism promised a new dawn, a revival of the glories of the past. To its followers the republic was a mere interregnum, a deplorable lapse from true German ideals, a wandering in the darkness of exotic liberalism, an apostasy that must be atoned for and wiped out.

The army, as of old, is again a symbol and a cult. The new Prussianism celebrated its advent to power by a solemn pilgrimage to Potsdam to pay tribute to Frederick the Great, hero and creator of the old Prussianism. President Hindenburg spoke his gratification that, in spite of the Treaty of Versailles, the "martial idea" had been maintained. Chancellor Hitler had said: "I am for force because in force I see strength, and in strength the eternal mother of rights, and in rights the root of life itself." An official Prussian decree recently said: "The joy of the duel derives from the fighting spirit, which must be promoted in our academic youth."

There is a movement—officially sanctioned, like everything in the new Germany—against what are called "American forms of sport," and in favor of "military sports and field exercises." Even the courts must reflect the "martial idea," for a recent Prussian decree announced that lawyers aspiring to become judges must undergo a term of "camp service," where they will be schooled in "martial sports."

In order to suppress Prussian militarism the Treaty of Versailles ordained that the German Army must be limited to a professional force of 100,000, with enlistment for twelve years. But twelve years is, after all, a short career. After that, what was the young officer or soldier to do? The new Prussianism, in the form of the Nazi movement, solved the problem. It created an unofficial army of its own, the "storm troops," and utilized this idle military talent. Napoleon once limited the Prussian Army to 42,000 men, but Scharnhorst, by rapid training during short enlistment, built up a huge reserve. Similarly, the new Prussianism got round the peace treaty by organizing an army which was none the less useful for being unofficial. This new militia, far greater than the official Reichswehr permitted by the treaty, carried through a revolution and now serves as the instrument by which the new Prussianism rules Germany.

Animated, like its progenitor, by the military ideal, the new Prussianism retains the old Pan-German aspirations. "The great German revolution (the Nazi uprising) is by no means at an end," said the editorial in the Voelkische Beobachter, Hitler's newspaper, recently. "Its dynamics carry it further on, and one hostile fortress after another falls before it. The first period of the revolution will be closed only when National Socialism has become the foundation of the thought of 80,000,000 Germans." (Only 63,000,000 live in the present Germany.)

"We begin where we left off six centuries ago," wrote Hitler in his book, "My Struggle." "We shall stop the German movement to the south and west of Europe and turn our eyes to the land in the east. * * * When we speak of new territory we think, first of all, of Russia and the border States under its rule. * * * Our mission is to bring our people to see that its future goal lies * * * in the labor of the German plow for which the sword supplies the ground." The old Prussianism began in the colonization of the Eastern Baltic; according to Hitler, the new Prussianism should expand—at least "first of all"—in the same direction. But this will not be its only preoccupation with affairs outside its frontiers. It must, says Hitler, "never tolerate the rise of two Continental powers in Europe." It must "regard every attempt to organize a second military power on Germany's borders—even in the form of a State capable of becoming a military power—as an attack upon Germany," and it must consider it as "not only a right but a duty to prevent the rise of such a State by every means, including arms." And if such a State already exists, it must be "crushed" ("zerschlagen"). For Germans, adds Hitler, must "never forget that the most holy right in the world is the right to land to cultivate, and the most holy sacrifice is the blood spilt for that land."

Just as liberalism was suppressed by the old Prussianism in 1848 and again in 1862 under Bismarck, so it has been denounced and crushed by the new Prussianism. In his Reichstag speech Hitler declared that nineteenth-century liberalism had paved the way for socialism and "communistic chaos." A cartoon in Simplicissimus recently showed a curious crowd gazing at two figures in a museum marked "the last German liberals."

It is an interesting historical fact that the liberal republic, which the new Prussianism has so ruthlessly wiped out, was to a great extent an American creation. There was no demand for a republic in Germany, and the country established one because President Wilson, in his telegrams replying to the armistice appeal, plainly insisted upon dealing with a representative government. He drew a sharp distinction between the imperial government and the people; he asked the Germans to change their government.

His words, says Philip Scheidemann in his memoirs, "fell like a bombshell; it was now clear that Wilson would deal only with representatives of the German people." So the revolution which led to the republic—the revolution which Hitler calls "the crime of 1918"—was instigated by Woodrow Wilson, who believed he was serving the German people as well as the cause of peace by freeing Germany from Prussianism.

The impression which the new Prussianism has made upon the outside world is similar to that made by the old. More than a century ago Canning called Prussia "a downright grenadier, with no politics but the drumhead and cat-o'-nine-tails." Lord Rosebery compared her to a pike in a pond, "poised for a dart when the proper prey shall appear." He added that her policy, "brutal as it is, requires genius, and Prussia has not been richly endowed in that way."

Rarely if ever in peacetime has the British House of Commons, with all parties speaking in unison, indicted a foreign State in the way it did in the recent discussion of the new Prussianism and its methods. Sir Austen Chamberlain, former Foreign Minister, referring to the "savagery" of the new régime, dared the government to "put another Pole under the heel of such government." Sir John Simon, the present Foreign Minister, said "the government would not be expressing the feelings of the country if he did not associate himself with what had been said." Commenting upon this judgment, The London Times observed that "Germany has forfeited in the last few weeks most of the sympathy which she has managed to regain during the last ten or twelve years."

The barrier which the old Prussianism created between Germany and the rest of the world was no greater than that by which the new Prussianism has again isolated the country. There is the same incomprehension of foreign minds, the same aggrieved contention that Germany is maligned and misunderstood, the same inability to conceive that German violence and expansionist aspirations might disturb Germany's neighbors.

Herr Hitler was much distressed by the speeches in the House of Commons—which German newspapers thought it best not to publish—and instructed his Ambassador to protest, as though he expected the British Government to silence the British Parliament as he had silenced the Reichstag. Herr Hitler said America had no right to protest against persecution of German Jews, since America's immigration law discriminated against certain races; as though he saw no difference between limiting the number of immigrants admitted into a country and taking away the means of livelihood from people whose ancestors had dwelt in the country for centuries. From Nazi headquarters came a warning to England of the "considerable growth" of British communism—which hardly exists.

These fantastic judgments of foreign opinion and events recall the German Government's expectation in 1914 that Ireland would so annoy England that she could not fight; the German belief that America would not enter the war, whatever the submarines did; the German confidence in 1917 that, though America had declared war, it would not matter because she would be unable to send an army across the Atlantic; the Zimmerman scheme to incite Mexico against the United States.

Only minds out of touch with reality, or obsessed by grandiose dreams, could entertain such conceptions. In this the new Prussianism is true to type. It has completely failed to appreciate how it looks to outsiders. In gauging foreign opinion it has been consistently wrong. Here lies one of its greatest dangers—for Germany and for Europe.

Germany Liquidates
Her Revolution

by Harold Callender

BERLIN

SPEAKING IN THE REICHSTAG twenty years ago, Herr von Oldenburg-Januschau made the now historic remark that the most effective political instrument in Germany was a "Lieutenant and ten
men." When Herr von Papen seized control of the Government
of Prussia in the approved soldierly manner, Herr von Oldenburg-
Januschau revised his earlier observation by noting that "a Captain and four men sufficed to break the resistance of Red officialdom."

It was a commander and some 160,000 Stahlhelm men—forming one of the three large "private" and unofficial armies of Germany—who proudly paraded recently before a distinguished
company that included the Chancellor, members of the Reich and
Prussian Governments, commanders of the Reichswehr, the navy
and the Prussian police, veterans of the Kapp uprising, the Crown
Prince, his brothers and former reigning princes and dukes. In
consequence of the presence at its annual reunion of so many
representatives of the old regime, perhaps it would be more ac-
curate to say that the Stahlhelm, of which President von Hindenburg has been an honorary chief since its foundation, now enjoys

From the *New York Times Magazine,* October 2, 1932, copyright © 1932,
1960 by The New York Times Company.

a sort of semi-official status by virtue of the marked favor of the government.

This cannot be said, however, of either the Nazi Army or the republican Reichsbanner, though each of these military organizations (like the Stahlhelm) far outnumbers the State's official army, the Reichswehr. Deprived by the peace treaty of the traditional privilege of universal military service, hundreds of thousands of German youths have joined these political or class armies. And von Hindenburg has just issued a decree establishing systematic physical training of German boys by military officers. So no German Government has cause to worry about a possible lack of the indispensable "Lieutenant and ten men."

That they are still regarded as of vital importance was emphasized again recently by a visit of General von Schleicher, the Minister of Defense, to East Prussia, when he assured the residents of that severed eastern province that the government would see that it was defended against its neighbors (its neighbors being Poland and Lithuania). East Prussia, the General said, was in especial danger. This was one of the reasons for Germany's demand for equal rights with the other powers as to armaments, a demand which will be the dominant issue facing the disarmament conference when it meets again within a few months.

In the formal note to France outlining this demand, the German Government remarks that it claims the right to establish a military system suitable to "the country." Millions of Germans, like General von Schleicher, genuinely believe that frontier regions such as East Prussia are really menaced and insufficiently protected, and that a larger army is necessary for security. Moreover, the recognition of Germany's equal status by removal of the military restrictions of the peace treaty is required, as they see it, to wipe out the stigma of inferiority that has wounded German pride.

But there would be obvious domestic uses also in the reorganization and strengthening of the Reichswehr which General von Schleicher has projected. A strong national government, seeking to unite a politically divided nation and to insure against disorder from any quarter, has need of its "Lieutenant and ten men," suitably multiplied. It would be in a happier position if it could, without violating a treaty, enlist behind the constituted authorities all or most of the military forces of the country which now follow partisan political flags. This would be particularly advantageous on the assumption that the government's ultimate goal was the creation of a State in which the army held the peculiar position accorded to it by Prussian tradition. In that case the reorganization upon which von Schleicher insists so strongly would be governed, not only by the assumed needs of frontier defense but by the "social characteristics of the country."

What has happened in Germany within the last three months has been a stubborn attempt to liquidate the revolution of 1918 and its consequences and to reinstate a type of non-democratic, military State more in harmony with the country's traditions. The principal rivals for power—the von Papen Government and the Nazis—both desired this familiar kind of State; the only question was: under whose leadership was it to be ushered in—under that of a politically inexperienced agitator from Austria named Adolf Hitler or under that of less picturesque but more business-like North Germans who, whether they had actually governed or not, were by reason of their inheritance considered born to rule and had grown up under the traditional Prussian system?

A considerable majority of the voters of the country, though divided on nearly everything else, seemed to agree in their pronounced aversion to "the system" (as the Nazis call it) built up since the revolution, and in desiring some kind of strong, if not dictatorial, government—aristocratic, industrial or proletarian. For in the July 31 election the Nazis (Fascists) polled 13,732,779 votes, the Communists 5,278,094, the German Nationalists (monarchists) 2,172,941—a total of 21,183,814 votes out of 36,845,-279 votes cast going to parties openly and aggressively opposed to the republic. The Nazis wanted a military, dictatorial regime backed by a Fascist militia; the Communists wanted precisely what Russia has; the Nationalists wanted something as near as possible to what Germany had before the war. But they all wanted a drastic change; they all wanted to do away with democratic, parliamentary government.

Hitler had skillfully organized a movement of nationalistic discontent which represented, if in a somewhat caricatured form, a genuine popular emotion of which any government must take account. He was a most successful trumpeter of Fascist revolution; he had done his job of inciting and organizing and drilling with an effectiveness indicative of genius, but he was not the man (as he himself appears to have realized) to create and administer the new State for which his dreams and his oratory had paved the way. Nor was Dr. Bruening, the unemotional scholar who underestimated the strength of the Nazis, perhaps because of his lack of sympathy. So President von Hindenburg—himself a life-long military man and servant of the monarchy who had wanted to put down the revolution of 1918 by force—turned, perhaps instinctively, to a set of leaders personifying the aristocratic and military traditions of his Prussian upbringing.

It was the mission of the new Cabinet to utilize, either with Hitler or without him, the "constructive forces" (as von Papen called them) of the Nazi movement; to enlist the fiery revolutionary enthusiasm of the Nazi Army and the Nazi voters in support, not of a Fascist State under the rule of an irresponsible visionary from Vienna, but of a solid, realistic Prussian State governed in the stern old-fashioned manner suggested by Herr von Oldenburg-Januschau's phrase about "a lieutenant and ten men"—the kind of State that the Germans, to judge by their history, prefer above all others.

Hitler shared this political ideal, so it was at first sought to enlist him as an ally, along with his storm troops and his followers. But Hitler refused to be enlisted. The counter-revolution, he held, belonged to him since he had done so much to organize it, and he declined to hand it over to a Cabinet of elderly country gentlemen with noble names, however genuinely Prussian they might be.

It did seem a bit unjust, in a sense, for the Cabinet was virtually saying to Hitler: "You have done a wonderful job in arousing a morally necessary national emotion—though you should not have mixed it up with socialism, as you unfortunately did. But you are not capable of controlling and directing it. For that, we need more mature, more practical, more northerly blood, not Viennese histrionics. So we'll pay you off for your good work with a seat in the Cabinet, and allow you to deliver over to us your excellent organization and following."

The Cabinet had done all it could—compromising its claim to

"impartiality"—to conciliate and favor the Nazis and to embarrass and undermine the Socialists.

One of the first things it did was to lift the ban on party uniforms and parades which Dr. Bruening had imposed in the interest of order. This cheered the Nazis a good deal and satisfied them for the moment. They immediately held a great demonstration in a working-class suburb of Hamburg, flaunting their Fascist uniforms before the eyes of unemployed men and Communists. Shots rang out and many were killed. The government, practicing what has been euphemistically called "spiritual differentiation" in favor of the violent Nazis as against the violent Communists, now turned accusingly upon the Prussian Government for not maintaining order (though it had maintained order very well before the ban on uniforms was lifted).

Here was an admirable opportunity to settle with the Socialist Government of Prussia, which had to be got out of the way before the liquidation of the revolution could proceed very far. So an emergency decree was prepared (under the conveniently elastic Article 48, of which the republican Dr. Bruening had availed himself so extensively during his two-year Chancellorship); and the "Captain and four men" took over the Prussian State, in the name of the Reich Government, with military dispatch. Thus the 10-year-old Socialist régime in Prussia (which constitutes about two-thirds of the Reich) was wiped out within a few minutes, the Prussian police were placed under the authority of the new Conservative Cabinet, and one of the principal results of the revolution was removed with surprising ease.

The Reich Government had another stroke of luck in foreign affairs which aided it at home. One of the things about which the Nazis had worked up most indignation was reparations. It had been obvious for at least a year that reparations payments would never be resumed and that all that remained was to get them formally canceled. A French election brought in a Left Government, and this, ironically enough, played into the hands of the ultra-Right German Cabinet by enabling it to be the government that actually got rid of reparations. It had to make the concession of a final payment, but a Right government can do many things that no Left government could do; it can make concessions to France without being accused of treason, as a Socialist government would be if it made such concessions.

A Right government can also speak out for a strong army in a more whole-hearted way and without the qualms and apprehensions that must beset any Socialist government, whose supporters have certain prejudices against military programs and the military caste. It can do this the more consistently since it stands for the re-creation of the military State which has played a dominant role in German history and can summon to its support emotions rooted in the past.

Though the present leaders of Germany are admittedly monarchists and the only party that fully supports the Cabinet is that of the monarchistic Nationalists, it is not now so much a question of filling a vacant throne, or even of getting rid of the republican Constitution, as of preparing the ground for a strong, centralized, non-parliamentary or merely nominally parliamentary régime with due military backing and permeated with the genuine Prussian spirit. The shell of the republic might be left standing for a long time, now that the Socialists and republicans have been shorn of power. A republic ruled by monarchists would serve quite well for the liquidation of the revolution. A republican Constitution containing the Heaven-sent Article 48—by means of which a "captain and four men," backed by the President's signature, can do almost anything the liquidators desire—is not a bad instrument for this purpose.

Modern Prussia was created by militarism and it in turn created the German Empire, the nearest approach to a united Germany that the nation has known. Consequently it is not surprising that the military State still is closely associated with the ideal (as yet unattained) of complete German unity, or that the dream of a stronger and more self-confident Germany, divested of the treaty-imposed inequalities, so readily takes a military form.

The new State might easily be a military one on the old model and at the same time, to a considerable extent, a socialistic one. Thus it might at least come much nearer the Nazi ideal of a "Third Reich" than the Nazis now seem to expect. "The real Prussian militarism," wrote Johannes Haller in his admirable book, "Die Epochen der deutschen Geschichte," "meant that every individual, high or low, rich or poor, belonged body and soul to the State, served the State, lived for it and died for it." What could be more socialistic than that? What more could even Stalin ask of his people? "The old Prussian spirit and the socialistic idea are one and the same," said Oswald Spengler. "We Germans are Socialists as no other people can be."

What could be more statesmanlike, or more consonant with the real Prussian spirit, than for the counter-revolutionary government to contemplate a measure of socialism by way of eventually conciliating the Nazis and the Socialists—the two greatest parties, both of them socialistic—and incidentally by way of amalgamating their already drilled and disciplined party armies with the "special militia for internal order and frontier defense" of which the German armament note to France speaks? Bismarck nationalized the railways and introduced social insurance; the protagonists of the Prussian ideal could, in these times, go a great deal further without violating their creed. Moreover, the German State has now such extensive interests in banks and industries and such wide authority over prices, wages, interest rates and trade that it has already gone a long way toward abolishing private capitalism.

This increasing invasion by the State of spheres of finance and trade hitherto left to private enterprise is largely the work of Dr. Bruening, a Catholic and an ardent exponent of capitalism, who felt himself compelled by circumstances to take such measures. For events of recent years have driven Germany toward socialism at a much more rapid rate than her traditional inclination would have dictated. If a capitalistically minded Chancellor can be induced by the pressure of an economic crisis to extend the powers of the State even to the point of fixing interest rates on existing securities, a nationalistic government which considers that it has a sacred mission to liquidate a revolution and save the nation from civil war need not be expected to prove excessively squeamish or doctrinaire. Prussianism is older than capitalism and might conceivably outlive it, especially if it allied itself with the forces that seem likely to dominate the immediate future in Germany.

Thus Germany is, perhaps, reverting to type; gradually sloughing off an alien-inspired and uncongenial political system established because the flight of her Princes had left a vacuum that had to be filled, and because Woodrow Wilson, by inciting the German people against their Imperial Government and by replying to the armistice appeal by saying he would deal only with a government representing the people, virtually insisted upon a revolution. The Germans made a revolution in order to get peace, not because they wanted a republic. They embarked upon a novel venture in democracy at the precise moment when faith in it elsewhere was at a low ebb and dictatorships were springing up on all sides, and at a time when they had plenty to do to reconstruct their war-depleted land without political experiments for which the country was not ready.

Now, in spite of the uninspiring record of the military State and its leaders between 1914 and 1918, they seem bent upon turning from the teachings of the idealistic President to those of the realistic Iron Chancellor who welded the disunited German States into a powerful empire. They are turning from the proportional representation and referenda and constitutional liberalism to something far more deeply rooted in history—the "lieutenant and ten men."

Hugenberg—Giant Shadow over Hitler

by Emil Lengyel

ALTHOUGH HE IS less in the public eye than are President von Hindenburg and Chancellor Hitler, Alfred Hugenberg may yet be known in history as the most powerful man in the Reich of this period. As Minister of Economy, Minister of Agriculture and Food and arbiter of wages in the Hitler Cabinet, he has been described as Germany's economic dictator. His present posts are not, however, the real gauge of his importance. That lies rather in the fact that he is the leader of the German National People's party, which for years has had the largest non-Socialist political group in the Reichstag.

In German conservative circles Hugenberg is described as the greatest constructive force of his nation; in liberal circles he is spoken of as the arch-enemy. He is known as the czar of the German press, the potentate of German films, as well as the dictator of the Reich's industry and chief monarchist. The real extent of his power has never been charted, but it is immense and reaches beyond the press, the cinema and industry into the fields of banking, agriculture and politics.

While Hitler has taken the world by surprise with his sudden ascent to a dizzy peak, Hugenberg has been climbing toward the

From the *New York Times Magazine,* February 26, 1933, copyright © 1933, 1961 by The New York Times Company.

top with dogged tenacity. It is predicted that long after Hitler's name recalls merely a passing phase, the name of his Minister of Economy will be remembered as a significant product of the age.

Hugenberg's appearance is not impressive. He lacks Hindenburg's massive form and the wiry tension of Hitler. His sixty-eight years are belied by his face and ruddy complexion. He looks more like a physician than a would-be tyrant. He speaks calmly as a rule, although he is capable of spasms of anger. "Behold the miracle," a Communist newspaper commented on one of his outbursts, "an iceberg is in volcanic eruption." He looks as if he had just stepped out of a fashion plate of the 1880s. It is especially his high-standing collar that stamps him as a man of the pre-war world, and of his mustache it was said that it is high treason against the republic.

Hugenberg's ideal is a Reich governed by a selected few—"not the elected but the elect." He does not conceal his belief that his success in many fields qualifies him as the super-dictator of the Reich. He is a monarchist, but a royalist restoration in the near future is not his aim. For democracy he has scant respect and under his rule universal suffrage would be discarded. "Germany's greatness," he has said, "was built on obedience and it should be the keynote of her economic revival."

Socialism and communism are his pet aversions; against them he is preaching a crusade of extermination. He holds the social legislation initiated by Bismarck one of the main causes of Germany's misfortune. He believes in higher tariffs than those in existence, and he advocates the doctrine of Germany's self-sufficiency, the much-discussed "autarchy," forced upon the Reich, as he sees it, by the nations who cut off her colonies and foreign markets.

In the foreign field Hugenberg holds the former Allies and the Treaty of Versailles responsible for Germany's recent political upheavals. Long before Hitler, he exhorted his countrymen to put under the ban the spirit of Versailles. He concentrated a barrage of criticism on the reparation policy of the Allies and carried on an implacable campaign against the Dawes and Young Plans. He would reunite the Polish Corridor and Eastern Upper Silesia with Germany, and would consult Alsace-Lorraine on whether it wanted to rejoin the Reich. He is the spokesman of those who insist on Germany's right to arms equality. He preaches the cult of heroism and old-fashioned nationalism. He wants to lead a political organization of strong men whose motto is: "We want a bloc and not a jelly."

What is the secret of the man who enjoys the reputation of knowing no failure? What was the magic that enabled him to rise both under the empire, to which he was devoted, and under the republic, to which he is opposed? How did he manage to thrive on inflated trillions, and to consolidate his possessions when deflation appeared? What was the key to his success, not only when Germany had her short day in the sun, but also after a calamitous tornado had hit the ship of State? What is the background of the man who at 68 is still driven onward by a daemonic urge—this veteran warrior who is entering the arena for a new battle?

"Herr Schatzrat" (Treasury Councilor) Hugenberg, Alfred's father, was nicknamed by his neighbors in the city of Hanover "Herr Schwatzrat" (Garrulous Councilor), not because he spoke much, but because he spoke little, minded his own business and led a retired life. Young Alfred was known in the family circle as "der Kleine," a serious youth, emulating his father in speaking little and working much.

Alfred was a "schwaermer," a dreamy youth who sought the solitude of the woods of the Eilenriede on the outskirts of Hanover. Remembering those days, Alfred Hugenberg wrote several years later: "The forests form the reserve of a people's strength * * * and they are the refuge of man in search of solitude."

His dreams were cast into shape in a slender volume, "The Quartet," which was well spoken of among friends, but which the world at large decided to ignore. This rebuff—the only serious one in the life of Hugenberg—induced him to turn his back on poetry and to seek solace in practical work. In deference to the custom of wandering scholars, he went from one university to another in quest of wisdom, and took his degree as a Doctor of Laws at the University of Strasbourg. His doctor's treatise was about the colonization of Germany's northwestern moorland.

Hugenberg then accepted a government office in the Rhineland, near the Dutch frontier, where he had a chance to display his organizing gifts. Next we find him a successful agriculturist and a member of the colonization commission of Posen. His chief of bureau asserted that his young assistant had the best political head he had ever come across.

With breath-taking rapidity Hugenberg was climbing the ladder of civil service. As an official of the Prussian Finance Ministry he visited the United States in 1905 and wrote a report about his observations. He found America's cities "esthetically repellent," built for utility and without regard for beauty. "In New York," he wrote, "one cannot get away from the impression of seeing a magnificent spot of earth, scarred and devastated." In the Middle West he studied the colonization of recent European immigrants and he recommended the application in Germany of some of the colonizing methods he found in this country.

Many State officials would have wished for nothing more than to reach the position he now occupied in the Prussian State administration, but Hugenberg had the inflexible principle of never resting on his laurels. After reaching the peak in one walk of life he immediately left it for more arduous climbs.

Marriage had brought Hugenberg into contact with the banking dynasties of South Germany, and with the assistance of his father-in-law, the Lord Mayor of Frankfurt-am-Main, he obtained important banking positions. He was not quite 44—five years before the war—when he was chairman of the board of the vast Krupp armament firm in Essen. He was now looked upon as an industrial virtuoso, a prodigy of quiet efficiency and of clear-sighted cunning. Three years later he was made the director of the coal and steel syndicate in the Rhineland and in Westphalia, the greatest honor the industry could bestow on a member. It seemed that in that field, too, Hugenberg had reached the peak. Where would he turn now?

Then the World War opened and the industrial leaders of the Reich began to whisper about the Hugenberg Line long before the Hindenburg Line was ever heard of. Alfred Hugenberg was now the head of an organization that employed nearly 200,000 workers, the manufacturers of great cannon—the "dicke Bertas"—and of other paraphernalia of destruction with which the Central Powers hoped to carry on to victory.

Before the war ended Hugenberg turned to the work with which he has achieved his greatest fame. Inspired by the example of Lord Northcliffe in England, he decided to put his energies at the disposal of Germany's war propaganda. With the aid of leaders of the steel industry he bought several newspapers and acquired the German Cinema Company. He wanted to be the generalissimo of propaganda. His resignation at Krupp's was accepted, however, only after the armistice.

Hugenberg rebelled against the social order that succeeded the monarchy. At the birthday party of the new Constitution he denounced the German Republic on the floor of the Weimar theatre as a monstrosity which must be put out of existence. He saw his mission in counteracting the influence of the Socialists and Communists, his mortal enemies. He convinced his former industrial associates of the necessity of what he called a "healthy press." While Germany was waiting for the new day, Hugenberg bade the sun to stand still.

And while the French were in the Ruhr, Hugenberg was preaching passive resistance. During the inflation he allied himself with Hugo Stinnes. While Stinnes was buying up the brawn of the Reich in the form of factories and mines, Hugenberg was buying heavily into the German soul through his acquisition of a chain of newspapers. But though the vertical trusts of Stinnes, veritable Towers of Babel of iron and steel, crumbled as if they had been built of cardboard, the paper realm of Hugenberg stood up against the vicissitudes of deflation.

Today Hugenberg is in control of the political opinions of about two-thirds of the German press. In Berlin alone he owns four daily papers, among them the well-known Berliner Lokal-Anzeiger. But his power as a newspaper Czar is greatest in the provinces, especially in the agrarian East, in certain sections of which he has a virtual monopoly in supplying the population with its political views. Through his control of the Telegraphen Union, one of the most powerful news services in Europe, he serves about 1,600 German papers. "Hugenberg is everything to the German press," a prominent member of the Reichstag said, "except its dry nurse."

About five years ago Hugenberg startled Germany by the purchase of the Universum Film A. G., known internationally as Ufa.

He acquired the company as the head of "twelve national men," whose identity was at first kept secret. The Opposition, suspecting that the "national men" were a group of counter-revolutionary plotters, forced Hugenberg to disclose their names. They were found to be leaders of the heavy industries, retired high public officials and a former soldier. Ufa is today Europe's largest film company, although at the time of its acquisition by the Hugenberg group it was on the verge of collapse.

Hugenberg's political opponents became more restless. Was this colossal juggernaut of publicity to crush liberal thought in Germany? Was the Reich's population to become the audience of a huge soapbox on which Hugenberg preached the religion of "Gott, Kaiser und Vaterland"?

In this field, too, Hugenberg had climbed as far as any man could go, and it was suggested that it would be difficult for him to find a new field of action. Then it was that his opponents realized that all his work was only preparation to reach the real goal of his life.

Until then Hugenberg had not appeared much in public, and he stood mostly behind the throne. Now he was ready to assume the responsibility of his position, and he claimed all the responsibility and all the power. In his newspapers he came out openly for the establishment of a dictatorship. He had his own candidate for the position—Hugenberg himself. For years he had been the motive power of the Nationalist party; now he claimed its leadership and obtained it. Everything was prepared for a Hugenberg dictatorship.

But Hugenberg seems to have forgotten that in these times even an anti-democratic move must be based on the consent of the masses. He had all the qualities demanded of a first-class dictator, except the power to fascinate a country. He could make an eloquent speech, but he could not make himself beloved. And then he came across Adolf Hitler, who was the admired leader of a nationwide revivalist meeting and who had the one quality that Hugenberg lacked. The "Pied Piper of Germany" could stir up the Reich; wherever he appeared he made converts by the million. What was more natural than that the two men should pool their forces?

Temperamentally the two men represent opposite poles. Hitler is a mystic, a genius of eloquence, while Hugenberg is a practical man of affairs, an efficiency machine. Hitler made his name as the spokesman of a new world order; Hugenberg considers himself the apostle of the old system.

The men have been both fast friends and relentless enemies in recent years. Hugenberg set the National Socialist avalanche rolling by throwing in the lot of his party with Hitler's in the Summer of 1930, with the result that at the September elections the Nazis scored a spectacular victory. A year later the two men met at Bad Harzburg and to the tune of martial bugles sealed their alliance with handclasps, repeated several times in the presence of a battery of newspaper cameras.

The partnership was soon broken, Hugenberg electing to stand behind the von Papen dictatorship and Hitler continuing his fight for a free hand for his Nazis. Before the elections of last Summer Hugenberg called upon his Nationalists to rally against the Nazis, whose defeat, he said, would be "the greatest boon to the Reich." When von Schleicher succeeded von Papen, Hugenberg turned a cold shoulder to the militarist, and when von Schleicher stepped out Hugenberg was ready at last to join with Hitler in their present alliance within the same Cabinet.

In the Hitler government Hugenberg occupies a position in which he can dictate to any dictator. His future line of action is therefore important not only for Germany but for the rest of the world. In a recent statement Hugenberg declared that after the elections of March 5 there would be no more elections in Germany, which clearly indicates a determination to carry on the business of the State as an open dictatorship. In another significant statement Hugenberg said that Germany would be forced into bankruptcy unless a new arrangement with her creditors was reached, which was interpreted as meaning his determination to reduce the interest rate on the Reich's foreign obligations.

It is still uncertain whether the influence of Minister Hugenberg is not stronger than that of Chancellor Hitler in the present partnership of Hugenberg and Hitler. Their two parties are fighting the electoral battle under the Hugenberg banner as "the fighting front of Black, Red and White."

To impartial opinion the alliance must appear unnatural. Hugenberg's party program of national capitalism can receive scant attention from the man who has popularized national socialism unless Hitler's enemies are right in asserting that the socialism of the Nazi leader is merely a bait to attract the despairing masses.

Hugenberg has never lost an important battle, and he seems confident that the time will come when Germany will invest him with full power as a dictator. Whether the tremendous antagonism he has aroused in the working classes will not be too much even for this strong man is a question which the future will answer.

The Average German Speaks

by Emil Ludwig

IN EVERY NATION there are a few persons who envisage the future shrewdly and a few who reflect with knowledge upon the past. Together these two classes amount, at most, to ten out of a hundred. The remaining 90 per cent have been brought up with a one-sided view of history; they misunderstand the past, they do not worry about the future, and therefore they live in a misty plain hemmed in by impassable mountains—a plain in which each individual has light enough to descry only his immediate environment. I venture to assert that most people know as little of the world about them as they do of their own personal character.

The Germans are less open than others to criticism in this respect, because—by reason of their geographical position, their methods of education, their knowledge of languages, and their widespread interest in foreign habits and customs—they are more familiar with the rest of the world than are many other nations. During the war a Turkish officer once exclaimed to me, with manifest distaste: "Oh, that is your German objectivity!" That the citizens of the smaller European States should speak foreign languages well is inevitable—they find it necessary to do so; but of the great nations—the four or five whose languages by reason of their literature and their strength have become world-languages —the Germans are by far the most polyglot. Only the most cultured class of Russians can be compared with them. Englishmen, Frenchmen and Italians are so seldom able to talk German to us that as a matter of course we Germans use their languages on our travels, in our reading and in our correspondence.

This German sympathy for the outer world was severely affected by the war. Today the average German's outlook has narrowed. But, before he is condemned for this, the reasons must be considered. At the beginning of the war he felt that he was being attacked, without justification, by an envious world intent on robbing him of the fruits of his industry. He knew as little about the immediate cause of the war as he did about the history of the preceding decades; he believed everything the German propagandists told him; he was convinced that the worthy "Michel" was being perfidiously threatened by evil neighbors, and, in consequence, he cast aside swiftly that sympathy which, until then, had bound him to one or another of the now hostile races. This attitude was intensified five years later by a peace by which he felt he had been grossly defrauded.

Along this line the German attitude has developed in the course of the last ten years. Immediately after the war there arose in Germany a strong conviction about the folly and the stupidity of the old régime; the anger against its disastrous blunders led to an inclination to believe in the new governmental forms. In this respect the six months of the armistice period, from Nov. 18 to July 19, were the most enlightened period; the republic in the earliest months of its existence received its strongest support from the great mass of the people because, first, it was marked by the innocence and promise of youth, and, second, because the faults of the preceding administration were still so fresh in memory. The flight of half a dozen kings and princes, the pusillanimous disappearance from the scene of twenty-two princely houses, the cowardice of a number of these fugitives, and then, to top it all, the greed of the unthroned imperial family, which was not ashamed to extort millions from the impoverished people—all this contributed to the enlightenment of the Germans and led them on toward the acceptance of the new ideas.

But the peace of Versailles did great damage. Even we, a small minority, who endeavored to construct the first bridges toward understanding, felt that we were defrauded—we, indeed, most of all, because we believed in a new Europe. The occupation of the Ruhr, four years later, destroyed completely the first faint feeling of confidence that had begun to shape itself, and the German outlook darkened more and more; it is easy to understand the bitter disappointment.

For I am dealing with the outlook of the average German. We must not allow ourselves to be deceived about the feelings of the great mass of the people by the circumstance that a minority of German men and women have sought zealously, by word and deed, to make good what we destroyed by the war. I want to make it quite clear that I am not here expressing my own views; they differ often from those which I am about to record. I am endeavoring to speak the mind of the average German, the type not so actively engaged in politics, a postal official, say, or a bank clerk, a landed proprietor, a farmer, an insurance agent, a commercial traveler or a school teacher. The outlook of this average German prevails also in the universities; there the old enmities are kept alive and all who endeavor to inculcate other feelings are regarded as traitors and enemies of the State. While individual philosophers and scientists in Germany continue to introduce splendid new discoveries and inventions to the world, the spirit in these "seats of learning" remains hostile to that outer world with which such services should be uniting us. During this last difficult decade no class of the German population has been so much at fault as the university professors; instead of becoming the spiritual leaders of the nation, piloting its youth to peace and freedom, the majority of them have become panegyrists of the splendors of imperial Germany and denouncers of the November-Verbrecher—the "November malefactors"—whom they accuse of attacking the "victorious German armies" in the rear. With a few exceptions (Berlin and Heidelberg, among them), the universities have been the strongholds of the Hitlerites.

The country most on the mind of the average German is, of course, France. It was in France that the peace was made; it was in France that the occupation of the Ruhr was conceived; it is

in France that the bitterness against Germany has persisted long-
est, because it was in France that the greatest material damage
was caused by the war. Naturally the first impulse of German
statesmen and men of letters was to try to bring about reconcil-
iation with France, and some Frenchmen responded. The German soldier who stood year after year in the Argonne or on the
Somme is Francophile in his sentiments, just as most soldiers speak
most sympathetically of the country with which they became acquainted during the war. For nations are not fundamentally either
good or bad; they are made up of citizens in whom are found both
good and bad attributes; the foreigner sees himself reflected in
them when he makes a long stay among them; he acquires confidence when he discovers that they are not very different from
himself. "The nations," wrote Voltaire, "should not be always
thinking of the small matters that divide them but of the many
qualities which unite them."

This feeling—for we have to deal with half-conscious feelings
rather than with clear-cut conceptions—is offset, however, by the
bitterness that is inherent in the relations between a debtor and
his chief creditor. "If he were to die suddenly," reflects the debtor,
"I should be free of all my cares. Why should he suck my blood
—he who possesses the richest land in Europe?" To this is added
the natural jealousy of a neighboring State which now possesses
the strongest army—a pre-eminence to which Germany formerly
could lay claim. The average German refuses to believe that
France stands in fear of a German attack; I myself did not believe
it until recently. When Stresemann, after years of imperialistic
tendencies, began to work for friendship with France, he lost the
confidence of the average German. Let a writer exert himself with
zest toward this end and any morning he may read in a newspaper that he has been in the pay of the French! There was little
idea of revenge in Germany in the first years after the war; in
these latter years it has become more pronounced. But I do not
think it is directed toward Alsace and Lorraine, or, indeed, toward the west at all. It is directed toward the east. The Poles are
the nation least loved in Germany. While France has fought her
own battles, the Pole, in German eyes, is a man who has had
German lands bestowed upon him by the victors. The chief de-

feats of the peace treaty are found in the east, and thus German bitterness is concentrated against those who occupy Upper Silesia and the Corridor.

This Corridor—a manifest makeshift, as any schoolboy can see from the map—for it divides German territory into two sections—constitutes, in my opinion, a danger to European peace, not by reason of the intrinsic importance of the region, but by reason of the strong feelings to which its loss has given rise in Germany. These feelings are intensified by antipathy against the Poles, whom most Germans regard as a people lacking in a sense of citizenship and of order and with a civilization of a type lower than their own. Scarcely any reasonable German would express such a view of the French.

The Czechs, the other neighbors of the Germans, stand much higher in their eyes. The three million Germans who live in the new Czechoslovakian Republic are considered to be better off than those who are under Polish rule; they are represented by two Ministers in the Czechoslovak Cabinet, and it is well known that President Masaryk does everything in his power to protect the German minority. Unfortunately, the Germans have ground for complaint there, none the less. Yet the Czech, who resembles the Prussian in his efficiency, is regarded in Germany as a dangerous rival rather than as a hated enemy.

Another point in the Czechs' favor is that they have poached on Austrian territory, not on German. If German sympathy with the Hapsburg monarchy was quickly dissipated, the explanation may be found in the artificial nature of the German-Austrian alliance. It was only in the course of the war that most Germans became aware that Austria-Hungary was made up of eight races; before that it had been thought of as an empire made up of Germans and Hungarians, and the claims of the other six races were dismissed impatiently. The Hungarians were always in favor in Germany and they are in special favor today because a dictatorship, as such, impresses the Germans. The war alliance with the Bulgarians and the Turks was forgotten the moment the war was over and has left all the fewer traces in view of subsequent developments in Turkey and of the fact that little Bulgaria has not much to do with Germany.

The change of feeling toward England is significant. During the war the Germans said: "We despise the Russians, we pity the French, we hate the English"; and the words *"Gott Strafe England!"* were to be seen in big letters everywhere. This indicated a feeling that Germany had been betrayed by her own kindred. Even today the average German believes that the World War was engineered in England with a view to the annihilation of her commercial rival. Hence the profound feeling of anger when the German fleet was to be handed over to the English and the decision to send it instead to the bottom of the sea.

However, the feeling of kinship came swiftly back, owing to the contrast between the conduct of the English and of the French in the sections of German territory occupied by each; by reason of the fact that England was in no considerable degree a creditor of Germany; and, more especially, because she did not take part in the occupation of the Ruhr. The friction between England and France was very welcome to Germany. An English traveler in Germany is now much more amicably received than a Frenchman.

The attitude toward Russia is less easy to analyze. The only enemy that took no part in the peace treaty, the enemy that, in 1922, was the first to enter into a compact with defeated Germany, the country which before the war had always been a peaceful neighbor and which was the natural foe of Germany's foes, the Poles—Russia was manifestly marked out to be Germany's ally and would doubtless have become so if—it is a big "if"—she had not been so disturbingly "Red."

The vicissitudes through which Germany passed in the Spring of 1919 have never been clearly understood by the mass of Germans. The circumstance that the Communists were against the peace treaty made it necessary for Germany to agree to it; Germany had only one ally against the dictatorship of Versailles, and this one ally she dreaded as much as the treaty. A bolder, more adventurous leader would at this juncture have confronted the world alliance against Germany with an alliance of Germany and Russia, and at least a long postponement of the victory, perhaps a dissension among Germany's foes, might have resulted. Lloyd George stood in fear of this during the Paris conference.

Even today the average German does not know what to think

of Russia. Whenever his dreams turn toward a war alliance with the Red Army, he is recalled to his senses by a vision of empty money-chests, of his beautiful home confiscated, of his children in the hands of the State. As Germany derives its main strength from the bourgeois class, it turns away from communism. The German workman is either a bourgeois or anxious to become one. A race of which only 27 per cent are peasants cannot have recourse to the same methods as a race of which 85 per cent are peasants. The average German does not speak Russian, and for the last thirteen years he has had no opportunity of seeing Russians with his own eyes: the fortress is closed and if one gets out of Moscow alive, he is a seven days' wonder. The nonsense talked about Russia all over the world is believed in Germany, just as it is elsewhere.

It is the Italians who, at the present time, are looked upon with the most favor in Germany. They were condemned only because of their withdrawal from the Triple Alliance. Even those Germans who (while they continued to eat it with relish) called macaroni "Treubruch-Nudeln" ("Disloyalty Pasta") are in ecstasies now over the discipline and order that prevail in Italy.

The centuries-old relationship between the two races has been resumed and German visitors are swarming into Italy as before the war. This has been the case more especially since Mussolini has called for a revision of the treaty. Taproom politicians, who would prefer an armed alliance to a mere friendly understanding, look toward Rome with shining eyes and indulge in visions of a German-Roman union like that of the Hohenstaufen era, in their ecstasy overlooking the fact that Switzerland stands in the way. The average German, in truth, holds nothing against Mussolini except the question of the South Tyrol, and this would be forgotten if the moment should come when the Germans, clad likewise in Fascist uniforms, took the field by his side against the common enemy, France.

Meanwhile there are in the world two powers which give the average German more cause for excitement even than the question as to which political party he should support or oppose. One of these "powers" is powerless and has its seat in Geneva. Stresemann's services to his country can best be appraised in connection with the change he effected in German public opinion with regard to the League of Nations. As the League was part and parcel of the peace treaty, it was bound to be unpopular in Germany at the start; it did not seem to show any development during the first years and it became an object of ridicule.

A man who is not black-balled at a club will see its weaknesses the more clearly and will rejoice over every opportunity for mocking at it. To bring the Germans into the League was the great achievement. Once they were in, they were bound to realize that, with their passion for organization, they could make use of it as an unparalleled tribunal from which to combat the peace treaty in sight of all the world. Three days before Germany joined the League, I happened to hear the League laughed at by a high German official in Geneva. Today when no German Government could exist without Geneva, the League is perhaps of greater value to us than to other countries, and the knowledge of this fact is steadily, if slowly, sinking into the mind of the average German.

The second power is the United States. After the war our first sympathies went to South America, where the German was amicably received. At that time the whole weight of German hatred fell upon President Wilson, by whom Germany felt she had been betrayed. The average German called attention to the fourteen points, in accordance with which our forces had downed arms. Even now he does not believe that Wilson no longer represented the majority of voters in the United States at the time of the treaty; he is barely aware that the United States did not ratify the treaty. All he knows certainly is that Wilson on June 19, 1919, did not stand by what he had promised on Oct. 18, 1918. Added to this is the resentment of the debtor against the principal creditor— the feeling that all Americans are very rich and that they need only to renounce a couple of dollars each from their income and then the whole question of war debts would be settled. All these factors, it seemed, were bound to make the United States appear as Germany's foe.

And yet this is not so. The average German feels toward the United States what he feels toward Russia, but for different reasons. He would like to live in friendly relations with these men against whom, theoretically, he has a grudge. The matter of their wealth is merely a single element in the problem; it is not the sole element. The German feels drawn toward the American because both move at the same pace. In Europe, the German is everywhere looked at askance because he goes ahead faster and is more efficient than his neighbors. In the United States he finds these characteristics applauded. In Europe the German has left war memories behind him everywhere because he penetrated deep into all the enemy countries. In the United States no German soldier has ever been seen, and what the Americans saw of Germany after the war was calculated to please them. Although it was the American who was the decisive factor in the defeat of Germany, he is thought of as a friend and helper who fought against the Fatherland for only a year. So, instead of holding the Americans more responsible than any of the others for their share in the war, the German absolves them for it, and all the more readily because he recognizes that they were impelled to enter the war through less material motives and that they sought no profit from it.

These considerations, which I feel I have no right to disguise, influence the average German in his attitude toward other countries. But there are different types of "average German." The citizens of the Hansa towns, for example, by reason of their geographical situation and their past history, are swifter to adapt themselves to the views of the outside world and to judge it more fairly. And the German workingman, by virtue of his political training, is able to look upon his neighbors more reasonably; and so he constitutes the strongest guarantee of peace and stability in Germany.

But these two classes do not represent the majority of the people and will not do so for a long time to come. On the contrary, under the pressure of the debt German prejudices are being strengthened rather than weakened, and a farsighted policy would favor a revision of the peace treaty, for it is in this that the German advocates of revenge still find their strongest arguments.

The Youth Who Are Hitler's Strength

by Alice Hamilton

HITLER'S MOVEMENT IS called a youth movement and during the first months of the Nazi rule, while I was in Germany, this certainly seemed to be true. The streets of every city swarmed with brown shirts, echoed to the sound of marching men and Hitler songs; there were parades, monster mass meetings, celebrations of all kinds, day in and day out. The swastika flag flapped from every building. In Frankfort-on-Main where I had spent, years ago, delightful student days, I went to the beautiful Römer Platz, only to find it unrecognizable, its lovely buildings hidden under fifty-three Nazi banners. Rathenau Square had been changed to Horst Wessel Square, for Wessel, the young organizer of storm detachments in the slums of Berlin, who died at the hands of Communists, is the new hero of Germany and his name has replaced that of respected adult statesmen—not only Rathenau but Ebert, Erzberger, Bülow, Stresemann.

The measures on which the government was then concentrating its attention were distinctly adolescent in character. It seemed more important to reorganize all the sport clubs so that Jews and Social Democrats should be debarred than it was to plan a program for the lessening of unemployment. There was more in the newspapers about the coming Olympiad than about the coming Economic Conference. The public speeches, the radio talks, the leading articles in the "cleansed" papers, all were directed to youthful minds, not to adult. The purified stage presented such plays as would appeal to the young, Jost's "Schlageter" (Schlageter was the hero of the French occupation of the Ruhr) and the incredibly dull and childish "Wanderer" of Goebbels which closes with a vision of the future storm troopers marching across the stage with swastika banners to the strains of the Horst Wessel song.

To understand Hitler's enormous success with the young we must understand what life has meant to the post-war generation in Germany, not only the children of the poor but of the middle class as well. They were children during the years of the war when the food blockade kept them half starved, when fathers were away at the front and mothers distracted with the effort to keep their families fed. They came to manhood in a country which seemed to have no use for them. Even compulsory military training was no more and there was nothing to take its place.

It is true that a number of movements were started by the younger generation, movements full of idealism, such as the volunteer service camps where both lads and girls gave months of unpaid, hard, physical work to the Fatherland. But hundreds of thousands of lads in the great industrial cities were not reached by these influences and grew up physically and mentally stunted, without hope or ambition or pride. A settlement worker told me that she knew families in which the children had come to manhood without ever realizing the connection between work and food. They had never had work, and food had come scantily and grudgingly from some governmental agency.

To these idle, hopeless youths two stirring calls to action came —one from the Communists, the other from Hitler; and to both of them German youth responded. Both appealed to hatred, both held out an ideal of a changed Germany, but Hitler's propaganda was cleverer than the Communists', because his program is narrower, more concrete. The Communist is internationally minded, his brothers are all over the world, his ideal State embraces all lands. Hitler repudiates internationalism; he is against all who are not German; his ideal State is a self-contained Germany, an object of fear to all her neighbors. The Communist is taught to hate a class, the capitalistic, the Hitlerite to hate each individual Jew. Many young Communists were brought under the banner of Hitler by appeals to national pride and race antagonism, but also by the ideal of a united Germany without class hatred.

Hitler made each insignificant, poverty-stricken, jobless youth of the slums feel himself one of the great of the earth, since the youth was a German, a Nordic, far superior to the successful Jew who was to be driven out of office and counting house to make place for the youth and his like. Hitler told the young men that the fate of Germany was in their hands, that if they joined his army they would battle with the Communists for the streets, they would see Jewish blood flow in streams, they would capture the government, deliver Germany from the Versailles treaty and then sweep triumphantly over the borders to reconquer Germany's lost land. He put them into uniforms, he taught them to march and sing together, he aroused that sense of comradeship and esprit de corps so precious to the young, and gave them what is even more precious—an object for hero worship. Life suddenly took on meaning and importance, with the call to danger, sacrifice, even death.

Among the hundreds of thousands who make up the audiences at Hitler's or Goebbels's meetings, and who seem to an outsider to be carried away by a kind of mass hysteria, there are many who are actuated by real idealism, who long to give themselves unreservedly to the great vision of a resurgent Germany. Being young they are of course contemptuous of the slow and moderate methods of the republic; they are for action, quick, arrogant, ruthless.

But their program calls for a changed Germany, one purged of all selfishness and materialism. They repudiate liberalism, for that means to them capitalism, it means the profit-making system, it means class distinctions, inequalities. The Germany the young are planning will have no division between the classes and will substitute the common good for individual profit. They really believe that Hitler will bring about a genuine socialism without class warfare and this part of their program is highly idealistic and fine, but, as is to be expected, it is mixed with the intolerance of youth, it calls for the forcible repression of opposition within the country and a battling front to be presented to the outside world. This is the outpouring of a student writing in the official organ of the Nazi students' league:

> A people organically united and filled with the spirit of sacrifice for the common good, strong and eager for battle. A people fused into an unconquerable fighting unit against a hostile world. This is what we must achieve in these incomparably important days. The millions who stand aside from our movement must be made to believe in it. He is a traitor who now holds back. Our revolution marches on, over saboteurs and counter-revolutionaries, whoever they be.

The students call for compulsory labor camps, to take the place of the voluntary six months' service which has been largely adopted during the last few years. They feel that the voluntary system is harmful, demoralizing, for it has in it the germ of an undisciplined spirit. What is needed is compulsory service, with strict discipline, and the groundwork for it is already laid; it is the fanatical will of the best of German youth to service for the nation and for the renewal of the Reich.

These labor camps are to be different from the old barracks, for here there is to be no distinction of social class, no more one-year service for the educated and two years for the sons of peasants and laborers; all are to be equal. They dream of a reform in the courts of justice which is to be brought about by requiring each candidate for the bar to serve for eight weeks in a labor camp, working shoulder to shoulder with men from all walks of life. In every way the barriers between workers and students must be abolished. "We must strive against intellectualism and liberalism which are Jewish. We wish to be red-blooded men. Students, show the peasant and worker that you are not intellectuals."

A typical appeal to German youth was made by the Reichscommisar for sport:

> Sportsmen and gymnasts! Fellow-countrymen of the same blood and the same home! Your hour has struck! Do not mistake the signs of the times, do not fail to join the powerful

forces of these historic hours in which we are now living. We have had enough of speeches and resolutions. Now for action, for battle under the stern discipline that deserves your confidence. Show that you recognize it as a holy duty to make free the road to unity among yourselves as also to unity in the nation. Embrace your German brothers who have been rendered rootless through the poison of Marxism.

But above all stands the command: The physical development of the people through sport and gymnastics shall not from now on languish under the weight of cowardly, slavish and internationally minded politics, but must aid in the struggle to make Germany a State powerful with the sword, and free to defend its boundaries within and without, a State that will win back its dignity in the eyes of the world. Adolf Hitler's Brown Shirts greet you, German sportsmen, and call you to common work for people and country.

And here is one of the songs which the boys and girls sing as they march through the streets.

Seest thou the morning red in the East, a promise of sun and of freedom? We hold together for life or for death, no matter what may threaten. Many a year were we slaves to traitor Jews, but now has arisen a son of the people—he gives to Germany new hope and faith. Brothers, to arms! Young and old flock to the hooked cross banner, peasants and workers with sword and with hammer. For Hitler, for freedom, for work and for bread. Germany, awaken! Death to the Jew! Brothers, to arms!

Never before had I been in a country where youth had taken the bit between its teeth and was running amuck—to mix metaphors. It is a rather uneasy experience. You may assure yourself that the youngsters in brown shirts are filled with devotion to their country, but you cannot help watching them nervously because you have no idea what they may do next, and if this is true of a foreign tourist, how much more is it true of German adults?

In spite of the strict censorship of the press, we heard many a bloody tale of the Storm Troopers, but we heard even more about their high-handed methods in business houses and in the universities. While we were in Berlin the struggle was going on between the Nazi students and the rector of the university. It was on the issue of academic freedom. The students had nailed up twelve theses in the entrance hall of the main building and refused to take them down at the command of the rector. These were the theses that called for the expulsion of all "non-German teachers," that demanded that Jews should write only in Hebrew and that repudiated "Jewish intellectualism."

One day during the Spring vacation, as students came and went in the big hall, I stood in front of the pillar and copied the theses in my notebook. It was a curious experience for an American. In one of our colleges the men and girls would have swarmed around the pillar, with eager comment, they would have called each other to come and read, they would have disputed noisily. These German students stole up behind me and read without more than a whispered comment, then slipped away.

It was only too clear that whatever group had put up the theses ruled the university, and there were proofs aplenty that this was true. The rector threatened to resign if the proclamation was not removed. He did resign and his successor declared himself to be unreservedly behind the Nazi student movement. The new "Cultusminister" soon afterward dissolved all student organizations and announced that there would be in the future one only, the Nazi students' league. He went on to praise the part played by the students in the revolution and to warn the faculties that they must no longer lag behind when youth led the way.

No wonder the students took things into their own hands, howled down the few Jewish professors who had received exceptional treatment because of war service, raided libraries, denounced suspected liberals right and left! The students of Kiel University demanded the discharge of twenty-eight professors. In Hamburg, when the university formally opened after the Spring holidays, a student arose and addressed the rector and faculty, telling them that any young Nazi was worth more to the Fatherland than the whole lot of them. His speech was received in silence.

Some two months later, also in Hamburg, a professor in the Medical School who was in the war and had declared himself an admirer of Hitler, was turned out of his position because a student reported that he had said something derogatory of the Nazis. The Berlin students undertook a "cleansing" of Magnus Hirschfeld's Institute of the Science of Sex. A procession of students in white shirts (for purity) drove to the institute in trucks bearing signs such as "German students march against the un-German spirit," and at a blare of trumpets they entered the library of the institute, seized books and pamphlets, threw them into the trucks and drove off. I suppose the books were consigned to the purifying flames.

All this seemed simply stupid and ugly and primitive to an American, an incomprehensible swing-back to a day when physical force was the only thing respected and men of thought shut themselves in monasteries and were not always safe there. But this is an aspect which the students with whom I talked could not see. They were passionately behind the new movement, the revolt against intellectualism, against scientific objectivity, against all that the German universities had stood for. The burning of the books was their work and they were proud of it.

This revolt of youth against modern education is a part of Hitler's program, for Hitler has long preached the necessity for a new pedagogy, one that is directed first toward physical prowess, then character training, while purely intellectual subjects are to be left for specialists. Herr Frick, Minister of the Interior, said while I was there: "The mistake of the past was for the school to train the child as an individual. This led, especially after the war, to the destruction of nation and State. We will supplant it by a training which will sink into the blood and flesh and cannot be uprooted for generations, a training which will fuse the German into his nation and bind him by the closest ties to his history and the destiny of his people."

The most important subject in the new curriculum is history, with the emphasis laid on German heroes, German inventors, German rulers, poets, artists. The German child must be taught that his nation is superior to every other in every field. Next to this comes politics and then everything that has to do with agriculture. Such subjects as mathematics and the physical sciences take a secondary place. Physical training and mental training find their culminating point in the last year, which is the year of compulsory service in labor camps. The training in these camps is military, for "defense warfare." For girls, education ends in a year of domestic service, with training for wifehood and motherhood.

Of course all the young men and girls accept Hitler's fantastic theories about "pure Germanism" and the superiority of the Aryan type, and that girl is most envied who can display two long braids of yellow hair. It is true that yellow hair and blue eyes are not as common in many parts of Germany as the Nazis could wish, but peroxide helps, and there is said to be a great demand for it now. It is a little ironical that the prophet of the Nordic religion should himself be black-haired and round-headed, a good example of the Alpine type he so despises.

In April, May and June youth was in the saddle in Germany, the Brown Shirts had their way with little interference; then, gradually, an effort to check open acts of violence began to be manifest, and now it is clear that independent action on the part of the Storm Detachments has been decidedly repressed. But they still constitute Hitler's army and are obedient to his voice; and this is not the voice of an adult man but of a youth who has never really grown up.

In his autobiography and in his voluminous speeches Hitler reveals himself as a man with the ambitions, the ideals, the crudities and the virtues of the adolescent. His physical courage and daring are those of the perfect soldier; he cares nothing for ease and comfort; he adores display, applause; he worships force and despises persuasion and mutual concession; he is intolerant of dissent, convinced of his own absolute rightness, and ready to commit any cruelty to carry out his own will.

It is this violent, fanatical, youthful despot, backed by some millions of like-minded youths, who now rules Germany. Truly it is a new thing in the world—a great modern country submitting itself to the will of its young men.

The Tune Hitlerism Beats for Germany

by Miriam Beard

THE OUTSTANDING FEATURE of the Hitler movement in Germany is not the emergence of a powerful personality, a new dictator for Europe; it is the practice in politics, on a scale never before witnessed in that country, of all the arts of mass-suggestion. And in this new technique, which, whatever the destiny of the "Nazis," will remain a permanent contribution of far-reaching consequences, observers detect a leaning toward Chicago as well as Rome.

In shirts, salutes and flags, of course, Germany's new national socialism resembles Italy's seasoned fascism; its standards are topped with Roman eagles; its leader, Hitler, was a former house painter, as Mussolini was, for a time, a mason. But such likenesses are accidental and merely picturesque; the differences are acute and fundamental. Though the brown of Hitler's apparel may seem close to the black favored by the Duce, a whole spectrum of divergencies parts the two leaders. Hitler keeps a picture of the Italian on his desk, but in his book, "My Battle," reveals long study of the speeches of Lloyd George, and American advertising and war-propaganda methods.

Not so mysterious as the word fascism might connote was the

From the *New York Times Magazine,* June 7, 1931, copyright © 1931, 1959 by The New York Times Company.

upset last September, when the National Socialists became the second largest group in the Reichstag. It meant that the village had been mobilized as never before in Germany; that small-town mentality, much the same the world over, met a master analyst; that a medley of disillusioned women, theological students, peasants, the growing hordes of big-city office workers, dispossessed "rentiers" and "white-collar" men, once the most stable and now the most insecure element, were fused together by new means. The earnest, solid arguments of everyday German politicians were outdone by a glittering array of orators, who worked on the public, through a tenor voice or a light blue limousine, and proffered a rainbow program to suit everybody. In this biggest show ever offered to German voters, learned Germans traced the precepts of Machiavelli, but others, more traveled, see the hand of Big Bill Thompson, or mutter "Barnum und Bailey."

Propaganda cannot be held responsible for all the Nazi success. This is perhaps a "crisis phenomenon" more like American know-nothingism than fascism and may dwindle, as it once before fell after the inflation period. And there are other signs that the German masses, so monumentally patient during hunger, inflation, invasion and accusation, are beginning to show human symptoms of strain. Some of these are startling to German observers, but familiar to the America of booms and revivals. There was a strange witchcraft trial. An alchemist, promising to make gold enough to pay off the war debt, caught the savings of hundreds. A revivalist, curing the faithful by prayer and cream cheese, swept Berlin. And at the head of masses already in motion Hitler had but to set himself, exclaiming: "The crowd is only there to carry the leader!"

The richest store of racial and local types of any one country in Europe is undoubtedly to be found in Germany; they range from the Baltic to the Bavarian, the Prussian to the Saxon and all shades between, including pure freak. But Hitler was the first to play so deftly upon so much of that diversity. He knew—and frankly explains it—that while some may be roused by earnest talks on finance and agriculture, many are set vibrating best by mention of Wotan and Valhalla, a denunciation of African jazz, or a crusade against flat roofs as symbols of insidious Orientalism among Germany's peak-tops.

Some are attracted by membership contests with cameras as prizes; some by brass bands, or slogans like "Heads Must Roll!" or "With Sword and Plow to Freedom!" Gooseflesh can be raised on many by whispers of Freemasonry and allusions to the cabalistic significance of the number of the radiowave over which Pope Pius XI spoke for the first time on the air. Others are more interested in the banning of cubism than of communism. To alarm yet others the ghosts of long-laid racial passions must be called forth to stalk again the dark lanes of medieval towns. And all parties, republicans and aristocrats, are pleased by the Nazi formula: "A good republic is better than a bad monarchy and a good monarchy is better than a bad republic."

Such a complexity cannot be represented by any one man, as Mussolini symbolizes Italy. Hitler, Austrian by birth, is southern in sympathy. Though his party's strength lies in the north, he seldom speaks there, shuns Berlin and prefers to live in the citadel of his clerical enemies, Munich, whose artistic atmosphere, he says, lends the glamour of a Mecca or a Rome to his movement. He himself has written a book on art, designs all emblems and badges for his troops and is renovating as party home the magnificent, costly Barlow Palace, called the Brown House now. Revolting Nazis, from the less genial Berlin, quarrel over the great expenses of the new mansion and assert that the dictator in Hitler is swallowed by the decorator.

The appeal of the Nazis is less personal, then, and more romantic than that of the Fascisti. While fascism exalts the State, the Nazis find a surer sensation in race and turn for source-material not to Italy but to the American Lathrop Stoddard to supplement their own professorial "race researchers." Though fascism accepts modern industry, the Nazis glorify the precapitalistic, hand-worker age. Hitler is nebulous; he sways enormous crowds not by programs but by sermons on love and destiny.

Whereas Mussolini evokes visions of ancient Rome and world-ruling Augustus, Hitler's slogan, "The Third Empire," recalls that folk-longing, through the war-torn Middle Ages, for a utopian unity and the figure of Barbarossa waiting in a mountain cavern, as legends say, for the millenium. Out of the past the Italian draws a challenge; the Austrian summons a nostalgia. The one refers to

a classic noonday; the other to a Nordic twilight. The one points
to a fulfillment and the other to a dream.

Sociological rather than political are many of the rousing con-
troversies Hitler raises. He has provoked a veritable inky storm
by his analysis in his book of the "analphabets" whom he despises
and, once in power, proposes to disfranchise. He proclaims his
own insight into the mass-soul, believing that, had his government
used him in the war, not at the front but behind it as propaganda
chief, he might have turned the tides. He promises "in the year
1931 to show what propaganda is." Maintaining that the masses
have never been properly understood and mobilized before in
Germany, he challenges the "ink knights," the theorizers, to combat. When four leading economists sent him a letter disputing his
financial schemes, he replied only: "Where are your storm troops?
Go on the street, go into folk meetings and try to see your stand-
point through. Then we'll see who is right—we or you." Proclaim-
ing a "revolt against reason," crying "Intellect has poisoned our
people!" the Nazis trumpeted activism, intuition as higher values.
"Who conquers the street conquers the State," announced Goebbels. "We need a superfluity of national fanaticism!" cried Hitler.
And the National Socialist Minister of Braunschweig boasted that
one could look in vain for reason and logic in the Nazi program.

Men—young men—swell the Hitler movement; three-quarters
of its Reichstag delegation are young. The schools, hot-beds of
politics, turn to him; recent student elections showed great Nazi
gains in every one of eighteen colleges. Bored farm boys are attracted; slum youths, better read, a survey shows, in Jack London
than Goethe; university students, chiefly of the first semesters,
who are not all solemn owls either. Indeed, the University of Er-
langen reports that the books most in demand last year at its library
were—another American touch—the Red Indian tales of Karl
May. To such, Hitler politics seem but a natural extension of
Pawnee warfare. And they are captured by a philosophy that rolls
the Superman, the Front Soldier, William Tell and Hiawatha all
into one.

Now that the guitar music of the comradely, sentimental Youth
Movement has died away, and now that "inflation period youth,"
more bewildered, more "thirsty for the deed," than the war generation, comes on the scene, the stage is set for the Nazis. For all

youth "out of a system" as well as a job, they offered activism, glorifying blind activity. Goebbels, the Berlin leader, describes in his semi-autobiographical novel a model refutation of an enemy propagandist: "Now I seize him by the gullet. I hurl him to earth. * * * I crash in his skull with my foot. And now I am free!" And Hitler caps it all by promising that in the Third Empire education will consist of religion, hero stories and gymnastics.

The redskins, thus urged, went on the warpath. They let loose white mice in theatres; crashed shop windows; ambushed political opponents with paving stones and pitchforks, leaving scores wounded; treated many an old Rathaus to scenes of inkstand-throwing; beat up a pastor and a few artists and helped roll up last year's total of 300 political murders. Great cities were terrorized until the recent emergency measures; even such a slumbering village as Grossgeschwenda was awakened by terrific booms to find youngsters experimenting in a barn with primitive cannon. Chair legs became a favored argument—at one Berlin meeting 500 chairs and several skulls were crushed—so that in some places all chairs are ordered lashed together at meetings. And the beer mug, once a symbol of German Gemütlichkeit, was turned to such a political weapon that some East German village elders ordered inn keepers to supply beer at all rallies only in papier-mâché mugs.

Especially villages have been awakened by the Nazis, a phenomenon portentous in Germany. Rural, not city, districts are their strongholds. Peasants from the Dutch to the Danish border rolled up their votes. More thoroughly than any party before, they combed the countryside. Many a village had never seen a political meeting till Hitler gave it one with a riot for side show. Plenty of places in Mecklenburg and Holstein, says a writer, had "only three links with the outside world—the telephone, the State forester, and the Nazi pamphlets."

But the ink-knights have taken up the gauntlet. Political oratory, never developed in Germany so highly as in England, is now to the fore; Social Democrats opened a school for training orators specifically to counteract the wonderful working forensics of the Hitler men. Pamphleteers, trying to write "popular" leaflets, ask themselves, "Can we reach the same masses without the same methods?" Articles fill the press on "The Unknown Folk," or the "subjectively under-conscious," which is the intricate German definition of what Americans, in their abrupt and hasty way, dismiss as "morons." For whatever the National Socialists have done, they have made the moron front-page news and political advertising an issue.

Most puzzling—as usual—is woman. Why does she vote for a group that intends to take the ballot from her? Why does she support anti-feminism? How are we to account for the fact that in nine cities where the sexes voted separately, last Autumn, more women than men voted for the Nazis? In Greater Berlin the proportion was 204,122 to 191,866.

Post-war disillusionment accounts for something. One woman spoke for many of her sisters when she expressed reaction against extreme feminism, glorifying sport and economic struggle; she was wearily glad to "sit back" and let the men lead on to the millennium.

The martial appeals to many types. Brown shirts seem more dashing now that uniforms are scarce in Germany; the Reichswehr members, in their twelve years of service, owing to lack of funds, find it difficult to marry. Women Nazis wear leather caps with chin straps, often receive the woman's decoration of the Red Swastika and learn to give the salute, "Hail, Hitler!" with outstretched arm.

Avowed enemies of feminist pretensions are the National Socialists. Perhaps the clearest statement of their position was made by the economic expert of the party, Gottfried Feder, who denounced sex democracy: "We young men must sally forth and slay the dragon, in order to return to the holiest thing that the earth knows—the woman who is maid and servant. The way, the will, the goal are called National Socialism."

Such arguments appeal readily to jobless men, wishing women's places in offices and factories. And they find echo in Denmark, for the National Socialist party founded last year in Copenhagen aims to exclude women from Parliament because, as the melancholy Danes declared, they "completely lack the naked brutality necessary for political achievement." What weighs more heavily in party councils is the restiveness of men who see what the enfranchisement of women, so greatly in the majority since the war, is doing to defeat masculine tastes.

Dreaming in their broad land of dikes and windmills, stood

the Holstein villages, with their huge, steep roofs of thatch and little blinking windows. Picturesque—and bored. Suddenly appeared a car of rollicking Nazi youths, with flaming placards, and made them a speech, cursing the high rates of interest, praising blue eyes, referring to Odin and "our boys lost in the war," and ending: "Germany ought to be more than a police-regulation machine, more than a State; it ought to be a home—sweet magic word, redolent with the fragrance of the furrow."

Small towns thrilled to the trumpets of the Third Empire. On them, not the proletariat, rests the Nazi movement; of the eleven most enthusiastic urban districts last September only one was a big city and the rest markedly non-industrial. And the program offered all a small-towner could very well ask: away with industry, away with big cities and their immoral habits, away with proletariat. Bind everybody by law to his home spot. Return to small towns and the handicraft age.

The élite of the small town was considered. Armyless officers were offered new folk regiments to lead. Evangelical pastors could join a large league. Teachers, in Germany chiefly men, were invited to become culture dictators in the Third Empire. Where the Nazis ruled for a time in Thuringia they ousted republican textbooks, banished modern art works from the museum as "not according with Nordic essence," and, in a Nazi pedagogical newspaper, planned the refashioning of Grimm's fairy tales as allegories of the oppressed dolichocephalics, thus making converts to Hitler in kindergartens.

Perhaps the Nazi master stroke was a solution of the building problem. Other parties have long wrangled over loans, subsidies, costs and legal entanglements—old-fashioned arguments that drove voters to despair. But a new day in propaganda dawned when the Hitler agitators, without harrying their audiences by such technicalities, simply and quietly handed out sheets printed with beautiful sketches and ground plans of the ideal two-family dwelling with six rooms, bath, garden and "attic space that may later be transformed into another room." Here was something tangible in the fog. The folk went home clutching the precious documents. And, if women outnumbered men in the rush to the polls, it was perhaps because they firmly believed that in the Third Empire there would be enough closet space for all.

Again Germans Look to the Reichswehr

by Emil Lengyel

FROM THE TOP of an omnibus on Berlin's Unter den Linden one
sees steel helmets bobbing up and down with machinelike reg-
ularity, beating the rhythm to the strains of a band that leads the
way. As the small detachment swings into Wilhelmstrasse the
young men in the ranks look like automatons, so perfectly are
their movements timed. A sharp command, and they thrust their
feet as high as if they were the ballet of the Berlin Opera. There
are proud smiles on the faces of those who watch the noontime
change of guards in front of the President's palace, for this is the
German Reichswehr, the country's pet and hope.

It was this Reichswehr which, after President von Hindenburg's
death, took the oath: "I swear by God this holy oath that I will
give unqualified obedience to the Leader of the German Government and the German people, Adolf Hitler, as commander-in-
chief of the army * * * "

What thoughts crossed Hitler's mind when the leading generals
of the Reichswehr pledged unswerving loyalty? Did he remember
that, nearly 200 years before, King Frederick II, known to history
as Frederick the Great, had received the oath of allegiance from
the Prussian Army? Did he recall the scene some hundred and

thirty years later in the Hall of Mirrors of Versailles Castle, when Emperor Wilhelm I received the homage of his army, and remember that among those troops was a young lieutenant of the guard, Paul von Hindenburg? Did Hitler also recall how he, a young Austrian and a volunteer in the Bavarian regiment "List," swore allegiance twenty years ago to His Royal Majesty Ludwig III?

Adolf Hitler must surely have remembered that August day in 1914 when posters appeared on Munich's walls with the word "mobilization." The call to arms may have been a dismal message for many but it was one of hope for the house-painter Hitler, anxious to escape from uncongenial surroundings. His heart in his throat, he drew up a "most humble application" to the Bavarian King for permission to enter his army, even though the petitioner was a subject of Austria.

And there must have come to Hitler, on this day of memories, a vision of the years he spent in the trenches as a private and lance corporal, known as "Mad Adolf" because of his ravings about the way he would conduct a war. If he had suggested to his comrades then that in two decades he would be commander-in-chief of all the German armed forces, they would have felt in duty bound to report a serious case of lunacy to their superiors.

While spurs rattled and heels clicked in his honor Hitler must have remembered that other rattling some ten years before in front of Munich's Feldherrenhall. It was the rattling of Reichswehr machine guns that mowed down his men as he led them in a demonstration of revolt. And the Führer must have recalled how the Reichswehr which now rallied to his rule had been protected for years from the contagion of his message and how some of its officers had been sentenced to prison for professing themselves loyal Hitlerites.

Backed by the Reichswehr, Hitler is Germany's undisputed master. He has command of the instrument of national will without which no German government is firmly in the saddle. It is only now that his régime has been fully legitimatized.

What is the Reichswehr? What accounts for its strength as the supreme court of national approval?

It is one of the smallest armies a great country has ever had, but it is the best-drilled army in the Old World and it knows how to obey. For Germany it represents great traditions and strong national will, the inspiration of the past and the promise of the future. It is the potential instrument of rebellion against the "shame of Versailles"—the sword of retribution. Germany, though an impoverished country, has lavished all she has on the Reichswehr.

If the entire Reichswehr were assembled on Berlin's Tempelhof airfield, it would cover only a small part of the vast area. The Treaty of Versailles limited its size to 100,000 officers and men, less than one-seventh of the pre-war German Army. The reserves —legal and illegal—are probably not more than 200,000 strong. This force is supplemented by the militarized State police, the Schupo, authorized by the Allies some years ago to deal with internal disorder. In recent months the Hitler government has been increasing the Reichswehr's strength, partly as a bid for its good graces and partly as a gesture of defiance to the victors of the war.

It is at the manoeuvres of the German Army that the havoc wrought on it by the peace treaty is fully realized. The roar of heavy cannon is merely stage thunder, the lumbering howitzers are made of wood. Tiny automobiles, the "Hanomags," are made to play the part of heavy tanks, the planes that dip and rise, seeking to elude spurious anti-air-attack guns, are commercial craft, dropping flour bags instead of bombs.

At the peace conference the Allies laid down the law that Germany could have no heavy artillery, tanks, military airplanes, anti-aircraft defenses or poison gases, and that she could have only a limited number of her machine guns and light cannon. The Reichswehr was to be stripped of its offensive power and was to be made into "reserves for the maintenance of order in the country and the policing of its territory." For sixteen years the Germans have rebelled against these provisions; Hitler's march to the summit of power was largely a result of this rebellion.

If the Germans had carried out the Allies' ideas their army today would be unwieldy, the Versailles treaty having weighted it down with too much cavalry, and harmless because deprived of modern material. But the Reichswehr of today is recognized as a powerful instrument of war. Its position has been achieved through the most careful selection of its members and through its strong organization.

General Hans von Seeckt, father of the Reichswehr, proceeded on the theory that the war of the future would be decided not by quantity but by quality. In a book on national defense he says that "folly of numbers" which immobilized millions of soldiers in the World War will not be repeated. Instead, the future war will start with an attack by air armadas. Their first object will be to render useless the enemy's airfields, their next to destroy his air force. After that the air fleet will strike at the capital and the principal railway junctions in an effort to prevent mobilization of the army.

Then a small but compact army will invade the enemy's territory with utmost speed. "The value of this army increases with its mobility." It will strive to destroy the opposing forces with a view to quick peace. While this action is going on a general mobilization of the masses can take place.

Now let us see how Germany is equipped for the method von Seeckt suggests. While she is denied military airplanes by the treaty, she has the best commercial air force on the Continent and would be able to use it for the purposes described. As to the mobile force that sweeps into enemy land and tries to force a decision by its rapidity and technical superiority, the Reichswehr is ideally adapted for the role. It is an army of highly trained technicians, with its men serving for twelve-year periods and its officers for twenty-five. After such a period of intensive training any member in its ranks could take charge of a company if need arose.

It was with a chuckle that Grand Admiral von Tirpitz remarked about the post-war German Army: "Whether our enemies like it or not, we now have an army of 100,000 sergeants."

Viewing the men of the Reichswehr, as they march past, some may feel disappointed. Where are the giants of the Potsdam Guard of whom King Frederick William I was so proud? The leaders of the Reichswehr found that gigantic stature does not always make a good soldier. Experiment showed them that the best soldiers were those of medium height; actually 5 feet 5 inches is the preferred height of the Reichswehr man.

But height is by no means the sole gauge of fitness of a prospective recruit. His environment is studied with care. Army detectives check his habits and his words. If he is addicted to expressing political opinions freely he is disqualified. His physical skill, power of concentration, reliability and loyalty are tested.

The competition to enter the Reichswehr is great. There are said to be twoscore applicants for every vacancy. That is not only because the privates of the army receive good pay—about 50 cents a day, as compared with 1 cent in the French Army; what counts fully as much is the social prestige. The Reichswehr takes village boys as a rule—because city boys may harbor undesired political thoughts—and in the countryside the value of a young man in the love and marriage market rises when he wears a uniform. Beneath a shining helmet he is no longer a mere human cipher; he is the bearer of the national will, a member of the élite.

In the imperial army the recruits were treated as human raw material that had to be knocked into shape—and the knocking was sometimes done literally. In the Reichswehr the newcomer is drilled not only in the arts and crafts of warfare but also in self-confidence. He is made conscious of his role as a potential leader in a fight for national glory. It was General von Seeckt's idea that the soldier must be treated as the most sensitive machinery of the army.

As an important investment of the nation, the recruit must have his efficiency increased. He is therefore trained in some technical science, so that when he leaves the service he may be an expert in his line. He is also instructed in some agricultural pursuit, so as to foster his connection with the native soil. The State makes him a non-commissioned officer before he is discharged and takes an interest in him ever after. The graduates of the Reichswehr form a corps of national leaders in the German countryside. They are often used for instructing their neighbors in military sports.

The officers are mostly the cream of the old imperial army. About one-fifth of them belong to the nobility; the other four-fifths would like to belong. Under the republic the officers were suspected of being monarchists at heart. If they served the Weimar régime it was because it gave them a livelihood and because no other possibility offered. Perhaps they are for Hitler for the same reasons.

The Reichswehr is what the officers make it. They have their own rules, one of which is that a gentleman does not stoop to politics if he can avoid it. Yet the interests of the army must be safeguarded and the Reichswehr has always maintained a certain supervision over all that was going on in Parliament and the Ministries. That accounts for the inability of radical government, in the past, to carry out their ideas.

Though the Reichswehr constitutes only a small armed force for a nation of 65,000,000 people, its prestige is enhanced by a strong German feeling for the military. King Frederick William I liked to hold forth on the superiority of the rough Prussian soldier over the silk-clad marquis of the entourage of France's Kings. His son, Frederick the Great, entirely of his father's opinion, startled the world by pushing his uncouth country—barbarous, in the view of the generals of Versailles—to the front rank of great powers. He foresaw, as no other European commander did, the coming of an era of collective valor as against the individual heroism of the past; and he trained his army to feats of courage. That lesson has stuck.

Most present-day Germans are convinced that the fear, envy and admiration with which the world regarded the second empire —born at Versailles and dead at Versailles—could be laid to its incomparable war machine.

The army has become the epitome of those national traits which children are taught to acquire. The goose-step gladdens German hearts with its decisive precision. It betokens order, discipline, community action. It means not merely the pounding of the pavement by strong legs, but also a form of "Weltanschauung," a philosophy of life.

What has been the Reichswehr's role since Kaiser Wilhelm II took a special train to the Dutch frontier and left his army to its own devices? The German military leaders were far from being in a hurry to swear loyalty to the new republican rule. They sent their spokesmen to Berlin to make known their terms, which were accepted. Even then they gave their support with bad grace. It was many months before the Reichswehr placed a guard before President Ebert's official residence.

Instead of trying to break the Reichswehr's power the Socialist and semi-Socialist governments curried its favor. It was with the army's help that the Socialist Minister of National Defense, Herr

Noske, crushed the Communist Spartacist movement. Encouraged by such open admissions of weakness on the part of the new masters, a part of the old army rebelled in the Kapp putsch early in 1920; the putsch failed only because the majority of the Reichswehr held aloof.

A large number of Germans refused to abide by the peace treaty and continued to go to war against foreign enemy as well as domestic foe. Illegal army organizations sprang up and carried their grudges against the world to the Baltic countries. There they fought the Bolshevist Russians and, in default of them, their own allies. Then they transferred their activities to Upper Silesia, fighting the Poles. Large detachments formed free corps and sought to crush the Communists in the valley of the Ruhr.

Discontent lay at the roots of the redoubtable Black Reichswehr, which sought to end the republic's rule five years after it had begun. The attempt was crushed by the regular Reichswehr.

In the same year Bavaria threatened to secede from the Reich. She was in open rebellion, and Adolf Hitler prepared to march on Berlin. In that hour of danger the President gave dictatorial powers to von Seeckt, as head of the Reichswehr. Bavaria was soon silenced. Hitler was captured and imprisoned.

Bavaria's neighbor, Saxony, had a government composed of Socialists and Communists, which the Reichswehr did not like. Von Seeckt's troops marched into Saxony and the radical government was wiped out.

Since those turbulent days the Reichswehr has kept more or less in the background. Still, it had a finger in every political pie through General von Schleicher until the general was assassinated during the recent "purge" of the Third Reich, and through Colonel Oskar von Hindenburg, son of the late President.

The army's support of Hitler gives him strength. It indicates that the prospect of a revolt on the Junkers' side has become more remote, since the army has nearly always been the Junkers' hunting ground. If a revolt occurs it will probably originate from below, when the majority of Germans become definitely convinced that Hitler's Third Reich holds little hope for them.

Extremes Meet–
Against Hitler

by R. G. Waldeck

BEFORE ADOLF HITLER attained power in Germany, and ever since, European political observers have been speculating on the direction that National Socialism would take. Would it go Fritz Thyssen's way? Or would it go the way of Dr. Otto Strasser? These two men have come to be looked upon as the extremes between which the destiny of the Third Reich hangs suspended. Herr Thyssen's way was the way of Big Business, of the "steel barons" on the Rhine and Ruhr, of all men of property. Otto Strasser's way was the way of "German socialism," as he himself called it, or, as some said, of sheer bolshevism.

For some time it appeared Herr Thyssen had won out. Nazism, so the observers said, was a capitalistic plot. Then again it appeared as if the Third Reich was on the verge of going Socialist after Otto Strasser's fashion. The case is not yet clear. To make it more puzzling and more ironically significant, both Thyssen and Strasser are now exiles from Nazi Germany.

Fritz Thyssen, Germany's most powerful rich man, was the most potent single factor behind Hitler's struggle for power. Not long ago, until he openly expressed opposition to "the war and present policies of the Reich Government," he held 15 per cent

From the *New York Times Magazine,* March 3, 1940, copyright © 1940, 1968 by The New York Times Company.

of the total capital of the Vereinigte Stahlwerke. This enormous mining trust rules over 75 per cent of Germany's ore reserves, 50 per cent of its coal reserves, 200,000 workers, 60,000 workers' dwellings, 52 square miles of property, a railway network from Paris to Koenigsberg, 14 harbors and 219 power stations. Besides, Herr Thyssen was a member of the German Reichstag, a Prussian State Councillor, leader of the Amalgamated Union of West German Industry, Supreme State Authority for the Whole of West German Industry.

Fritz Thyssen's political creed fits into his belief in a strong Germany. This strong Germany, in his view, must be capitalistic, anti-Bolshevist and friendly with Great Britain. A war which pits Germany against England and which, as it proceeds, may possibly bring the Russians to the Rhine goes against his grain.

Herr Thyssen told the Fuehrer he believed that the outcome of this war could only be "Bolshevist chaos" all over Europe. In consequence Hitler presented him with the alternative of exile or a concentration camp and possibly violent death. Thyssen went to Switzerland, where he would be free to fight Hitlerism and try to organize a crusade against bolshevism. The Nazis confiscated some 300,000,000 marks of his German property.

Thyssen is now 66. Tall, dark, loosely hung, with heavy-lidded eyes, a slow shy smile, good hands, he does not look much like a tycoon. He looks like a grand seigneur with charm.

The tycoon of the family was Fritz Thyssen's father, August Thyssen. He built an industrial empire out of nothing, and lived in a forbidding castle which he peopled with enormous Rodin statues. Of his three sons, only the second, Fritz, was close to his heart. When, in 1926, he succeeded the old man, Fritz Thyssen was 53. No castle with Rodins for him; he lived in a serene villa of mere bourgeois proportions, bought works of art quietly and with taste. He would travel all the way from Muehlheim to Berlin to hear Furtwaengler conduct the Fifth symphony. He would write his friends in longhand. He had what the French call, "mesure," except that his fierce love of Germany knew no bounds.

Fritz Thyssen was the first of the big industrialists to join the Nazi party and to admit it. That was in 1929, and it was a daring thing to do. Thyssen believed in Hitler and liked Goering. These, he felt, were the "new men" to make the strong united Germany for which he longed.

"None of *us* can get the country out of this mess," he would say defiantly to apprehensive fellow industrialists. Smilingly he shrugged off that part of Hitler's program that advocated the persecution of the Jews and the churches. Hitler himself didn't mean it, he assured them. As to Hitler's socialism: Well, a leader of the masses on the make had to say many things. The revolution was to be a strictly national revolution, not a social one. He had Hitler's word for it.

Thyssen's persuasiveness smoothed Hitler's way in quarters which were naturally adverse to revolution. Hitler might have won against these quarters, but it was easier to win with them. By the time the Presidential elections of 1932 were under way the big industrialists contributed to Hitler's and not to Hindenburg's election funds. When, in November, 1932, the National Socialist party lost 2,000,000 votes and was broke, the big industrialists footed the bill for a last-minute effort. Fritz Thyssen alone is reported to have spent 3,000,000 marks on the Nazis in 1932.

Soon after Hitler reached power the reorganization of the Vereinigte Stahlwerke was carried out, in the course of which the Reich's holdings of Vereinigte Stahlwerke stocks were reduced from 80 per cent to 22 per cent. The liberals and radicals and especially Dr. Otto Strasser said that this just showed that Hitler had sold out to Fritz Thyssen.

Actually the move was a euphemistic gesture. Hitler wished the capitalistic world to believe at the time that Germany had sacred respect for the rights of property. The sight of a few very rich men, Thyssen among them, would make the illusion more complete while not changing the fact that in a totalitarian State everything belongs to the State whether the State has a financial stake in it or not. Hitler was not ready to divest the industrialists of their money, but he took their power away. Thyssen, though officially the economic dictator on the Rhine and Ruhr, was a glorified government clerk.

Eventually there were rumors of trouble. In 1936, when Thyssen spent some time in South America, some thought he had left Germany for good. His departure, it was said, followed an interview at which he and other big industrialists had handed a memorandum to Hitler. The Fuehrer was reported to have trampled the memorandum under foot and shouted angrily, in effect: "Did you saps really believe that I would go to all this trouble just to make Germany safe for the steel barons?"

It is a likely story. But it was not the government's heavy hand on the German economy that Thyssen resented so much as it was Hitler's persecution of the Jews and the churches. Fritz Thyssen had Jews among his friends and close business associates, and his father had been a devout Catholic. To Hitler's industrialist friend religious and racial persecution seemed a stupid and unnecessary degradation which was losing Germany the good-will of the world. He constantly warned of this. Hence he incurred Hitler's displeasure, which increased when Thyssen became too vocal against the Nazi-Soviet pact and the bringing on of war.

Dr. Otto Strasser, unlike Herr Thyssen, was among the earliest refugees from Nazi Germany. Recently the Gestapo, by alleging that he had organized the Munich bomb plot against Hitler, tried to put him in the light in which Stalin had placed Trotsky in Russia—that of a conspirator against the revolution.

Strasser, at 42, is a square, mild-mannered Bavarian. With his hair cropped close on his big, egg-shaped head, he is a German stepped out of a Low cartoon. He comes from a family of small officials and was a lieutenant in the World War.

Brought into the Nazi movement by one of its founders, his beloved and admired brother Gregor, Otto Strasser quarreled with Hitler in 1930, founded a secession movement, the Black Front, and prudently fled Germany after Hitler came to power in 1933. Gregor's death in the June purge of 1934 stirred him to white heat. He swears that the Black Front, still strong inside Germany, is a real danger to Hitler and that he, Otto Strasser, will be the leader of the "second revolution."

In the dramatic discussion between Hitler and Otto Strasser which preceded the secession, Otto Strasser accused Hitler of having betrayed the revolutionary aims of the party, and Hitler exasperated, shouted at Otto: "What you call socialism is pure Marxism, and your whole system is a writing-desk job and has nothing to do with real life." He also accused Otto of being "troubled with humanitarian feelings" and added that the masses wanted nothing but bread and amusement.

The part of Strasser's program that aroused Hitler's wrath and formed the basis of the Black Front was his concept of "German socialism" as a production-for-use economy which abolished private property and gave to all "Volksgenossen" a share in the ownership, direction and profit of the total economy according to capability and worthiness. Otto Strasser also believed in autarchy, which at that time Hitler thought could not be realized in a hundred years or so. Strasser favored an alliance with Russia, on the ground that, since it was interested neither in capitalism nor in the status quo, it was the natural helper of Germany. At that time Hitler believed in friendship with England.

Yet there was much in which Strasser saw eye to eye with Hitler. He shared, for instance, the concept of a German Middle Europe which was to include Austria and the Sudetenland and to form a customs union with Hungary. Nor did the thought that this German Middle Europe couldn't come about except by a war against the powers of Versailles keep him awake at night. "A people never wins its freedom back in any other way than by war," says he.

Strasser's view of the racial question was basically the same as Hitler's. He, too, considered the Jews as foreigners in Germany who had to be segregated from German life, but, contrary to Hitler, he was unaggressive about it. Lately, under the influence of world reaction to Hitler's anti-Semitic policy, he has favored giving the German Jews minority status and has even ventured that a few, a very few, Jews might "pass" into the German people.

Strasser insisted strongly on the need of revolution. Yet he had a way of devitalizing the revolution so that it struck his hearers as an eminently reasonable enterprise. It was this way of his that, in the two years before Hitler came to power, made him the Horst Wessel of the literate.

"I'm afraid we'll have to shoot you, Mr. X," Otto Strasser would say at a soiree, bowing politely in the direction of a famous Jewish lawyer. And Mr. X would beam back at him as if he had been promised a medal. You just couldn't see this nice Bavarian, who could talk like a Heidelberg professor, making heads roll.

A dialogue today between Fritz Thyssen and Dr. Otto Strasser, both in exile, might contain the following:

Strasser: That alliance between Big Business and Nazism was a mistake, wasn't it?

Thyssen: It certainly was. Say, it must be hard on you to see that Hitler carries out all your Bolshevist ideas, but in his own way.

Whether Herr Thyssen or Otto Strasser or both will ever play a role in Germany again depends on the development of the Nazi revolution and on the peace. The Black Front, which absorbed many malcontent Nazis of the revenge-for-Roehm variety, may come into its own if and when the Nazi revolution should slip from the hands of the present leaders and make a left turn.

Recently Strasser's name figured prominently in the speculations of refugee-politicians and even of conservative British and French circles who worry about a successor for the Fuehrer. This serves as another illustration of Otto Strasser's strange charm for the bourgeoisie.

As for Thyssen, he still is the recognized leader of German Big Industry. For the present terror may prevent his opposition from becoming the signal for the revolt of the "steel barons" against the regime, but any new regime, unless it is Bolshevist, will call him back to Germany.

Meanwhile, both men, from their knowledge and experience, could make a useful contribution to the struggle against Hitlerism. Is this not the era of the renegade? Former OGPU agents become Crown witnesses of liberalism. Former Fascist and Communist fellow-travelers tell it to Mr. Dies. There is no limit to what can become of two sadder and wiser Nazis.

The Man Who Backed Hitler

by George N. Shuster

I PAID HITLER. By Fritz Thyssen.
New York: Farrar & Rinehart, Inc. $2.75.

FRITZ THYSSEN is no doubt one of Hitler's most spectacular victims. Deluded, disillusioned, self-exiled, and now probably dead at the hands of the Gestapo, this powerful German industrialist of yore supported the Nazi movement not merely with money but also with considerable idealism. He was a conservative Catholic gentleman—no empty-headed, vainglorious adventurer like Franz von Papen, but a person of substance and some wit, who had a seat of honor in both church and State. What induced him to support the Nazis? And what caused him ultimately to turn over to Emery Reves a volume of memoirs which, for all its faults, is one of the most effective indictments of Hitler so far published?

The essentials of the story are soon told. Together with his abler father, Thyssen witnessed the revolutionary turmoil which followed the defeat of 1918. This upheaval was a piddling affair, but there was always the danger that it could develop into something truly portentous; and fear lest it might, that "Bolshevism" was just around the corner, was so mighty in Thyssen's soul that he believed everything he heard about it, even in the end Goering's story of the Reichstag fire. The Social Democrats were, he thought, too weak to cope with such a menace. In addition there was the threat from the outside. Thyssen was a die-hard. The Treaty of Versailles should not have been signed. Germany could fulfill neither it nor the stipulations of the Dawes and Young Plans. When the Center party bowed to the inevitable, Thyssen left it and veered to the extreme conservative right. He took a large part in the organization of "passive resistance" in the Ruhr Valley following the French "invasion" of 1923. Characteristic of this period were his patriotism and his inability to grasp anything of what the labor groups were trying to do. When he discusses the resistance to France in the Ruhr, he takes all the credit and does not so much as mention the fact that the trade unions bore the lion's share of the burden. This is not dishonesty or mere egotism. It was sheer inability to realize the fact that trade unions exist.

Then in 1928 Thyssen met Rudolf Hess, having been introduced by old Herr Kirdorf, a coal magnate who combined a truly Gargantuan ignorance of politics with a sublime faith in his recipes for Germany's political improvement. Thyssen paid off the debts outstanding on Hitler's Brown House in Munich, getting from Hess an I. O. U. which that gentleman never honored. He was introduced to Goering, and financed that gentleman's household. It seems to have been Goering who presented Hitler, thus paving the way for the Fuehrer's historic speech of Jan. 27, 1932, which so charmed the assembled Rhenish-Westphalian industrialists that thereafter the Nazi war chest was filled to the brim. Thyssen says that he himself gave the Nazis a million marks—at that time about a quarter of a million dollars. Other magnates were similarly generous, but prior to the final triumph of the party most of the sums passed through the hands of Herr Hugenberg, then the majordomo of the Conservatives.

In performing these deeds of almost incredible generosity, Thyssen was actuated by a desire to set up a corporative society in Germany, since in his view this was a panacea for all ills; and he quite naively fancied that nothing was dearer to brown-shirted hearts than just such a society. The memoirs are unfortunately incomplete at this point, but it is possible to make out that the dream which haunted Thyssen's mind had been created by Professor Othmar Spann, a Viennese professor who expounded a grandiose theory of "organic" social organization. The man who initiated Thyssen into the mysteries of the Spann State was, ironically enough, arrested when Austria was annexed and is still languishing in a concentration camp. From the beginning, however, men high in the Nazi party had little use for either Thyssen or Spann. Probably they, in particular Hess and Goebbels, saw to it that Thyssen did not attend the fateful dinner at the house of Von Schroeder, the Cologne banker, which afforded Papen his chance to manoeuvre Hitler into the Chancellorship of Germany.

When the Nazi victory was finally assured, Thyssen was rewarded with a seat in the new Reichstag and a promise from Hitler that the corporative system was to be established "within eight days." But nothing came of it, and Thyssen gradually awoke to the fact that he had been fooled. The rest of the book is concerned with expounding the magnitude of his delusion and with the spell which was cast on others. It is easy to shake one's head at the narrative of imposture and banditry which is unfolded, but the man who wrote these pages dipped his pen into his heart's blood. Thyssen had, for instance, known Goering when he lived with his first wife in a small Berlin flat. And he was to know him also as the man who finally won unlimited access to Hitler's presence by murdering scores of men in the purge of 1934; who rifled museums, stores and private homes of art treasures with which to grace his numerous establishments; and who finally turned the Prussian State into his own private concern, badly managed and riddled with graft. Nevertheless, Goering remains, as so many have remarked, the best of a bad lot.

It was what happened to religion, however, that most deeply wounded the extraordinary man who writes this book. The pogroms, which nobody wanted; the assaults upon the Protestant faith; the weakness of some industrialists and other influential men, who abandoned the church because they fancied the Nazis wished them to do so—all these things surprised and angered Thyssen. But how could he witness with anything short of despair the systematic attempt to destroy the Catholic faith of the Rhineland? I should imagine that on this subject he is a bringer of unimpeachable testimony. Other observers may be dismissed as liberals, political exiles, intellectuals and whatever other title is convenient. But here is a delightfully arch-conservative pillar of society, who wanted to be a Nazi and could not because in addition to being a manifestation of bottomless cruelty and stupidity, Nazism was a sacrilege.

Finally, with war threatening and his son-in-law dead in a concentration camp, Thyssen left Germany. He dispatched a letter to Goering demanding that his vote as a member of the Reichstag be cast against war, destined in his view to destroy the Fatherland. But the intermediary official who was supposed to deliver the missive was afraid to do so. Instead Dr. Albert Voegler of the United Steel Works and Hitler's inner circle, came to Switzerland in the hopes of inducing Thyssen to return home and destroy all copies of his letter. The answer was negative. Believing that Germany must inevitably lose the war, Thyssen was fated to witness the crushing defeat of France and to be left with his back to the wall somewhere in a region combed by the Gestapo. Thus ends as amazing, as interesting and as characteristic a tale as our tragic era has produced. It is the story of a Europe which has gone forever because it sacrificed its many virtues to its narrowness of mind. I shall add that these memoirs would have been a better gift to the world had they not been wrapped in the cloths which encumber them. Of Mr. Reves's introduction one can say only that most of it should never have been written, for reasons which will probably be obvious to the reader. And concerning the "Historical Notes" I shall say only that their quality is well illustrated by the fact that the former Chancellor of Germany is referred to in them as "Hermann" Bruening.

Man of Steel Who Looms Behind Hitler

by Emil Lengyel

BEHIND THE DRIVE on the Nazi radicals, which so recently stirred
the world, there looms the figure of Fritz Thyssen, one of Germany's most powerful industrialists. In the conflict between Right
and Left, the Nationalistic and Socialistic aspects of the National
Socialist party, his view has won. Hitler's Third Reich is Thyssen's Germany. Thyssen's gifts are those of the will rather than
of the intellect, and so obstinately can he pursue his way and so
effectively can he impose his views on the nominal leaders of the
Reich that Hitlerism today cannot be understood without refer-
ence to this industrial magnate.

As head of Germany's most powerful industrial concern, the
United Steel Works, Thyssen is in good years the ruler of 170,000
workers. He is a personal friend of Adolf Hitler, of whose views
he was the first sponsor among the owners of Germany's heavy
industries. On the Nazi roll of honor he is the only prominent
living industrialist, "a pioneer and champion of New Germany."
As the economic dictator of Rhenish Westphalia's coal and iron
realm, he wields a large executive power. As a member of the
Reich's Grand Economic Council and Prussia's State Council he
is officially a Nazi brain-truster. But his influence is said to be

From the *New York Times Magazine,* July 22, 1934, copyright © 1934,
1962 by The New York Times Company.

even larger in the shadow of the throne, where whispers count for more than shouts and a hint avails more than a word of command.

Thyssen walks with an academic slouch and he has an air of meditation. Addicted to shutting himself up in his ivory tower even in the midst of company, he looks more like Germany's fabled absent-minded scholar than like a leading industrial magnate. His eyes, under broadly arched brows, look surprisingly candid, though it is not easy for outsiders to establish contact with the mind behind them. His neutral smile—his subordinates say—has a way of turning sour without intermediary stages. He likes to sink into himself and his lips are chary of words. But when he does speak, his words are dry and categorical—a sentence on a judge's lips.

He spends endless hours in his office at the headquarters of Vereinigte Stahlwerke (the United Steel Works), in Muehlheim, on the Ruhr. His desk is clear, his calendar exact, interviewers come and go on schedule. A word, a telephone call, settles thorny questions; efficiency and promptitude are the mottoes prominently displayed. A heavily padded conference chamber is the inner shrine, where Nazi chieftains drop in and lower their voices to words of confidence. Fritz Thyssen is not the typical magnate of the Ruhr Valley, covering countless pads with figures of tons of steel. He is the statesman-industrialist, who deals in politics and also in war and peace.

Is he a man of supreme intelligence to have achieved such prominence? He has "Bauernschlauheit," peasant's cunning, neighbors will say, and of course, as all the world knows, his father, August Thyssen, was the genius of the Ruhr. From his father he inherited an indomitable will to power and a bent of mind that refuses to acknowledge defeat. To the fact that Thyssen is a single-minded man is attributed his success so far. Beset by such difficulties as he faced three years ago, a man with more imagination would have thought his plight hopeless. Thyssen did not, and he acted accordingly. In Hitler he saw a man whom he could guide in the maze of economic problems in which der Führer—according to his own admission—was completely lost. Thyssen expected rich rewards for being the financial adviser of the Nazi Third Reich.

This industrialist is just past 60. Until a few years ago he lived his life in the shadow of the powerful personality of his father. August Thyssen was "der alte Herr," the old gentleman, to thousands of his employes, but to the world he was a giant of steel, one of the great pioneers of German industry, a missionary of efficiency and rationalization.

Starting with little, August Thyssen built the powerful Thyssen concern, of which at first he was not only the owner but also director, stenographer, bookkeeper, technical expert and commercial traveler. On a cow-house in an outlying part of Muehlheim was written the proud word: "Contor." There the iron and steel work empire of the Thyssens had its humble origin.

August Thyssen was considered an eccentric. He was prodigiously thrifty, and as he did not want to spend money on street cars he had the heels of his shoes reinforced with iron to prevent their being worn off. Day or night made little difference to him; he was continually at work improving processes of production. First he began buying up coal fields in the Ruhr, then iron-ore concessions in German Lotharingen, in French Lorraine, in Northern France. He branched off into Normandy and spread southward as far as Morocco and Algiers. He was a devotee of the "vertical" concern, which exploits its own raw materials and carries them through to their final stage in its own plants. He had his own cement factories, electric power stations, railway lines and vessels. In less than half a century the number of his employes had risen to about 25,000.

He was now Germany's steel king, and so proud was he of his power that he refused to have dealings with the German court. Although he was jealous of the Krupp works, Germany's official ammunition makers, he made no effort to replace Friedrich Alfred Krupp in the Emperor's affection. To suggestions that he present himself at court he liked to answer that his clothes were shabby, and when it was said that he could well afford to buy new clothes he simply answered that the thought had never occurred to him and there the matter rested.

Of August's three sons Fritz was the only one to show an interest in business. After finishing his university studies he got a high chair in the factory "Contor," and a salary of 50 marks a month, with nothing for overtime. His regular work over, Fritz was called into his father's combination study and experimental shop to learn the intricacies of the business.

The workers called him now "der junge Herr." The old gentleman, the young gentleman and the thousands of employes led a patriarchal life. August Thyssen was the father of his workers, which in an old-fashioned German home meant that he was an autocrat. He had houses built for them, but he would not tolerate socialism, which he considered a criminal movement. He and his son ate "wurst" and drank cheap beer in the company of their workers. On Sundays they went to mass in one of the churches he had built.

The World War boomed the Thyssen steel works, which became one of Germany's principal ammunition factories. Then came the morning after, and the French marched into the Ruhr. The industrial magnates of the region decided to compromise with the inevitable, but not so the Thyssens. The head of the firm was now past 80, but he was still packed with energy and vigor. The Thyssens refused to comply with French commands and Fritz was court-martialed. Before his French judges he proclaimed his faith in Germany's cause and refused to bow his head to the military masters. He was sentenced to a prison term and when he was led away by armed guards his father told him loudly that this was the proudest day of his life.

The Ruhr occupation over, Fritz became the sole master of his father's realm. The new ruler was of a different cast and so were his subjects. Fritz Thyssen no longer ate wurst and drank beer in the company of his workers. It was in a motor car that he was driven to his Castle Landsberg on the Ruhr. This large Wilhelminian structure on top of a hill symbolized the Thyssen power.

Nor were the subjects of the Thyssen realm like those with whom old August had trudged to church. A revolution had swept patriarchy out of the way, and Germany was a republic. The factory owner was no longer the father of his flock, but the capitalist whose power had to be shorn in the interests of social justice, labor's representatives said. Factory councils now claimed a share in the management and social legislation stripped Fritz Thyssen of August Thyssen's old autocratic power. He tried to stem the tide with tight-lipped obstinacy, and thereby he aroused much resentment. If business was bad it was because of the Socialists, he insisted. "They are our greatest enemies," he told his colleagues, the magnates of the Ruhr.

Thyssen now went into politics. Many of his neighbors were supporting the People's party, which stood for the republic and peace with honor. Thyssen began a drive both on the republic and peace. In the Weimar régime he saw the perpetuators of the "shame of Versailles" and the upholders of what he called the Socialist and Communist rule.

The French he had never liked, especially after the courtmartial at which he was sentenced. He transferred his personal grievance to the nation and demanded a strong-hand policy. In the resurrection of imperial Germany he saw hope for a new age in which the capitalist would be the master and the Socialist outlawed. He joined the Nationalist party, which was monarchist and reactionary, as strong an advocate as he of stamping out the Red danger. He became an angel of the nationalistic Stahlhelm, steel helmet organization, which believed in war as a cure for German ills.

Conditions went from bad to worse. Some of Germany's largest steel companies merged in the "Vereinigte Stahlwerke," of which Thyssen was the nominal head. The economic tornado hit Europe, steel was blown out of its place of prominence, and Thyssen's position in the steel union was jeopardized. Other men, more elastic and productive of new ideas, were contending for his place. Otto Wolff, an upstart in Thyssen's eyes, used his connections with the then ruling Catholic Centre party to bolster his position.

The crash of 1931 brought German industry to the brink of bankruptcy. Thyssen was even harder pressed than his competitors because of family reasons. One of his brothers, Heinrich, demanded settlement of the estate and Fritz took over his share at a high price. Meanwhile, the Bourse collapse had caught steel in its vortex and Thyssen found himself in a desperate situation.

It was then that he embraced National Socialism. He speculated on the success of Hitler and was ready to give him a helping hand. The masses were turning to the Austrian spellbinder for exactly the same reason—they had tried nearly everything and here was a new device. If Hitler could get the industrialists behind him, who could stop his march to victory?

To many magnates of the Ruhr, National Socialism was a suspicious spiritual fare. In what respect would they be better off if they exchanged a vigorous National Socialism for a tame international socialism? Did not the Hitlerites preach the end of the capitalistic era?

Thyssen sought to dispel these fears. "It is the national aspect of the movement that is important," he said. He saw the battle between the Socialist and the Fascist State; he regarded the Fascist State as one that in a crisis would take measures to bring order and then restore economic freedom when the crisis had passed.

Hitlerism promised to scrap the Versailles treaty. It preached defiance against the former enemies. It depicted the peacefulness of the republic as cowardice and the belligerence of the coming Third Reich as courage. A Hitler government was bound to arm Germany, and that would be good business for the steel barons. It would be an authoritarian government, and that would be bad business for the Socialists. Hitler knew nothing about economics and to advise him in such matters would be good business for any one quick enough to grasp a golden opportunity.

It was thus that National Socialism penetrated the padded doors of the boards of directors of the Rhine and Ruhr. Quietly, with dispassionate intensity, Thyssen explained to his colleagues what they might expect from Hitler's rule. There was conviction in his words and he got together a group of capitalists that contributed millions to the election treasury of a so-called Socialist party.

In January of last year a supposedly secret conference took place in the house of a friend of Thyssen's in Cologne. The participants were Herr Hitler and Herr von Papen. Here they agreed on a common policy, which practically assured der Führer's appointment as Chancellor of the Reich. President von Hindenburg held out until he was shown that heavy industry, represented by the Thyssens and the Hugenbergs, was back of the Nazi-Nationalist cooperation.

But what would the Nazi rank and file say to a Third Reich that was no more socialistic than the Weimar Republic against which they had revolted? Would it put up with Thyssen's domination? At the beginning of the Nazi reign the radicals did, indeed, make an effort to redeem socialistic party pledges by raiding the managerial rooms of the industries of the Rhine and Ruhr.

But Hitler made good his word to Thyssen. At the head of the Ministry of Finances, of the Ministry of Economics and of the Reichsbank there stood the stalwarts of capitalism, to whom the Nazi movement represented a New Deal to the extent that it was a departure from the peaceful policy of Weimar.

Herr Thyssen once more occupies the leading place in the Ruhr. He has beaten his competitors, and the bloody Saturday which claimed some of the lights of the Nazi party as its victims has assured nationalism for the present at least, as the paramount power in the National Socialist movement. Thyssen had not deceived his colleagues when he assured them that socialism was merely window dressing.

Thyssen enjoys the same serenity and patriarchal quiet which his father found so stimulating in his work. Factory councils are stripped of their power and Socialists do not dare to open their mouths. This is the Third Reich of Herr Thyssen, the defiant, nationalistic, anti-social Germany, for the realization of which he was striving for years.

But what fate awaits Thyssen after Hitler? His espousal of the Nazi cause may yet bring new troubles on his head. He may plead that his actions were guided by lofty motives of patriotism, but will his rivals accept his apologies? Will they not want to pay him with his own currency? Fritz Thyssen may yet learn the true wisdom of his father in keeping away from the court of the mighty because of his shabby clothes.

The Fabulous Farben Empire Faces Trial

by Delbert Clark

FORTY-THREE years ago half a dozen industrial chemists seated themselves around a table in Ludwigshafen in southwestern Germany and pledged themselves to an association. Out of that almost unnoticed meeting came an organization that was to be the backbone of the national war economy in two great world conflicts. Today twenty-four successors of the half-dozen are in prison at Nuremberg, awaiting trial as war criminals.

The six principal chemical firms in Germany that formed the trust in 1904 planned to eliminate domestic competition and to dominate the world market in synthetic dyes. By 1926 their number had increased to eighteen. Their fabulous—and infamous—organization bore the name Interessen Gemeinschaft Farbenindustrie Aktiengesellschaft which, freely translated, means Associated Dyestuffs Industries Joint Stock Company.

This is I. G. Farben, the huge combine that helped the Imperial German Government to fight the first World War and then helped Adolf Hitler to plan and fight the second. This is the gang of industrialists who through bribery, blackmail and espionage gained a stranglehold on the world's chemical industry and set about to make Germany master of the world.

From the *New York Times Magazine,* August 10, 1947, copyright © 1947 by The New York Times Company.

Farben executives were not indicted because they made synthetic dyes or because they dominated the world's chemical industry. They were indicted because they formed an alliance with Hitler. They are charged with "planning, preparing, initiating and waging wars of aggression and invasion of other countries; deportation to slave labor of members of the civilian population of the invaded countries and the enslavement, mistreatment, terrorization, torture and murder of millions of persons"; with plunder and spoliation "pursuant to deliberate plans and policies"; with plotting the rise of Hitler, with espionage and many other things that go far beyond the making of munitions.

Count 3 of the indictment, entitled "slavery and mass murder," relates with horrible exactitude the enslavement and wholesale killing of forced laborers in work camps organized and managed by and for Farbenindustrie.

"In its plants Farben accepted and appointed as its security representatives men designated by the SS and the Gestapo, and in the administration of its plants adopted the policies and practices of the Gestapo. Although the Farben plant manager was responsible for the morale and discipline of its slave workers it was standard policy to call in the Gestapo to enforce discipline.

"Farben was aggressive in the acquisition of slave laborers. * * * Subhuman standards of living were the established order. * * * Poison gases manufactured by Farben and supplied by Farben to officials of the SS were used in experimentation upon and extermination of enslaved persons throughout Europe. * * *"

Such in outline is the nature of the indictment. Let us turn now to the development of this huge empire and to the men who did Hitler's bidding. First let us look at the ostentatious citadel of Farben in Frankfort. That building, spared by bombers, is now the headquarters of the European command of the United States Army. It is a huge structure, with spacious approaches, and is faced with creamy travertine. As one walks up the front steps and enters, there is a sweep of stairways leading to office floors and straight ahead an enclosed terrace merging into an open terrace and lawn with fountains. On the upper floors are handsome offices with fine furniture and heavily padded soundproof doors. Today the terrace is a snack bar for soldiers and civilian clerks and the offices are occupied by American Military Government officials.

It was not always so. Here in these very offices the shadowy figures about to be tried for war crimes ruled a vast and insidious empire. They were shadowy, indeed. For German industrial leaders, especially those closely integrated with the regime, did not court publicity. These Farben men were powerful, they knew the source of their power and what they were about.

Years before World War I a Heidelberg University student, who later became a distinguished American chemist, asked a professor why German chemical research was concentrated so heavily on coal-tar dyes.

"Young man, some day this work will save the fatherland," was the reply.

The six companies that fathered I. G. Farben were engaged exclusively in the production of dyes and had but one immediate objective—to suppress competition among themselves and to destroy it in other countries. The years passed, and the development of aniline dyes advanced, always with the German "Big Six" in the lead. But a major problem had to be met—how to make use of the various by-products of dye manufacture. Extraction of dyestuffs from coal tar left other derivatives for which there was no known use. This resulted in a high manufacturing cost for the dyes themselves.

Then under the impetus of the inexorable drive toward war on the part of the Imperial German Government, a research chemist of "Big Six," and obscure university professors subsidized by them and by the Government, discovered new uses for these by-products which had no relation to the color of a lady's gown.

Early in this century the German chemists realized the military significance of trinitrotoluene, which is readily made from coal-tar by-products of dye manufacture. Better known as TNT, it is an important ingredient of many high explosives. Abruptly the chemists ceased research for new colors and let stockpiles accumulate for the coming war.

Parallel to this development the "Big Six" determined to thwart development of a coal-tar industry in the United States or anywhere else. There was no objection to attempts to produce dyes so long as coal-tar products from which the dyes were made came from Germany. But there must be no opportunity on the other side of the Atlantic for the development of a coal-tar munitions industry. At one time during this period, when three American manufacturers of heavy chemicals tried to start production of aniline oil and get away from reliance on the German product, the "Big Six" sent emissaries to the United States with a demand that the production of oil be stopped and offered to repay American firms for expenses already incurred.

When Congress put a 10 per cent duty on aniline oil the Germans cut prices below American cost of production. This was not trade, it was war.

Research went on apace, and economic penetration of other countries continued, with branches and agencies set up in the principal countries of the world. Dyestuffs now were distinctly secondary and medicines from coal tar began to assume an increasing importance, but always in the background were munitions of war. It was in the interest of Germany's monopoly in this field that I. G. Farben resorted to espionage, bribery, legislative corruption and disguised ownership of subsidiary companies abroad.

In 1911 the storm broke in the United States and by 1913 more than thirty court actions under anti-trust laws had been started against members of the "Big Six" and their agents. So well were they defended by an American attorney that all the suits were dismissed by the end of 1916, but not until after several large cash settlements had been made.

American indignation at bribery by "Big Six" representatives reached such heights that steps were taken to taper it off, but a bit later members of the cartel in convention assembled adopted this resolution:

"Resolved that henceforth bribery shall be abolished except in the United States and Russia."

With the outbreak of World War I Americans became acutely conscious of their dependence on German dyes, a circumstance which led to President Wilson's protest against the British blockade and to sharp diplomatic exchanges with the nation whose ally we later became.

Before the United States entered the war the "Big Six" were very active in trying to corner supplies of munitions and ingredients, to prevent their sale to England, while at the same time German propagandists sought to arouse American indignation against England for blocking shipment of dyestuffs from Germany to America.

By the end of the first World War the prestige of Germany's chemical leaders had not diminished at all—they had led no armies in the field and had lost no obvious battles. On the other hand, they had established chemistry as an essence of modern warfare. They had developed the TNT industry, planned and executed the use of poison gas, and by extracting nitrogen from air had made their country independent of the natural nitrates of Chile. They were top dog and continued so.

In 1916 two more chemical firms joined the "Big Six." Nine years later the Badische Anilin und Sodafabrik, kingpin of the trust, moved to Frankfort on the Main and changed its name to I. G. Farben Aktiengesellschaft. Five other firms identified with Badische came in, and still later several other firms joined the trust, including Germany's five biggest manufacturers of explosives. The pattern was laid out for the next German try for world supremacy.

Even Germans accept the fact of Farben's complicity in Hitler's war plans. In 1932 Farben considered abandoning research in synthetic gasoline, but asked Hitler if his party would support such research. When Hitler agreed Farben cast in its lot with him. And when Goering asked for money to replenish the party treasury Farben tossed in 400,000 marks, the largest contribution of any single firm. Thus Farben headed the German industrialists who prevented the Nazi collapse in 1933.

In the diplomatic maneuvering that led to war Farben stood ready at all times. Hitler absorbed Austria and Farben took over the Austrian chemical industry. A week before the Munich pact the German Ministry of Economics advised Farben that its plans for seizure and operation of the Czech munitions industry were acceptable. After Munich Farben moved into Czechoslovakia. And fourteen days after the invasion of Poland, Farben received the "trusteeship" of major Polish firms.

Americans who recall the notorious structures of public utility holding companies during the Twenties and Thirties may be under the illusion that I. G. Farben somehow resembled those corporations. That is not correct.

While Farben's corporate structure rivaled those fantastic crazy quilts in magnitude, it was not a case of piling one holding company on another, with no operating functions and no purpose other than to inflate stock values and make unearned profits. I. G. Farben was tightly integrated.

At its pre-war peak I. G. Farben was an impressive organization. In 1937 it had a net worth of six billion marks and a capitalization of 1.40 billion marks. It had active participation in some 400 industrial concerns in Germany and in nearly 200 outside Germany valued at about one billion marks. At this time it employed directly more than 200,000 persons, a figure which was doubled during the war.

Strict care was taken to insure continuous control of the trust. About 35 per cent of the capital stock was held directly by I. G. Farben, about 52 per cent by other German corporations and individuals. The remaining 13 per cent was held abroad. Swiss interests accounted for 3.57 per cent; British, for 2.93 per cent; Dutch, for 1.09 per cent, and American, for .71 per cent. This, of course, does not take into account widely scattered subsidiaries of I. G. Farben in other countries, including the United States— firms whose ownership was usually carefully concealed.

The top organization of Farben was direct and uncomplicated for so vast a structure. The board of directors—"Aufsichtsrat"— was composed of fifteen men. Most of them had been originally the heads of concerns which had been merged to form I. G. Farben. Their function appears to have been largely honorary, once they had been chosen as members of the management group —Vorstand—who really ran the cartel.

Below the Vorstand, or a part of it, were various research or administrative committees, and on down the line were operating departments. These central groups handled all matters of general policy and administration pertinent to I. G. Farben as a whole. Under them were the individual manufacturing plants subject to direct and autocratic control from the top group.

Carl Krauch, chairman of the Aufsichtsrat and also a member of the Vorstand, Herman Schmitz, Georg von Schnitzler, Max Ilgner, Heinrich Gattineau, Heinrich Buetefisch, Heinrich Oster, Otto Ambros—these are some of the top Farben men who will face the court at Nuremberg. All of them and their fellow-defendants were active in Nazi affairs.

Schmitz was a member of Hitler's Reichstag and bore the honorary title of War Economy Leader. Schnitzler, wealthy and ambitious, especially socially, was known in and out of I. G. Farben as a big Nazi. Ilgner was Director of Industrial Espionage. He belonged to nearly everything and was president of the Carl Schurz Foundation. Gattineau was head of the Economic Policy Department, especially created for him.

Buetefisch and Oster were primarily technicians and could have kept out of politics. But both of them leaped headlong into the Nazi stream, and Buetefisch belonged to no less than seven Nazi organizations. He also belonged to the Himmler "circle of friends" and had two high Nazi honors bestowed on him. Ambros was chairman of the Rubber and Plastics Committee. He was also manager of the Farben plant at Auschwitz, where slaves were worked until they could work no longer and then were sent to the gas chamber.

If American prosecutors at Nuremberg can convict these men and a decartelization law can prevent a resurgence of this vast trust, it will be an accomplishment that many have said was impossible. And to some extent it will vindicate the hopes of the men who fought and died to break German predatory power.

Part 2

FASCIST TOTALITARIANISM AND SOCIAL POLICIES

FASCIST RESTRICTIONS on personal freedoms were difficult to disguise or explain away, and could not be hidden by false statistics or fine-spun rhetoric. Journalists easily detect limitations on free expression in the mass media as well as the prevalence of official propaganda. It is essential to note, however, what is often overlooked. Such restrictions were more than denials of the abstract freedom of expression; they were policies enforced to stop all potential dissent from the left.

The social policies of fascism in power were not well understood in the thirties and forties, and little was then written that is worth preserving. Indeed, it is still difficult for scholars to glean data relative to the distribution of power, wealth, and social status among groups and classes under fascism. Fascist leaders hoped to convince the world that they were just to *all* classes, and especially favorable to the workers. The opposite was true, of course, but the mountains of false statistics issued by fascist governments obscured the favored treatment of the propertied. For this reason, perhaps, until recently scholars have been reluctant to grasp the conservative nature of fascist regimes.

Channeling the
News for Nazis

by Junius B. Wood

BERLIN

GERMANS ARE AVID newspaper readers, and their "newsboys" are
many. On city street corners one sees men and women, each in
a uniform and cap supplied by some newspaper, selling the latest
editions. Day and night and in any kind of weather other "newsboys" make their rounds, trudging on foot or cycling from one
cafe to another and finding customers.

But Germans, eager as they are for news, have difficulty in
satisfying their curiosity about what is going on in the world outside. For their government, through its controlled press and radio,
tells them only what it wants them to know and in a way to influence their thoughts in a common direction.

A set formula is consistently followed. Every day the newspapers are informed on government policy. They receive and follow
instructions on what to print about it. In addition, they get the
report of the official news agency, the Deutsche Nachrichten Bureau, whose version must be used—in part, if the editor chooses—
for decrees, speeches and many other things. A speech by Adolf
Hitler, for example, cannot be reported freely; it must be tran-

scribed, approved by the speaker, and then released by the official agency.

As that agency recently put it, in a time of international crisis the German press, radio and all avenues of information should be mobilized, like the army and industry. It should not, by any indiscretion, embarrass the home officials responsible for negotiations. In brief, the Fuehrer must at all times be depended upon to decide what is to be printed, and how, and when.

In the Third Reich, therefore, when a citizen is unsatisfied with his morning paper account of an important political happening he does not—as he might in a democracy—rush out to find what a rival paper is saying. He can be certain that all German papers are printing the same thing.

He may wait until noon, when foreign newspapers arrive from London, Paris, Switzerland, Holland or the Scandinavian countries, to get a less stereotyped version and form his own estimate of happenings. But this method has limitations. The citizen may find that street sales of the foreign paper he wants to buy have been banned, either temporarily or permanently.

At least two papers from New York, four from Switzerland, two from England, three from Paris, one from Sweden and possibly others are under the permanent ban. If the citizen asks for one not in this list, a whispered "verboten" from the newsboy may inform him that it has been suppressed because of an article in that day's issue.

The usual method, then, of satisfying one's curiosity is to talk with neighbors or, in a more cautious way, with strangers in a restaurant or street car. "What have you heard?" has become a substitute for the "I saw in the paper" of most other countries. The amount of news that circulates by word of mouth is amazing and, as might be supposed, so well embroidered in the repeating that it is nearly impossible to distinguish between fact and fiction.

"What does the Strasbourg radio say?" may be safely asked if one knows one's informant fairly well. That station across the border broadcasts its news report in German as well as in French.

Or, "Did you hear the Moscow radio?" may even be asked among close friends. The Moscow sender talks to the world in many languages, its messages varying accordingly. Science has not found a way to keep it out of the air over Germany, nor has it been possible to enforce completely the law punishing any one who listens to it. How it gets its information is a mystery, but it often is up to the minute with names, addresses and timing on incidents that have happened in Germany only a few hours past.

There is one other method of getting uncensored accounts of political happenings. It is to accept the clandestine newspapers which uncaptured Socialists and Communists run off in secret printing plants.

Germans who depend entirely on the regular press for their news get a great deal of staid and serious information. Some dailies specialize in finance and trade. Nearly all devote much space to editorials and to a wide variety of subjects including such as books, architecture, the theatre and the latest fashions.

A Berlin newspaper will have about eight department editors, who also do the reporting. It may have several times as many correspondents abroad or in other cities. The sports editor covers the best sports event of the day and the official news agency covers the others. Other editors will cover courts, city affairs, police and other "runs" in much the same manner.

No single subject, however, gets as much space as in a large American newspaper, and details are often lacking. A report of an airplane accident, for instance, says six were killed but gives no names. And some of the news appears to come from odd places. On a recent day a "cable" giving Argentina's reaction to the Pan-American Conference at Lima came from Milan, in Italy. On the same day the funeral of Kemal Ataturk in Turkey was described in a telegram from Paris. A dispatch from London told of a fire in California. A dispatch ostensibly from New York told of a lynching in Mississippi under the caption "Humanity"—a suggestion of the official agency which was carried by all newspapers.

One might get the impression from the papers that German Government and party officials devoted all their time to dedicating new buildings, receiving tributes from the populace or their colleagues, or issuing decrees and making speeches.

The Voelkischer Beobachter, the Hitler and party organ published by Alfred Rosenberg, and Der Angriff, the Goebbels publication, may be taken as the most official of Berlin newspapers. (The Beobachter is published also in Munich, Vienna and Cologne.) On a recent morning more than one-fifth of what was classed as news in the Beobachter consisted of speeches by party leaders, and more than a quarter of all the reading matter was about Jews, the principal topic at the time. In the Angriff, on the afternoon of the same day, two-fifths of the news was a speech by Propaganda Minister Goebbels, and there were reports of other speeches.

Two methods frequently used, in the interest of Nazi policy, are the suppression, delay or distortion of important news and the directing of a bitter press campaign against some foreign nation.

The editors often direct their wrath at the newspapers of republics, referring to them as the "Hetze-Presse" (baiting press). Thus, in the issue of the Angriff just referred to, the headline across the front page over a cable from New York was "Murder Baiting in the U. S. A. Against the Third Reich." Yet the German press itself almost always seems to have a "Hetze" on about happenings in one foreign land or another.

Russia, with its communism, is standing material for a German "Hetze." Czecho-Slovakia, at the time of the Sudeten issue, felt the "Hetze" in extreme measure. So did Great Britain a little later. After a group of Rumanian Nazis, called Iron Guardists, were killed by their Rumanian guards, the direct "Hetze" was withheld for political reasons; instead the press reprinted only foreign comment attacking the shootings—a sort of reflected "Hetze" for which Germany was not primarily responsible. At the present time the "Hetze" is turned against the United States.

For an understanding of how the German press works let us trace some events beginning with the Czecho-Slovakian crisis.

The first of two messages from President Roosevelt during that crisis, containing a general admonition for peace, was delayed from twenty-four to forty-eight hours in Germany. Before it appeared, "in part," Chancellor Hitler at a Berlin mass meeting declared his hopes for peace. The delay deprived Mr. Roosevelt of any "scoop" in Germany on the peace idea—as Minister Goebbels later explained was intended.

The second message, in which Mr. Roosevelt laid on the Fuehrer the responsibility for peace or war, was not published in German papers, although it was in the foreign papers that entered Germany.

Moreover, the mobilization of the British fleet toward the end of the crisis, which might have dampened the German ardor for forcible measures, missed press mention.

After the Czecho-Slovak crisis came the concerted outbreak throughout Germany of window-smashing, store-wrecking and synagogue-burning on Nov. 10, following the shooting of a German diplomat in Paris by a young Jew named Grynzspan. Newspapers in other countries gave great space to the details, but the Berlin papers printed only vague accounts.

The next morning a ninety-word statement from Minister Goebbels appeared, together with a 175-word official news agency explanation of the reasons for the "spontaneous national uprising." These statements were unaccompanied by any details or summary of what had happened in the country. Outside of Berlin a few newspapers carried local stories, and the official agency sent out a report for use abroad—but not inside Germany. In the official New Year's summary which every newspaper printed of history-making events in Germany in 1938 there was no mention of the outburst; the event recorded for German history on Nov. 10 was the death of the President of Turkey.

Every one in Berlin had seen some part of the property destruction, and in the absence of adequate newspaper accounts the news traveled swiftly by word of mouth. Within twenty-four hours after Field Marshal Hermann Goering had decreed a 1,000,000,-000-reichsmark penalty against the Jews for the Grynzspan crime every one who had ventured out of doors had heard the latest.

"Who is the greatest alchemist in the world?" was the question.

"Goering," was the answer, "because he made a billion in gold out of Gruenspan." (Gruenspan, the German spelling for Grynzspan, as a common noun means verdigris.)

Some German newspapers attempted to connect Winston

Churchill and others with the Paris assassination. The British Minister to Berlin made a formal protest. The papers did not report it. Instead, they turned their guns toward America, and the "Hetze" against the United States was on in a mild way. The reaction of American newspapers toward the Nov. 10 "uprising," expressing sorrow or horror at what they regarded as a German lapse from civilized law and order, was attributed to Jewish influence and, it was said, justified further repression.

The departure of the American commercial attaché from Berlin, following the return home of the American Ambassador, went unreported. Several American Congressmen who had criticized the "uprising" came in for a baiting, however, although the German readers were not told what they had said.

Then Secretary of Interior Ickes made his Cleveland speech in criticism of the affair and the "Hetze" reached its boiling point. A large scrapbook could be filled with attacks on Mr. Ickes made by the press in recent weeks. These may have puzzled German readers, for the reason that Mr. Ickes's sharpest digs were not printed.

The facts that the German Embassy in Washington made a protest against the Ickes remarks, and that this protest was promptly rejected by the State Department, were not printed here until ten days later, and then without the most pointed comments in the rejection. The newspapers contended that if Mr. Ickes had stayed in his office at Washington instead of making speeches the recent drug company and smuggling scandals in New York could not have occurred. Just how the Secretary of the Interior could have stopped these activities which did not fall in the jurisdiction of his department was not explained.

Both scandals got a big play in the German papers. The fact that several Jews were named in the smuggling case was always kept in the headlines, while the fact that the principals in the drug-company swindle were of Italian ancestry was ignored—for news must harmonize with politics.

Press sermonizing, it seemed, was sometimes more important than the facts. One could read in a German newspaper that Mr. Ickes is a United States Senator, or that Benjamin Franklin was a former President. Senator Pittman, who recently said that the

American public did not like the German or Japanese Governments, was advised in the German press to go West to get the sentiment of real Americans—although he could not move many miles in that direction from his State of Nevada without reaching the Pacific.

Along with the "Hetze" on the Jewish issue has gone a campaign against American efforts to build Pan-American solidarity against totalitarian encroachment. Before the Lima conference the German newspapers devoted space to the reputed sinister intentions of the United States in the western continent. The outcome of the conference was described in the German press as a fiasco for Washington.

Unlimited theorizing is possible on the effect of all this on the German people. In a country where newspapers express different views the people think and argue and are free to form their own conclusions. In Germany the older generation—among trusted friends—expresses and argues its opinions quietly. The younger generation is being trained to follow the party line and never to question. Nazis believe that this is the only method to create a united nation which will fulfill the slogan: "One leader! One people! One Germany!"

Goebbels Edits the Popular Mind in Germany

by Albion Ross

BERLIN

THE JAPANESE CALL their combination of propaganda and censorship "thought control." It is an expression that throws a great deal of light on what has been happening to the Germans since the arrival of the totalitarian State.

Totalitarianism has taken time to establish itself. The nationwide organization known as the Propaganda Ministry, with thirty-one subordinate offices in all corners of the Reich, is just beginning to appear in proper perspective. The thoughtful German is slowly realizing what Dr. Joseph Goebbels means in his daily life and that of his fellows. Even the foreigner living here experiences the necessity of resisting the all-pervading influence of that central mind in the Wilhelmstrasse weaving daily the warp of propaganda and the woof of censorship. If he is honest with himself, he feels sometimes a desire to flee the country, because combined propaganda and news suppression seem to be getting all life and the whole world out of focus.

Thought control pervades the atmosphere. It stares out of every printed page. It accounts for the music that you hear on the radio. It crops out in every conversation. It is like the fixed idea that torments a neurotic. Even while you are resisting, the propagandists are exercising their influence on you.

The means employed to obtain this result can be listed and described, but thought control itself can only be experienced.

A good editor, says the journalistic proverb, is to be known not by what he puts in the paper but by what he leaves out. The complicated publicity organs of the government are engaged today in editing the public mind.

Humanity is fickle. The propagandist seeking power is chiefly interested in changing people's minds. The propagandist in power is faced with the psychologically more difficult job of keeping people from changing their minds again. He proceeds on the principle that what the public does not know will not hurt it.

The technique by which "bad" information or opinion is suppressed is simple. The jobs of all newspaper men, radio men, film men, lecturers and the like are dependent entirely upon retaining the good-will of the Propaganda Ministry and its subordinate organs, such as the Reich Press Chamber, Reich Cultural Chamber, Reich Film Chamber, and so on. Any newspaper man, for example, can be dismissed from his profession, not only his job, instantly and for good, by a word from the Propaganda Minister. Instructions are issued and instructions are obeyed.

Crude as some of his propaganda may appear, Joseph Goebbels possesses a devious and subtle mind. Mere suppression does not appeal to him. He has demonstrated that he knows thought control is a curious marriage of censorship and propaganda and that the public must never be left unoccupied.

It is no easy job to spoon-feed 65,000,000 minds. Neither Adolf Hitler nor Hermann Goering could do it. Neither is so highly civilized as Goebbels. Neither is so genuinely Machiavellian. The man who does this extraordinary job is not a strong man, a hero in shining armor, a mystic crying in the wilderness. He is not filled with blind peasant hatred of his natural opponents.

Goebbels is an unusually well-educated man. He reads Virgil for relaxation. He delights in the company of artists, musicians, actors, playwrights and an occasional scholar. In society he is disarmingly attentive, though perhaps a little too much given to irony. While others were at the front during the World War young

Goebbels, against his will, was studying the fine arts, history and literature in the universities.

He has been lame since birth. Such an infirmity as his has accounted for a great deal in the lives of other historic figures— for example, Talleyrand, likewise lame. In Goebbels lameness, as in Talleyrand, seems to have sharpened his faculties, hardened his will and inflamed his ambition.

The comparison with Talleyrand should not be exaggerated. Joseph Goebbels is no "grand seigneur." His father was a factory foreman in the rather depressing industrial town of Rheydt, on the lower Rhine. His mother was the daughter of a smith.

That is to say, Goebbels represents a definite class of ambitious young men in modern German life, the academic sons of the industrious and saving small bourgeoisie. Many of these young men became involuntary members of the so-called "academic proletariat" after the war. They had an education that separated them from their origins, but no assistance, no "pull." Full of ambition, and expected by their parents to do great things, they resented bitterly their lack of opportunities and became agitators of one sort or another. Post-war life probably hit them harder than any other class. They either fought back furiously or went under.

Young Goebbels studied for a long time. Restless, he shifted from one university to another almost every semester: first to Bonn, then in turn to Freiburg, Wurzburg, Munich, Heidelberg, Cologne, Frankfurt and Berlin. Finally he took his doctorate at Heidelberg in 1921, writing a half philosophical, half literary thesis on "The Intellectual and Political Tendencies of Early Romanticism." The new doctor was not prepared to earn a living in any ordinary profession. His education had been interesting but impractical.

This point is significant in the career and character of Joseph Goebbels. He never had a profession. He never earned his living at any routine trade or business. The only profession in which he ever engaged is propaganda. Before that he was what is euphemistically known as a "writer." He sold occasional feature stories or political articles, done at his own risk, to the newspapers. In plain English, such people are engaged in the lugubrious industry of turning out "pot-boilers." It is a miserable way of earning a living.

Restless, unhappy, Goebbels wandered from his home town, Rheydt, to Cologne and from there to Berlin and Munich. In 1922 he became acquainted with Hitler and began to make speeches to students' mass meetings. He had found his calling. The French entered the Ruhr. He went into the Ruhrland as an agitator. In 1924 he became editor of a weekly journal in Elberfeld devoted entirely to nationalist and racial agitation and without journalistic pretension.

Soon he was made district commander for the National Socialists. He had become a regular party functionary. In 1926 he was transferred to Berlin to organize and run the National Socialist party in the capital. His success against immense odds established his reputation as the greatest of National Socialist agitators.

Meantime he had become propaganda director or campaign manager of the party, with headquarters in Munich. Goebbels, in other words, is a politician not only by conviction but also by profession. Before the party came into office Goebbels was the Jim Farley of National Socialism. His methods and the purposes of his party were different, but his job was essentially the same.

The pure art of politics consists simply of inducing people to act as you want them to act. To this art Joseph Goebbels is passionately devoted. Writing of a pre-1933 election he has recorded: "The election campaign in Berlin will outdo every previous one. I await it as eagerly as if it were a festival."

The office of Minister for the People's Enlightenment and Propaganda, which he now occupies, is of paramount importance in the structure of the totalitarian State. The fundamental idea of the modern totalitarian State is to achieve complete national unity and maximum force by creating complete uniformity of opinion upon all essential issues in life and politics. The purpose of propaganda is to convince some one that there is only one side to a question.

Goebbels's principles of propaganda or "thought control" are found more especially scattered through two books he has compiled or written, one before and one since he became Minister. Both, in the style of Hitler's "My Struggle," are autobiographical.

One is entitled "The Struggle for Berlin." The other, allegedly a diary of the twelve months before Hitler became Chancellor, is entitled "From the Hotel Kaiserhof to the Reich Chancellery."

"Propaganda in itself," Goebbels says in "The Struggle for Berlin," "has no fundamental method. It has only a purpose—the conquest of the masses. Every means that serves this end is good." The means which Dr. Goebbels employs are based upon his ideas about mankind. These he explains in scattered references, but at some length. He says:

> The ordinary man hates nothing more than two-sidedness, to be called upon to consider this as well as that. The masses think simply and primitively. They love to generalize complicated situations and from their generalization to draw clear and uncompromising conclusions.
>
> Our agitation has often been called unintelligent and primitive. Certainly National Socialist agitation is primitive. However, the people think primitively.
>
> The intelligence is subject to a thousand temptations, but the heart always preserves its steady beat.
>
> In the long run the average man is only impressed by force and discipline.

Speaking of the National Socialist editor, he writes:

> He consciously assumes as a priori truth the proposition that he in reality intends to prove to the reader and develops from it his conclusions.
>
> Bourgeois newspapers are satisfied to present more or less objective news reports. The National Socialist press has a much greater and more decisive duty. It draws the consequences from the information which it receives. It does not allow the reader to come to conclusions according to his own tastes. The reader, on the contrary, is to be instructed and trained accordingly to the newspaper's purpose and tendency.
>
> The National Socialist newspaper is only a part of National Socialist propaganda. It has a definite political purpose and must not, therefore, be confused with a bourgeoise organ of information. The reader of a National Socialist paper is to be

strengthened in his conviction. He is being consciously influenced. The whole of the reader's thought and feeling must be drawn in a certain direction.

Referring to the annual party congress the Propaganda Minister writes:

> The party congress presents no opportunity for fruitless discussion. On the contrary, it is intended to present to the public a demonstration of the unity and unbroken warlike spirit of the party.
> The intellectuals say that the more often a theme is presented the less interested is the public. That is not true. When one possesses the talent to find ever-new forms of proof, ever more Draconic and sharper arguments, then the public will not lose interest. On the contrary, its interest will increase.

In general, National Socialist propaganda is still based upon the principles cited. It still consists largely of the repetition of primitive slogans. Signs of opposition or a mere tendency to differ are still shouted down with cries of righteous indignation.

Huge meetings, parades and demonstrations of all sorts remain the staple diet of the German masses. The Berlin press reported during 1936 seventy-two major propaganda events in Berlin or the Reich. Crowds varied in size from the 18,000 functionaries of the Reich Air Defense League addressed by Goering to the 2,000,000 Berliners addressed on May Day by Hitler.

Since shortly after the Olympics, Germany has been living intellectually on a rather primitive political theme song in three parts. A: The Bolshevist pirates, robbers and murderers are trying to destroy European civilization for the benefit of the Jews. B: Democratic States are weaklings ready to be devoured by the Bolsheviki. C: National Socialism and fascism alone are strong and prepared.

This is good domestic propaganda, if not very novel. It has, however, a very definite foreign purpose. The 65,000,000 Germans are being employed primarily as a drum upon which the propagandists of the Reich are pounding out their theme song for the benefit of the world abroad.

Minister Goebbels declared at the last party congress in Nuremberg:

"We are convinced that we shall eventually succeed in opening the eyes of the world to make it see the true face of Jewry and bolshevism, just as we have succeeded in convincing Germany of the perilous parasitic character of that race. In the meantime we shall not tire of pointing to this fatal danger and calling the attention of all peoples who are undergoing terrible crises and upheavals to the fact that the Jews are to blame.

"We speak the language of the people and, therefore, hope that the people of outside nations will understand us. * * * For the world must have its eyes opened. * * * Therefore we take the opportunity of this party congress to ring the alarm against this world danger."

This campaign started after the signature of the Franco-Russian agreement and has gained steadily in intensity. It is intended to eliminate the old threat of enemies on two fronts by frightening the French peasant and middle class into abandoning the Soviet alliance and by preventing the British from eventually making the Franco-Soviet pact a new triple entente.

For the moment, the Reich propagandists seem to be employing the wrong technique. They are applying to sovereign foreign peoples the sensationalist, threatening tactics which were effective under the ill-founded German Republic. But if the Propaganda Minister is let alone he will probably find a way to work better abroad. He has himself said: "The nature of propaganda is quite unlimited. It adapts itself to the person for whom it is intended."

Spurring a Nation: The Nazi Way

by Otto D. Tolischus

BERLIN

THE GERMAN NATION goes to the polls today to endorse, with practical unanimity foreordained, Adolf Hitler and all his works and, incidentally, to elect a new Reichstag chosen by him to shout approval whenever such demonstration is deemed advisable.

Taken at face value—as the world is supposed to take it—the spectacle of a great people being at last welded into national unity through the struggle for resurgence from defeat, and for freedom from foreign encroachments upon their sovereignty, is not without grandeur. For though the election results will require careful analysis to discern the drift of German public opinion, nevertheless the majority is bound to remain so overwhelming that Hitler will still be able to repeat with a show of justification the taunting challenge he flung out at foreign statesmen during the election campaign:

"Behind me stands the whole German people. Who stands behind you?"

But even more awe-inspiring is the spectacle of a nation of 68,000,000 putting its fate into the hands of one man for better or worse. This spectacle becomes truly alarming when viewed as

From the *New York Times Magazine,* March 29, 1936, copyright © 1936, 1964 by The New York Times Company.

what it really is: namely, the result of the skillful wielding of the weapons of propaganda backed by the persuasive power of force.

This is no new combination. It was Machiavelli who pronounced the dictum that armed prophets conquer while the unarmed perish. But the use of this combination on such a vast scale as we see exemplified today in Fascist Italy, Soviet Russia and National-Socialist Germany is entirely a modern phenomenon. And the greater of the two weapons is propaganda.

Propaganda has made possible the modern dictators, who no longer sit on bayonets alone but are able to cushion their seats with the genuine and contagious enthusiasm and loyalty of such large masses as drag along, in decisive moments, the even larger mass of the discontented and indifferent, until visible opposition becomes negligible. Force is indispensable in crushing avowed opponents and discouraging secret antagonists, but it is propaganda which mobilizes the millions who shout themselves hoarse for "the leader" and finally go to the polls to cast valid "yes" ballots when it would be just as easy to vote "no."

Judged by results, the National Socialists generally and Hitler in particular are perhaps the greatest propagandists of modern times. They have conquered the German people more completely than either Stalin or Mussolini conquered theirs; they dare, therefore, to submit to the rule of popular vote oftener and in a more genuine election test than any other dictatorial régimes can, and be more confident of the result. To all outward appearances there is something to that "ennobled democracy" of which the National Socialists boast, giving point to Hitler's exclamations: "I don't want to be a dictator! I want to be your leader, and you are my judges!"

To the Western mind this "ennobled democracy" may seem rather warped because at best the established tyranny of the majority makes even that majority artificial by annihilating all parties and organizations which might overtake the government, thus confronting voters with a choice between the existing régime and possible chaos.

But as an election steamroller the National Socialist system must arouse the envy of election campaign managers everywhere. For, as Reich election director, Goebbels has a complete monopoly of all election propaganda and has furthermore at his disposal an organization which is unsurpassed in its striking force, a variety of methods that nobody dares criticize and funds that are unlimited.

There is only one legal party and only one ticket. Names on the ticket do not matter, inasmuch as they are all determined by the party machine, anyhow, and only a few of the top ones are mentioned at all. The ticket is not so much an election ticket as an expression of faith in Hitler. The election itself is not so much a Reichstag election as a plebiscite, which Napoleon also knew how to employ, frequently with good effect.

There is no opposition. The formation or attempt to form any other party outside the National Socialist party is forbidden by law; so is all criticism of either the régime or its representatives. Even dissent from party doctrine may often lead to the loss of one's job or even become the subject of a Gestapo investigation.

The entire State apparatus, with its monopoly of patronage, public relief and police powers, is put at the service of the National Socialist party's election campaign. This includes not only the vast body of government officials and employes, from Cabinet Minister to rural mailman, but also all social, business and cultural organizations which are under party control. All of these issue urgent appeals—now is the time for all good men to come to the aid of their party; stand by the leader; let the Reich show the nation's foreign and domestic enemies what's what. Count Helldorf, Berlin's police president, frankly instructed his police force: "You must be propagandists of the National Socialist idea. Helpers of the Fuehrer must see to it that every man and every woman follow the call of the Fuehrer and go to the polls."

It is difficult to imagine a German who will stay away after that; and nine times out of ten a voter brought to the polls is a voter for the government.

Finally, all the means of influencing public opinion—press, film, billboard; above all, radio, and even the pulpit—are converted into vehicles of National Socialist election propaganda. In the official press the periodical German press is frankly told that it is an instrument of political leadership and must devote every page, from first to last, to election propaganda, which can be only

National Socialist. Yet by Hitler's dictum, by National Socialist experience, the greatest instrument of propaganda remains the human voice, provided it is employed amid appropriate surroundings, with proper oratorical skill and lack of scruples. Through oratory the National Socialist movement first became a power.

A talent for oratory is therefore a first requirement of every aspirant to National Socialist leadership. The flood of election oratory poured out upon the German people is, therefore, assuming unprecedented volume; and since the Germans never before have had orators worth mentioning, they are virtually helpless before the flood, and will be until they are able to revive their critical faculties and thus develop their powers of resistance.

Radio, which in Germany is owned by the government, has extended the range of the human voice to embrace the entire nation simultaneously and has so created a new political force for good or ill which is revolutionizing political practice not only in Germany but in other countries as well.

Still, in organizing, in trimming the contents of election oratory so as to make it most effective, National Socialism surpasses perhaps every other propagandist organization in the world. It is especially remarkable that Hitler's book "My Struggle," written at the age of 34, is still the standard work on organizing "legal revolution," as Lenin's works are on organizing illegal revolution. At any rate, the National Socialist propaganda machine still follows its maxims, not to its loss.

The first of these maxims is that oratory is most effective at big mass meetings held in the evening amid a carefully created atmosphere of both solemnity and enthusiasm. In his book Hitler recounts how he learned this maxim by painful failures in his early attempts to stir crowds with speeches in broad daylight; how he came to realize the three conditions of successful political oratory. The big mass meeting, he explains, is necessary because in it an individual feels safe and courageous; the crowd produces its own spirit, which feeds enthusiasm and carries the individual along. In the evening, he continues, everybody's resistance is lowest and the mass succumbs all the more easily to the suggestive power of a stronger will.

Finally, says Hitler, he learned in the Catholic Church that twilight cathedrals in which incense burned amid solemn ceremonies created an atmosphere which made the words of the priests most effective; he determined to employ an equally appropriate atmosphere for the propagation of his own doctrine.

So far as possible these methods were employed during the National Socialist struggle for power; the attainment of power put at the disposal of the National Socialist régime unsurpassed facilities for enlarging upon them. Today the régime not only has a monopoly of oratory but also control of all meeting places, all State party organizations, which enables it to assemble mass meetings as large as desired.

It mobilizes for election purposes such huge organizations as the Storm Troops, the Schutzstaffel, the labor service, the Air Defense League, the Women's League, the Hitler Youth and, above all, the German Labor Front, with its shop organizations embracing almost every worker and office employe. Sometimes tens of thousands of the most loyal supporters are shipped by special trains to points where they can do the most good in leading cheers and creating enthusiasm.

In staging such mass meetings no bets are overlooked. There are flags, banners, bunting, magnesium lights, bands, songs, trumpets, fanfares and torchlight parades. A regal atmosphere surrounds the main speakers, who often operate their own spotlights from their desks. Not least is the ceremony of the solemn opening, which usually consists of "the trooping of the Nazi colors" into the meeting amid the silent salute of all present; and the chanting by a male chorus of the anthem of heroism, hate and heart-burning devotion, which puts the audience in a proper frame of mind to applaud anything from an abstruse dissertation upon National Socialist Weltanschauung by Alfred Rosenberg to a ribald attack on the Jews by Julius Streicher.

How large mass demonstrations can become is illustrated by the fact that some 300,000 assembled in Therese Meadows in Munich to listen to Hitler; the opening speech of the present election campaign, delivered by Goebbels, was heard by even more hundreds of thousands assembled in 230 of Berlin's biggest halls, interconnected by loud-speakers.

But this concentration of technical organizational machinery, however imposing, would remain an empty shell and, therefore, ineffective if the Nazis didn't know how to fill it with the living breath of the effective word uttered at the right time. It is here that they display their real mastery. And here again they merely follow the precepts of Hitler's book.

These precepts may briefly be summarized as follows: In order to be effective, propaganda must be of a popular order, and to be popular it must be primitive. For, says Hitler, the mass itself is primitive. In overwhelming majority, asserts the Fuehrer, are people so feminine that their thoughts and actions are determined not by sober reasoning but by emotions. Therefore, he holds, propaganda must appeal first of all to the emotions. Its intellectual level must be gauged to the lowest intelligence among the mass it is designed to reach, from which it follows that the larger the mass to be reached the lower must be the intellectual level of propaganda.

Oratory must therefore deal primarily with such primitive emotions and concepts as love, hate, right, wrong, patriotism, treason, without forgetting the material interest. All this must form the foundation for a few central ideas which must be hammered into even the dullest brain by constant repetition.

Above everything else, propaganda must have courage, fanatical one-sidedness which paints only in black and white and knows only heroes and villains. For, says Hitler, "If even a shade of justice is admitted for the other side, the foundation is laid for doubt in the justice of our own cause."

All this is nothing new to the authors of good old-fashioned melodrama, to demagogues and yellow journalists and war propagandists, from whom, in fact, Hitler learned his trade. But the application of their principles to politics on such a "totalitarian" scale as that adopted in Germany has rarely been paralleled. It is particularly remarkable in a country which has always made a religion of its Kultur. Yet with that "trancelike surety" with which he feels Providence is guiding him on his way, Hitler knew that the mere employment of cynical principles would be insufficient for ultimate success; he tied them up with what to Germans must appear a noble cause—namely, national racial unity in a bigger Germany—and made it seem plausible that in the service of such a cause the end would justify the means.

By their nature these principles are fighting principles, and fighting is proclaimed to be the essence of Nazi life. But to assure victory it is advisable to pick carefully both the enemy and the issue. In this respect Hitler is likewise following his own precepts. Concentrate on one enemy, he advises in his book; if necessary, lump even widely differing enemies into the same category. He proceeded to do so successfully in both domestic and foreign politics. All enemies of National Socialism are today lumped under the general category "bolshevism." This category includes such diversified elements as Jews, international finance, the Catholic Church and, as a potential new member, the French nation or any other nation standing in Germany's way. They are all being fought in the name of a crusade against bolshevism. This in turn explains why National Socialist elections are timed so that they can be connected with a vital issue of foreign politics such as Germany's bolt from the League or the scrapping of Locarno through military occupation of the Rhine.

But there is yet another fighting precept laid down by Hitler. That is challenging the enemy by appropriating his colors, his symbols, his slogans. He employed this precept so successfully that he was able to merge colors, symbols and slogans of both the Nationalists and the Communists with his own and, finally, to annihilate both Nationalists and Communists.

This precept was in the foreground of the election campaign, placed even above the injunction to concentrate on a synthetic enemy. According to instructions issued by Goebbels, the election battle was waged this time for something, rather than against somebody. Ordinary enemies, like critics of the régime and the reactionary grumblers, even the Jews and the still uncoordinated churches, were therefore sidetracked. The National Socialist orators appear in the role of crusaders for peace, freedom, law, order, "ennobled democracy," everything that is good, true and beautiful.

They do not so much denounce unconverted rascals; rather they emphasize the actual and apparent accomplishments of the régime. They stress their assertion that Hitler saved Germany from chaos and bolshevism, clad her in "shining armor" that enables her to take equal rank among the big powers and to defy all enemies.

They paint in glowing if too glaring colors how he provided work for the unemployed, vacations for the employed; how he increased wages, savings and profits; how he fed the hungry, clothed the naked from a 300,000,000-mark Winter relief fund raised by the National Socialist party in the best Tammany style; how he sent workers in their own ships to cruise the seas and visit such blessed islands as Madeira; how what has been done so far is merely a beginning, with bigger and better things to come.

In line with this "positive aspect" of the campaign, words and concepts like comradeship, honor, decency, heart, soul, faith, truth —and lately even God and the divine grace that attends rulers like Hitler—play a dominant role. The conflict between the German God and the Jewish Jehovah is buried for the present, along with the church fight. But if perchance the "positive aspect" of the campaign should fail to convince some of the hard-boiled enemy, Nazi orators leave little doubt that if necessary other means of persuasion will be found for "a cur who denies the Fuehrer his plea for a 'yes' vote."

Yet the biggest argument of the National Socialist régime, ranking high above all else, is Hitler himself. In German eyes he is already beginning to assume the stature of both superman and saint—a demigod who, like Atlas, is carrying worlds on his shoulders. Not only can he boast remarkable achievements, the reverse side of which is hidden from public view, but he is also the best campaign speaker the Nazis have.

Again he has been barnstorming the country as he did during his struggle for power. The fact is that this "man of the people" has proved himself the unsurpassed conqueror of men, the master player on the keys of human emotions. Goebbels may glitter among intellectual fireworks; Goering may thunder like Thor; Streicher may exhibit himself; but when Hitler speaks, with that dark voice of his and fanatical sincerity in everything he is saying at the moment, he imbues crowds with his own zeal. When he stands before a vast audience against a background of many banners, when with mingled pride and self-compassion, but also with amazing self-confidence, he recounts his own struggles, sufferings and accomplishments, he seems to his listeners the personification of the whole German people and their destiny—a man in a trance, from whom radiates a strange magnetism that escapes foreign observers but which apparently grips all Germans present, stirs them to both heroics and tears.

In short, Hitler is his own best propagandist; as long as the spell of his propaganda is coupled with the show of success, he will continue to dominate Germany.

In a Nazi Labor Camp: A Spartan Routine

by G. S. Cox

THE OBJECT of the German Youth Labor Service is to give the youth of Germany schooling and hard physical work in camps run and disciplined on military lines. There are already more than 1,000 of these camps—Arbeitslager—in existence, with some 280,000 trainees in them.

Some of the camps are for women, but the majority are for young men between the ages of 17 and 25. The service is still nominally voluntary, except for students who must do six months' manual labor in the service before they can enter the university. In practice it becomes compulsory for others as well.

Any young unemployed man refusing to serve in a labor camp would lose the dole; moreover, employers are required, in granting work, to give preference to applicants with a work-pass showing that they have served the required period in a camp. For youths between 18 and 25 six months' service is sufficient, those between 17 and 18 must remain a full year. As soon as funds permit, it is intended to make a year's labor service compulsory for every young German.

The camp in which I served was one of the ordinary camps in the Hanover district, situated on the edge of a lonely village on

From the *New York Times Magazine,* October 28, 1934, copyright © 1934, 1962 by The New York Times Company.

the heather moors. I speak German, and I served under the same conditions and the same discipline as the other trainees, who were all Germans. They were mostly young unemployed and workers from Hanover City and the Ruhr. I wore their uniform and swastika armband, slept in the barracks with the other members of my troop, did the same work and drill and played the same sports.

The camp itself consisted of low-roofed, wooden barracks, painted red and black and grouped round a sandy parade square. The living conditions were Spartan enough, but adequate. Sixteen men slept in a barrack room, each man having his own bunk, with a straw mattress and a locker to himself. He was supplied with everything necessary except his personal toilet gear—two uniforms, boots, sports shoes, sports clothes, eating utensils, bedding, overcoat, towel, even underwear and socks. The working uniform was a drab affair of field gray, but the parade uniform was of khaki, with a leather belt, black shoulder tabs, and a peaked cap resembling that worn by the Italian infantry.

For dining and living room we had one large room with trestle tables and an old piano. Its walls, and the walls of the barrack rooms, were hung with flags, photographs of Hitler and other Nazi leaders and slogans such as "Germany needs you, as you need Germany"; "Labor Service is the Honor Service of the German Youth"; "The Saar Remains German." One camp I visited near Berlin had a framed quotation from a speech of Hitler's: "The Jew is not a German but merely a trader; not a citizen but an exterminator."

On the opposite wall from this was, ironically enough, a quotation from Kant: "Have the courage to use your reason."

The camp day began at 5 A.M., with ten minutes' physical exercises in the open. Breakfast—coffee, bread, jam and margarine —came at 5:45. Then came flag parade, after which the various work sections marched off, arriving at the work place usually about 7 o'clock. Work—digging ditches to drain the swampy moorland, or cutting undergrowth for ditch bottoms—went on until 9:30, when we had a half hour's spell for a further breakfast of bread, sausage and cheese.

We never worked particularly hard, and there was always a

chance when the foreman was in another part of the work place to take a few minutes' rest in the sun. About 1 P.M. we knocked off and began the march home to lunch. Lunch consisted usually of a big bowl of stew. The food was good, and one could always get as much as one wished. After lunch came an hour and a half's compulsory rest; from 4:30 till 6 there was sport or drill. Another flag parade, followed by supper of bread, sausage and coffee, came at 6:30. The evenings were free, or used for lectures or singing. Lights were out at 10 o'clock.

Pay was very low, only 25 pfennigs (about 10 cents at present exchange rates) a day, and from this boot polish and soap had to be bought before anything was left for tobacco or other extras. Leave was, however, plentiful. Each man serving a full year received a fortnight free during that time. Every Wednesday afternoon was free from 3 o'clock until midnight and leave could also be obtained from 3 on Saturday afternoon till 2 on Monday morning.

The living conditions and food in this camp were, according to men who had served in other camps, better than the average. This difference was chiefly due to a difference in the quality of our leaders. One of the difficulties the camp faces at present is a lack of good camp commanders. Many camps are in charge of old members of the Nazi party who have received their posts rather because of their faithfulness than because of their efficiency.

Quality of the leadership is all important because the camp is allowed only 2.20 marks a day for each man, to cover all the expenses of upkeep, food, salaries, clothing and so on. A camp commander gets 160 marks a month, his keep and his uniform—a heavy salary in Germany today. The money comes partly from a government grant made out of the unemployed relief money which would have been paid out to the men had they not been drafted into camp, and partly from the peasants on whose land the work is done. The work is almost entirely agricultural improvement.

What was the attitude of the trainees themselves to this Labor Service system? On the whole they accepted it cheerfully enough as their duty. Some, usually students, resented the intellectual meagerness of the place—the library, for instance, consisted of about forty books. Others who had learned skilled trades were weary with the monotonous unskilled work. But most of them were genuinely happy. They were in splendid health, with plenty to eat—a luxury some of them had not experienced for years—and they were kept too busy to have time to criticize.

Political ideas of Nazism, which were presented to them by lectures and wall placards, they accepted more or less unquestioningly. They were, with a few exceptions, undisturbed even by the notice over the cook-shop door. "Thy People is Everything; you are Nothing" ("Dein Volk ist alles; Du bist nichts"). On the other hand, not many of them showed a burning enthusiasm for Nazi principles. Their attitude was one rather of personal faith in Hitler than of devotion to the details of his policy. Their view was that Hitler himself had once been a workman and therefore would not betray the workers. Moreover, those who were critical of National Socialism were usually of a conservative or nationalist opinion. Of Communist views I could find little trace.

Their national feeling, too, was very strong. They had been taught, and believed, that if war came it was their duty to follow the government into it unquestioningly. They declared, as every one in Germany declares, that they did not want war. In this they were quite sincere; but if Hitler called on them to fight they would do so enthusiastically.

Their faith in Hitler was, unfortunately, not supported by a very sound knowledge of international affairs. Many of them were surprised to hear that there were unemployed in England or America. They had been taught so long to blame all Germany's evils on the losing of the war that they thought that Germany stood alone impoverished in the midst of a group of rich, victorious countries. The inference, that winning a war is the way to prosperity, was not difficult to draw. Moreover, what instruction we had in the camp stressed the glories of war, and the opportunities it gives for manly development, and never its horrors or hypocrisies.

The teaching of such an outlook toward war is, of course, not peculiar to the labor camps; it can be found in any German school. Only in so far, however, as it is present in the camps can they be said to be definitely militaristic. Certainly the camps are conducted on soldierly lines. The uniforms; the heel-clicking and saluting; the sentry, spade on shoulder, by the gateway; the ceremony, morning and evening, of saluting the labor service flag —a flag resembling the Nazi banner but with the emblem of a spade and two ears of wheat instead of the swastika, and the five to six hours' drill a week give the whole camp a military appearance.

But these things the Germans defend as "soldierly" ("soldatisch"), meaning smart, disciplined, manly; as distinct from "militaristic" ("militaerisch"), which has the meaning of being actually trained in the use of arms. They openly admit that the labor camps are soldierly, while vigorously denying that they are in any way militaristic.

If one accepts their definitions, there is no doubt that in this they are stating what is the truth. There was in this camp no attempt to give actual instruction in the technique of fighting. The drill we did was merely elementary squad work in marching, turning and goose-stepping, with training in a sort of small-arms drill with spades—"Shoulder spades!" "Present spades!" and so forth. The only "militaristic" thing was the throwing, during the sports hour, of dummy hand grenades, and this is part of the Defense Sport ("Wehrsport"), which is played in every German school.

But even if no arms training is given in the labor camps, no one can deny that the general effect of their drill and organization is to provide Germany with a disciplined body of men who will form a ready basis on which to erect, if the need arises, a fully trained army. However, the German is very sensitive to having this fact pointed out to him. With his genuine love of drill and uniforms—many of the trainees in camp preferred, for instance, to do drill rather than play football in the afternoons—he regards marching and training quite sincerely as a sport.

The danger of this whole question of militarization is that militarization, being the most spectacular aspect of the labor service, has caused other and more essential features to be neglected. What is of paramount importance about the German Youth Labor Service is that it is no solution of the problem of unemployment.

It does ease the strain on the labor market by providing the camps as a buffer between school days and the search for employment. It does recondition and discipline the young, and give the brain worker some understanding of manual labor. But after his training period the young worker is still faced with the problem of finding a job. Moreover, he has received in camp no instruction in a skilled trade which would make the search for work easier. The unhappiest men in the German Labor Service today are those who have served their time and yet wait on in the camps, afraid to leave the security there for an outside world where, as unskilled laborers, they could not earn much more than they do in camp, where their food, lodging and clothing are provided for.

It is one of the defects of the present service that not enough attempt is made to encourage the initiative of the trainees or to deepen their interest in the work. There is no Five-Year Plan, no discussion of weekly or monthly output. All decisions are made from above, in accordance with the leading principle (Fuehrerprinzip) which dominates German life today; all that each man knows is that he must dig so much ditch or cut so much undergrowth on that particular day. In this respect the present German system is radically different from that of the voluntary camps out of which it grew, and which were all largely self-governing.

The women's camps are much better in this respect. For the women trainees work on the neighboring farms, serving both in the fields and the house, and learn a wide variety of duties. The system, as a result, is much more popular with the women than with the men. The main drawback of these women's camps (Frauen Arbeitslager) is, according to an American girl student who worked in one of them, their isolation and primitiveness.

All these criticisms, however, strike one only when one is thinking over the system in detail. When I was actually in the camp, the healthy work, the sunshine, and, above all, the cheerfulness of my fellow-trainees seemed to me to be powerful arguments for the system. The labor camps do undoubtedly achieve their main object of providing the young with at least temporary work and of obliterating class distinctions by making every trainee, whether rich or poor, serve under the same conditions.

But the success of the camp is only in its own specialized environment, which has to be built up outside of the main stream of the economic and social order and is not gained through the usual workings of that order. What is needed is not an extension of labor camps but a diffusion of their principles throughout the whole economic system.

On the Cultural
Front the Nazis Drive

by Elizabeth Wiskemann

BERLIN

AFTER MORE THAN a year of Nazi rule it is beginning to be possible to make at least a tentative estimate of what the new movement is doing and promises to do to Germany's cultural life. Very early in the Nazi régime it was made plain that what Herr Hitler and his followers had in mind was not only a political and economic but also a cultural revolution. The sentimentalism, internationalism and individualism which had run riot before the World War were to give way to qualities more suitable to the nature of an authoritarian and nationalistic State. The "pure Aryan" was to have his innings in the arts as well as in business and politics.

Republican Germany had given birth to a bold artistic experimentalism in an atmosphere of cosmopolitan freedom. There were Piscator's experiments with theatre and film, Erich Mendelsohn's architecture sprang up, Leonhard Franck wrote "Karl und Anna" and Döblin wrote "Alexanderplatz," while Marc, Klee, Nolde and Barlach became prominent in the modern galleries. Some of these were Jewish names.

The influence of Paris and Moscow was great, but though men like Emil Ludwig were accused of an alien superficiality it would

From the *New York Times Magazine,* May 27, 1934, copyright © 1934, 1962 by The New York Times Company.

have been absurd to deny the traditional heritage of Berlach and Thomas Mann. The majority of the educated classes were hostile to "Bolshevist" experiments, but they were richly supplied with the classics in theatre, opera and concert hall.

In contrast, one's first impression of cultural life under the Nazi régime is one of blank destruction. Klee and Thomas Mann are in exile and Toller is forbidden; picture galleries like Flechtheim's (a famous Jewish firm) are closed; there is nothing running at the highbrow cinema Die Kamera in Berlin, where many of us first encountered the art of Eisenstein; and the Querschnitt, once a serious literary magazine, is reduced to publishing travel photographs. If one looks at a list of the plays being given in Berlin or Munich or Frankfort, there appears to be a long array of silly comedies; only at Hamburg are the classical plays performed.

One gains the impression that the authorities wish to keep the people trivially amused, above all to keep their minds off their troubles, and solemn articles appear in the press on the value of laughter. Even the obedient journalists of today complain of the dearth of new plays. In the opera houses there is a tendency to give easy music, not Wagner so much as the nineteenth century Italians.

This general impression of nothingness is, however, misleading. On the one hand some of the cultural life of republican Germany, now that the first violence of the political change is over, is going quietly on; while from the National Socialist side passionate efforts are being made to establish an organic national culture, based, in accordance with Hitler's gospel, upon racial instinct as opposed to human intellect. For in the ideology of the Nazis the association of intellectual life with esthetic impulse is a Renaissance superstition.

The cultural aim of the Nazis, while esthetically unattractive to most foreign observers, has at least been amply and constantly defined, and by no one more adequately than by Hans Friedrich Blunck, who has been made president of the Reich Literary Chamber. In the new monthly magazine, The Inner Reich, which first appeared in April, a statement from Blunck on "German Cultural Policy" appears. Every kind of art, he holds, should concern itself with the race, its life and tradition. Recent research, he says with enthusiasm, shows the continuity of German racial development since about 1800 B.C., the beginning of the Bronze Age in the north. He even hopes that further revelations will show an unbroken evolution since the Stone Age.

Secondly, Blunck welcomes the establishment of the new State Chamber of Culture; he rejoices in State control on the one hand and guild organization on the other. Both seem to him truly to express the Germanic race; the new Germany is an expression of a "blood inheritance." Together with the rest of the spokesmen of national socialism, he wishes German art to be utterly autochthonous, to rule out all alien influence and base itself upon the glorification of blood and soil. (It will be observed that the conception of beauty has no place in the definition of Nazi art.)

Another leading figure in the Reich Literary Chamber, Theodor Fritsch, made a speech the other day in which he propounded the rest of the cultural doctrine of the Nazis. Art exists, he said, to express the soul of the race, but the "cultural bolsheviki" of the postwar period, because they were Jews, had twisted art into something between an acrobatic feat and a commercial product. But blood and soil will save the situation, as Professor Schultze-Naumburg, the art expert of Weimar, is also convinced. And Herr Darré, the Minister of Agriculture, has just written a book in which he sets forth the doctrine of the cult of the peasant as the purest representative of "blood and soil."

In every branch of cultural life one sees the attempt on the one hand to give life to the Nazi conception, and on the other hand an effort to preserve that independence of spirit which the pre-Nazi artists deemed essential. All artists—writers, painters, actors, musicians, whatever they may be—are, of course, obliged to join what is in fact a State guild, and in doing so to pledge themselves "to work in the spirit of the national government" and to carry out the orders of the leader of their section.

The obedient bookshops of Germany, whether in the towns of Bavaria or the Rhineland or in Prussian Berlin, are already filled with works upon early Germanic types and their racial significance. Wilhelm Schäfer, author of "The Thirteen Books of the German Soul," has also published a pamphlet pleading for medievalism, and it is characteristic that the German late medieval mystic, Meister Eckehart, is having a new vogue. This earthy medievalism is closely associated with the cult of the hero, and this again with war and chauvinism. The bookshops are crowded with books on the Caesars, and with biographies of Cromwell, Napoleon and Frederick the Great. Mirko Jelusich, a successful biographer of Cromwell, has recently portrayed Don Juan as well, but this must be regarded as a discrepancy. In general, no foreign influence but that of Italy is recognized. There is a conspicuous sprinkling of books which claim the restoration of Germany's African colonies, and always in books and war exhibitions a harping on the theme of "A Whole World Against Us," as one of the newer books is called. Erich Czech-Jochberg has rewritten German history in the spirit of national socialism, and his book is much in demand.

Every bookshop is, of course, richly stocked with works by all the Nazi leaders: Goebbels, Göring, Röhm and Rosenberg have all contributed to the party literature. But while Hitler's "Mein Kampf" has undoubtedly been widely read by friend and foe, the works of the other leaders make upon the casual observer the impression of compulsory window-dressing.

Three typically Nazi plays have recently been produced. First there was Blunck's "Land in Twilight"; it is laid in Iceland in 1480 and handles all the Nazi themes—peasants, revenge, faith, and so on. The play revolves around the heroic figure of a Governor of Iceland, who discovered America twenty years before Columbus—thus achieving a Nordic victory over the Latin, one of Blunck's favorite themes. The theatre where "Land in Twilight" was given was nevertheless quite empty at the third performance.

A play by Friedrich Forster-Burggraf, called "All Against One, One for All," on the theme of the emancipation of Sweden from Danish rule, has been put on in various provincial towns and appears to be popular. A different, yet essentially Nazi, theme is that of a play called "The Hour of Sacrifice," by Hellmuth Unger, which came on in Berlin on the same night as "Land in Twilight." This deals with a woman who, on discovering that there is insanity in her family, renounces love, marriage and reproduction in the interests of the race.

The unhappy financial condition of most of the Berlin theatres has attracted attention of late, and this has provoked an official statement on the theatre question. The Reich is taking over entirely the Charlottenburg Opera and three other theatres. Of these, one, which used to be Rheinhardt's Grosses Schauspielhaus, has become a people's theatre and is being used by the Labor Front as part of the new Kraft Durch Freude (strength through joy), or after-work organization; a Bavarian mystery play has already been given there. Another theatre has been transformed into a "House for the Education of the People."

On the whole, the cinema provides the most satisfying entertainment in Germany today. The photography and acting remain of a high standard. The period of strictly Nazi stories appears to be over, though the Horst Wessel film is still on in the provinces. A very popular film at the moment in Munich, Berlin and other towns is a war story, "Stoss Truppe 1917," played mostly by Storm Troop young men. The last new Ufa film, called "Gold," is a typical product of the period; it shows the noble German engineer (Hans Albers) avenging the death of a friend by the destruction of an unscrupulous capitalist.

The wireless, that mighty engine of the Propaganda Ministry, is moderating its patriotic transports; Dr. Goebbels had reason to fear that people were getting bored. But programs still include a judicious mixture of drill for different sections of society, interspersed with homage to the German race.

While the political revolution has affected the world of music and opera comparatively little, the fate of painting and architecture in the new Germany has been less happy. A tremendous attack has been leveled, especially by the book-burning students, against the "decadent and un-German" work of the post-war period. Even before the Nazis came into power, when Dr. Frick was in the Thuringian Government, he removed pictures from the Weimar Gallery which he and Professor Schultze-Naumburg considered un-German. They admired the famous medieval sculpture of Bamberg and Naumburg and approved the monotonous work of German painters in the nineteenth century.

In all the arts and crafts the present régime is exerting itself to supply a stimulus by awarding prizes for competition. A prize was recently offered for a large painting to illustrate the theme of the glorification of German labor. The first prize was awarded to an anonymous candidate, who subsequently proved to be Professor Gies, a man who had been condemned by the Nazis. A similar incident took place very recently at Hamburg.

While post-war painting in Germany did not, to be sure, achieve great importance, the post-war architecture of Germany won the admiration of Europe. Buildings are, moreover, very much more difficult to conceal, and Fahrenkampf's "Shell-House," which was only finished just before Hitler came in, reigns in insolent triumph over the War Office quarter of Berlin. We learn that these "bolshevistic" buildings are not to be destroyed, but that nothing of the kind is to occur again. A man who wished to build himself a house with a flat roof the other day was refused police permission until he had introduced an inconspicuous but slanting line to the roof.

The Chancellor himself takes a technical interest in architecture, and his taste is illustrated in the Brown House he designed, where the Nazi party has its headquarters at Munich. Hitler dislikes Berlin and regards Munich as, at any rate, the cultural capital of Germany. Accordingly, he has arranged for a big building program there, by which some more party buildings are to link up the Brown House with the art galleries which lie close at hand. He has chosen as the responsible architect Paul Ludwig Trost, and the style of the whole plan, as of the Brown House, far from introducing Gothic features, is that of the neo-classical buildings erected by King Louis I of Bavaria in the early nineteenth century. In the centre of the new buildings there is to be a big open space where the great national festivals of Nazi Germany may be suitably staged.

These great pageants, held on Labor Day, Party Day, and so on, are thought by some people to be the form in which national socialism, with its mastery over mass emotion, will make its chief contribution to Germany's cultural life.

The march of the Nazi culture is not, of course, uninterrupted. Some remnants of the older culture survive, and there are some divergent tendencies. The great S. Fischer publishing firm (which is itself Jewish) still finds it worth while to issue the works of Jews like Hofmanstahl and Wassermann and the latest novels of the exiled Thomas Mann, together with a number of translations from foreign writers.

Mann's new books are reported to be selling well. Hans Carossa continues to be read, and young novelists like Hans Fallada and Manfred Hausmann, who have been writing in non-political fashion for some years, are much in demand even among the Storm Trooper university students.

Fallada, like Richard Billinger, whose "Stille Gäste" is probably the best play to be seen in Berlin at the moment, has been attacked by the Nazi press as "sentimental." So has Sudermann, one of whose plays was recently condemned. But there still seems to be a lingering popular fondness for "sentimentality"; witness the fact that the opera houses are giving nineteenth-century Italian opera and that Wagner has had to give way to Weber, the harmlessly tuneful author of "Freischütz" and "Oberon."

On the whole, however, the Nazi revolution has certainly succeeded in injecting political bias and censorship into every important aspect of the country's artistic and cultural life. It has curtailed or destroyed much, if not quite all, of the fruitful creative activity of republican days, and the narrow racial-nationalistic culture which the leaders of the new régime aspire to establish has not yet found anything to put in its place.

Part 3

FASCISM AS AN INTERNATIONAL PHENOMENON

FASCISM IS the result of an ultra-conservative counterattack against liberals and radicals. It occurs in rapidly modernizing societies where old conservative power elites are strong enough and yet threatened enough to mobilize lower-middle-class violence against the left. It follows that in all societies there is a fascist potential, however weak. All the trappings and symbols of Italian and German fascism will not, of course, be present—each society has different national traditions to conserve, and different symbols for those traditions. The use of force and the urge toward totalitarianism to defend those threatened traditions and values will, however, be present, and will generate ideas and practices similar to those of European fascism.

The "threat from the left" will also vary from country to country. To select some examples at random, in America the civil rights movement led Southern whites to adopt essentially fascist attitudes toward black Americans. In South Africa, embattled white supremacists have already adopted many of the ideas and some of the practices of European fascism in their increasing attempts to maintain apartheid. In the future, feudal elites and neocolonialists in underdeveloped nations may find fascist policies attractive as democratic nationalism, socialism, and communism spread among aroused peasants.

Fortunately, the semi-feudal ultra-conservatives of the "third world" do not preside over mighty industrial powers, as did Hitler and Mussolini. This means that they have no accessible means of creating fascist terror and totalitarianism as they struggle against progressive social change from below. The only danger will come, perhaps, from the West. For example, caught up in the anti-communist mythology of the Cold War, the United States did its best to provide arms, troops, and funds to the potential fascists of the Saigon regime in Vietnam.

There is no way of knowing whether fascism has a future except through a study of its past. The following articles suggest something about the international impact of fascism in the twenties and thirties, and enable us to judge the future potential of revolutionary conservatism.

Sparks That
Light Revolutions

by Walter Duranty

REVOLUTION—A fundamental change in political organization or in the government or constitution; the overthrow or renunciation of one government or the substitution of another by the governed.—WEBSTER'S DICTIONARY.

THIS DEFINITION IS sufficiently general to cover virtually all revolutions that have occurred in history, with the exception of what are known as "palace revolutions," which involve no greater change than the overthrow of an Oriental monarch or a South American President by a rival in his own entourage. Today, however, the word "revolution" commonly implies a far-reaching social upheaval such as happened in Russia in November, 1917. The Bolsheviki, indeed, go so far as to say that there is no real revolution which is not accompanied by a transfer of power from one class to another.

Lenin did not explicitly state that such a transfer must be from the possessing classes to the workers—in fact, the Bolshevist encyclopedia admits the revolutionary character of the Cromwellian movement which transferred power from the English Crown and aristocracy to a body of middle bourgeois republicans—but his writings show clearly that no revolution, in his opinion, is complete until so radical a shift in power is accomplished. With characteristic logic Lenin argued that any transfer of control from one section of a ruling or possessing class to another is more apparent than real, and that if the remnants of feudalism, aristocracy, monarchy, or in more modern times high finance and big business, are allowed to remain in existence, it is more than probable that they will gradually reassert their rights and that the revolution will be only a partial or temporary change.

That proved true of Cromwell's revolution, which was succeeded by the Stuart restoration. It was true of the great French Revolution, which swung away from the proletarian lines of Marat and Robespierre to the Napoleonic Empire. It may be true in Spain, where the forces of reaction are now trying to reassert their rights in no uncertain manner.

At this point it is necessary to make a distinction between different types of revolution. The American Revolution, for instance, did indeed create a fundamental change in political organization; it involved the overthrow of British authority and the substitution of an independent government by the population of the former Colonies. But in reality this movement was a successful rebellion rather than a revolution in the true sense of the word.

The same might have been said of the war between the States had the Confederacy been able to achieve its independence. It is significant that the Federal soldier's term for the Confederates was "Johnny Rebs," which indicates that the people of the North regarded the Southerners as rebels rather than as revolutionaries, just as the English and the American Tories had regarded Washington and his army.

To some extent the Nazi movement in Germany was also a rebellion against the restrictions and impositions of the Treaty of Versailles, which every German considered to be a cruel and iniquitous treaty, and which, it must be remembered, was only signed under the direct threat of armed invasion by French, British, American and Czechoslovak troops in the Summer of 1919.

Thus, the Nazi "revolution" in Germany has a parallel with the American "revolution" of 1776, in that both were based upon the natural desire of a virile people to rid itself of a foreign yoke. True, the Treaty of Versailles did not actually force alien governors upon the German nation or dictate its policy and impose its taxes, but the pressure of Versailles upon the German people was no less great, no less unwelcome, and no less wounding than the pressure of English government upon the American Colonies.

A second type of revolution is a military dictatorship; Persia, Turkey and Poland under Pilsudski are the most conspicuous examples. In Persia and Turkey there were genuine revolutions, according to Webster's definition, in that Riza Khan and Kemal each overthrew the existing government, expelled the monarch and—virtually in the case of Kemal, actually in the case of Riza —assumed his power and prerogatives. Pilsudski's rule in Poland was somewhat different. He obtained power by constitutional methods, but then proceeded to rule in an unconstitutional manner. The same may be said of Hitler, who insists that his accession to power was also a revolution.

The Nazi movement in Germany and the Fascist movement in Italy might more accurately be termed counter-revolutions, and the same may be said of the uprising in Spain. Each of the three was presented as an effort to check or crush a proletarian revolutionary movement.

Mussolini had some justification for the claim that this was the goal of Black-Shirt policy. The growing chaos in Italy in the immediate post-war period, and the attempt of the Communists to seize factories in the northern industrial cities in 1921, gave more than a semblance of truth to Mussolini's assertion that he was rescuing his country from the forces of disorder.

On the other hand, few dispassionate observers will agree that the Germany of Stresemann, Bruening or von Papen was in any great danger of proletarian revolution. Hitler used this alleged danger as a means of propaganda with the middle and smaller bourgeoisie, and as a device to obtain financial support from big business, finance and industry. But, as I said before, the real key to Hitler's victory was his successful appeal to the wounded national pride of the German nation. As far as Spain is concerned, it is difficult at present to estimate whether the counter-revolutionary uprising is an attempt by ambitious generals to establish a military dictatorship, or a movement, similar to that of Mussolini, to forestall a proletarian revolution. Such facts as are available suggest the former theory, because the existing government of Spain, elected by a popular vote, was not much more "Left" than the present government of France or, for that matter, than the German government of Stresemann or Bruening.

The government at Madrid was trying to redress some of the more obvious grievances of the mass of the Spanish people. It had a liberal or, if one prefers, a Leftist policy, but no more than that, which is a very different thing from a revolutionary policy. It seems, therefore, that the forces of reaction which sponsored the present uprising have little more justification than Hitler had for saying that they were "saving the country from anarchy, chaos and bolshevism."

The same argument, or nearly the same argument, has been used against President Roosevelt by certain reactionary circles in the United States. A comparison between Moscow and Washington was deliberately made by an eminent public man who had been his party's standard-bearer in a hard-fought election, but it missed fire because the facts of the case proved it to be grotesque. In Spain, however, it is probably true that the government was making a more serious and energetic attempt to curb the powers of privilege than President Roosevelt ever dreamed of, and this, although it may not provide justification for a counter-revolutionary movement, at least has given the counter-revolution a platform on which to stand.

It is not difficult to deduce the technique of counter-revolution. It consists in declaring as loudly as possible: "Our aims are to save our beloved country from anarchy and bolshevism, from nationalization of women, from attacks upon religion and the home, and from the blood-stained hand of Moscow."

Such an appeal has proved successful in Italy and Germany. It would probably succeed in America should a similar situation arise—which seems unlikely. Whether or not it will succeed in Spain depends upon the internal circumstances of that country; which brings me to an analysis of the basic principles of revolution.

Before beginning to discuss them it is necessary to understand that there is all the difference in the world between liberalism and revolution. Hitler, Mussolini and General Franco may pretend that they are trying to save their country from the "horrors of bolshevism" and may use this bogy as a means to scare the big and little bourgeoisie into supporting them against a danger which in reality is more or less imaginary. In such a case these bogy-raisers are making a criminal assault upon democracy and the rights of human freedom.

In reality they are not fighting bolshevism at all; they are fighting liberalism. They are fighting the old fight of a privileged minority and of the "vested interests" against the mass of their fellow-countrymen, because it is not true, as reactionaries throughout the world are trying to suggest, that a liberal government is necessarily a prelude to revolution.

The prime and essential condition for a revolution is that a majority of the population—not a small majority, but a large majority, say 80 per cent at least—is so dissatisfied with the conditions in which it lives that it is prepared to fight in order to change those conditions. That is what the Bolsheviki call a "revolutionary situation"; it is the product of time and circumstances, but not of any one's wishes, nor even of propaganda, however adroit and pervasive. Such circumstances existed in France in 1789 and in Russia in 1917; perhaps they exist in Spain.

From this there follows a second requisite, that the régime against which popular discontent is rising in revolt is not itself too strong. Lenin always maintained that revolution was not a chaotic upheaval like an earthquake but a historical process which could occur only when the privileged minority had become extremely small and the discontented majority extremely great.

It is a dogma of Marxist theory that no possessing class will abandon its privileges without a struggle. If, therefore, the possessing class or bourgeoisie is numerically considerable, it is more than probable that it will be able successfully to defend itself against any popular movement because it has the initial advantages of power, money and superior education.

This proved true in Italy and Germany. It would doubtless prove true also in the United States or Britain, but it was not true in Russia. And I do not think it is true in Spain. The Spain of 1936 and the Russia of 1917 are rather similar in that the majority of the population of both countries was an impoverished peasantry, industrial development was only in its early stages, and there was no large middle class to bridge the gulf between the discontented masses and the highly privileged few.

Though the first requisite for a revolution is popular support, this support may be only potential and may require the energizing force of the third requisite of any revolution—leadership. The American Colonists were growing more and more restive under the policy of the British Crown, which may be summed up in the phrase, "taxation without representation." The Boston Tea Party and the action of a group of courageous leaders fired the spark of popular discontent and an explosion followed. In the same way Lenin and the Bolsheviki made dynamite of the mass discontent of the Russian people and used it to blow Kerensky's flimsy régime to pieces.

The Bolsheviki maintain that, given a true "revolutionary situation," leadership will be provided, as one might say, almost automatically; that the occasion calls for the men. That is a Marxist doctrine with which I am compelled to disagree. I would go so far as to say that without Washington the American Revolution might easily have been suppressed, that without Lenin the Bolsheviki would never have won power in Russia, that Napoleon changed the course of French history just as Hitler and Mussolini have changed the history of Germany and Italy.

The fourth requisite for a revolution, as the Bolsheviki found in their abortive struggle of 1905–06, is that the army should not be opposed to the revolt. From the time of Sparticus until today it has been a truism that disciplined soldiers will beat undisciplined revolutionists. It was never so true as at present when poison gas and machine guns have put an enormous advantage in the army's hands. In the case of Russia in 1917, the army had been broken by a foreign enemy and discouraged by the knowledge that its leaders were incompetent or worse. When the decisive moment arrived in 1917, the army failed to intervene against the revolution as it had done in 1905–06.

One thus reaches the conclusion that there are certain requisites for a revolution or a counter-revolution, but it must not be forgotten that requisites are not by any means the same thing as technique. To sum up briefly, the requisites for a counter-revolution are as follows: A numerically strong bourgeoisie, the support of the army and the police, and intelligent leadership. The requisites for a revolution are great popular discontent, a numerically or morally weak bourgeoisie, the neutrality if not the support of the army and, once more, intelligent leadership.

The technique, both of revolution and counter-revolution, is almost exactly the same. It lies in the effective mobilization of forces that are potentially favorable—that is to say, in applying the combined effects of propaganda and organization. Unorganized or partly organized workers can make an impressive demonstration and may terrify a weak government into surrender, but as the Bolsheviki found in July, 1917, no demonstration, however numerically impressive, is much good against machine guns handled by determined men.

Propaganda, therefore, is not alone sufficient. It can rally supporters and make them understand what they are fighting for and give them the enthusiasm to fight, but that alone does not insure victory unless there are the weapons to fight with and the ability to use them effectively. The process of arousing the enthusiasm of potential supporters, of training them and arming them, may be defined by the single word "mobilization," which in its military sense means no more than the preparation of a striking force. It is a military axiom that any army which is mobilized, which has assembled and equipped its forces and concentrated them at the most suitable points for offensive action, has nine chances out of ten of beating an enemy which has failed to mobilize or whose mobilization is not completed. The same is true of revolutionary movements.

According to Bolshevist theory a revolution is the culminating point of progressive social disintegration. This sounds well on paper and can be defended logically, but it fails to explain the success of fascism in Italy and nazism in Germany. Here surely the key to victory was the combination of propaganda and organization.

Finally, there is an additional factor of cardinal importance, and it is this which compels me to put so much stress upon the question of leadership. I refer to the choice of the psychological moment for action, whether it be revolutionary action or counter-revolutionary. In any form of human conflict, from boxing to war, what is known as "timing" has a paramount value and will decide the issue if other things are equal.

The Bolsheviki "mistimed" their action in July, 1917, and had Kerensky been more resolute they might have paid dearly for their error. Mussolini, on the other hand, gauged accurately the timing of the Fascist march on Rome, just as Lenin gauged accurately the most favorable moment for action in November, 1917.

The story goes that Lenin made this decision against the advice of the majority of his closest supporters, many of whom wanted to wait and "let the situation ripen," as they expressed it. Lenin said: "No, tonight is the time to strike; we cannot wait any longer." He then, I have been told, lay down on a bench and wrapped himself in a cloak. "You go ahead and argue," he said, "and meanwhile let me sleep, because I'm tired. Wake me when you have reached the conclusion that my arguments in favor of immediate action are unanswerable."

In an hour or two his supporters woke him and said: "We still think that action is premature, but we can find no answer to your arguments." "All right," said Lenin, "the revolution begins now." And it did.

This story may be apocryphal, but it illustrates the essential quality of leadership, which must combine a knowledge of where and how to strike and of the moment when the blow should be delivered. Another quality, little less essential, is ruthless vigor, the will to hit hard and to show no mercy until the adversary is beaten.

Behind the Fighting Fronts in the Two Clashing Spains

by Virginia Cowles

IN SPITE OF numerous and conflicting political terms used to classify the Spanish conflict, the fundamental issue lies neither between republicanism and fascism, nor between communism and monarchism. Mainly and simply it is a war between the proletariat and the upper classes.

The proletariat comprises 80 per cent of the people of Spain. Within this group approximately 60 per cent of the whole people are with the Popular Front, while the remaining 20 per cent, under the influence of the church, have thrown in their lot with General Franco and the privileged classes. Thus as regards numbers the sympathies of Spain are fairly evenly divided; a comparison of life on the two sides, however, affords a striking contrast.

One enters Valencia, which until recently served as the republican capital, to find a city of drab confusion. The only people in the streets are working-class people: peasant women with black shawls tied round their heads; laborers with unshaven faces and dusty boots; soldiers, some in the regulation khaki, others in sweaters and corduroy trousers; and platinum-blonde girls whose hair is growing out very black owing to the fact that all the peroxide has been confiscated by the hospitals.

From the *New York Times Magazine,* January 9, 1938, copyright © 1938, 1966 by The New York Times Company.

Hotels are overcrowded, there is a shortage of food, and petrol is so scarce that traffic is confined to army trucks, evacuation lorries and Ministry of War cars blazing with official stickers. Waiters, elevator boys and tram-car conductors are not attired in uniform, nor do the women of Government Spain wear hats, for paraphernalia such as these are considered a sign of the upper classes.

To travel from this world to Nationalist territory is to find strikingly different conditions. Upon crossing the International Bridge on the French Basque coast and driving into San Sebastian, one enters a city enjoying most of the luxuries of peacetime. Expensive motor cars glide through the streets; dinners are long and elaborate, hotels comfortable, and cafes and restaurants crowded with officers in well-cut uniforms and smartly dressed women laughing and sipping their cocktails. These conditions are not merely confined to San Sebastian. It is Nationalist Spain's proudest boast that except for frontline sectors one would not even know that a war was going on. Villages are quiet and orderly, shops are well-stocked and there is an abundance of food and wine. There is no shortage of petrol and even the railroads are running, trains carrying de luxe sleeping cars.

War propaganda is based not so much on the regime to come as on the campaign against "bolshevism." The people in enemy territory are represented as living beneath a tyranny of murder and anarchy; the authorities are always alluded to as the "hordes of Valencia," and when Franco captures a city his victory is not referred to as a "conquest" but as a "liberation."

That there are many White sympathizers in the towns held by the republic cannot be denied. When Santander fell, hundreds of Franco's supporters who had been trapped in the city for more than a year crowded the streets, laughing and crying. I saw many of them tearing down republican flags, while dozens of balconies were draped with red and yellow mantillas forming the royal colors of Spain. Automobiles blazed with Monarchist and Fascist flags, while pictures of Franco and Mussolini were plastered on the buildings.

It would be an exaggeration, however, to agree with Nationalist newspapers that Santander was "overwhelmingly pro-White." One had only to wander along the wharves to see the thousands of refugees, their bundles and bags piled up beside them, who gazed on the celebration in bewilderment; or to see the cold, aloof stares of waitresses, elevator boys and charwomen in hotels and restaurants; or the long columns of women and children patiently lined up before the jails which were bursting with militia men.

In the working-class quarters doors were closed and window shades pulled down. The streets were almost empty save for children who sat forlornly on the curbstones, and housewives who hurried to their homes. High up on many of the buildings were old, frayed signs which said: "Vote for the Popular Front." When one of Franco's generals, Queippo de Llamo, visited the city several weeks later these signs had not yet been removed; he delivered a radio broadcast decrying Santander as a "disgrace."

Upon the capture of a city, tribunals are immediately established; government leaders, army officers and men and women accused of betraying Whites are tried before a court-martial and the majority sentenced to death. When I inquired of one of Franco's officers why the penalty should be so severe, he informed me that it was merely in accord with Spanish tradition; that if one was wrong in politics one paid with one's head. To bolster his argument he explained that when Philip II had wished to have a Catholic Spain he had found no way more effective to rid the country of Protestants than to kill them; his method was so effective in fact that 300 years later only 35,000 of them existed in a population of 22,000,000. "It will be the same way with the Reds," he finished.

Although towns and cities burn with a patriotic fervor in their show of banners, their parades, speeches and radio broadcasts, the villages seem completely detached. Life in the country goes on as usual, with peasants working in the fields, donkey carts moving slowly along the roads and ragged children playing in the dust.

There is little doubt, however, as to the autocratic rule which has been imposed upon the country. While officials state that Spain is anti-democratic, anti-liberal and anti-parliamentarian, the "denouncing system" takes care that those of other opinions are confined to jails. The most casual remark may cast one in the role of suspect. The crusade against bolshevism has swollen in its bitterness to include any form of rule other than an autocratic one; to speak in defense of a parliamentarian government is sufficient to brand one as Red and leads inevitably to a denunciation.

Although the church is one of the leading Right Wing elements of Spain, strangely enough many of its members are suspect. A great number of its priests have lived in the villages, close to the working-class people, and, while at the outbreak of the war they suffered at the hands of Left extremists, some have been accused on the Franco side of having instigated class feeling. In more than one case priests have been placed under arrest, charged with espionage and sabotage.

While the dissenting views of Republicans, Socialists, Communists and Anarchists banded together under a Popular Front government have been widely publicized, little is known of the wide discords in the Franco ranks. These discords are deep and bitter. From one end of Nationalist territory to the other one sees two predominating uniforms: that of the Requetes with their khaki shirts and bright red berets and that of the Phalangists in navy blue with crimson tassels swinging from their caps. These groups represent Franco's main political parties. Aside from the fact that they have united to win the war in a common determination to set up an anti-parliamentarian government, their views are stubbornly placed at opposite poles.

The Requete party was organized in 1830 in support of Don Carlos, the pretender to the Spanish throne. As the Carlos line has been extinct for some time, this party was of little importance when the civil war broke out, but summoning the support of clergy and aristocracy under the slogan of "God, King and Country," it has grown into a strong political force. It advocates what in Spain is known as traditionalism but what in reality, its opponents say, is nothing less than a return to the feudal system. Its members consider the Phalangists a dangerous and radical organization.

Their feeling is not hard to understand, for the Fascist program spells the doom of Bishops and grandees. In favor of a supreme centralized government, they stand for land reform and separation of church from State.

I have heard Requetes argue that the peasant should stay on

the clod of land on which he was born, that his happiness did not lie in education but in the security the great landowner could give him. A Phalangist leader, commenting upon these remarks, shook his head emphatically. "That is the way they talk," he said. "But when the war is over there won't be any great landowners."

The attitude of the Requetes toward Republican prisoners is uncompromising; they demand that prisoners be placed in road-building gangs and forced to rebuild bridges and towns which they have destroyed. The Phalangists, on the other hand, insist that efforts must be made to win the enemy over to a Fascist point of view. When Santander fell and the roads were crowded with prisoners who had been cut off by the Franco forces, I saw innumerable Phalangist food trucks roll up with supplies, while many young officers jumped out, to laugh and talk with the men. Later I learned that thousands of these prisoners had been given Fascist uniforms and drafted into the ranks.

Although there may be a humanitarian element involved in such attempts at consolidation, it is equally plausible to assume that the Phalangists are eager to swell their power against the Requetes. When I discussed the situation with a Requete leader in Salamanca he held up his hands in horror and said that whereas Requete loyalty was unquestionable, half the Phalangists were nothing but Reds. In indignation he added that in the north many of them were giving the Popular Front salute and talking about their brothers in Barcelona.

Franco has made persistent efforts to bring Phalangists and Requetes together. In April he consolidated the two factions on paper, declaring that uniforms and symbols must become merged in one. In spite of his declaration, red berets and dark-blue caps continue to flourish individually; each party continues to maintain its own flag and its own national anthem, and as recently as October hostilities became so bitter that street fights broke out between the two in Saragossa and San Sebastian. In the mind of this reporter there is little doubt that when the war is over the Phalangists will get the upper hand. Their organization numbers almost 3,000,000, as compared with some 800,000 Requetes, while their political force is aided by the Nazi party.

The 10,000 Germans in Spain, aside from those who act as air pilots, operate the radio and telegraph, mark out the roads, check up on the water supplies, act as engineers on the bridges, direct the railroads, and are represented in almost every department of State administration. They encourage the Fascists in obtaining bureaucratic jobs, and thus arouse the resentment of the Requetes, whose fear of coming home from the front to find all the key government positions held by the Fascists is the subject of continual heated discussion. Evidence that their fears are well grounded is shown by the fact that only recently a National Phalangist Council was formed, composed of fifty leading party members, who described it as a move to give "a more permanent shape to the political structure of Nationalist Spain."

The Fascist salute is given from one end of Nationalist territory to the other, and no effort is made to obscure the fact of a Fascist affiliation with Italy and Germany. Hotels, bars and restaurants are decorated with the swastika and the colors of Savoy; many of the shops bear signs of "Man Spricht Deutsch," while numerous buildings shout "Viva Il Duce." Every midnight crowds all over Nationalist territory gather in central squares to listen to loud-speaker reports of news at the front. At the end the national anthem is played. Alternately there are Requete and Phalangist hymns, during which the crowd stands at attention, arms raised in the Fascist salute.

Needless to say, on republican territory fascism produces a very different reaction. To the Loyalists it represents a murderous tyranny equal only to that which bolshevism represents to the Nationalists. Madrid, Barcelona and Valencia blaze with posters showing the marching feet of militiamen crushing the Nazi swastika, while war circulars declare that fascism will dig its tomb in Spain.

It must be pointed out, however, that fascism is decried less as an anti-parliamentarian form of government than as a symbol of upper-class oppression and a perpetuation of the old regime. Fascism to the Loyalists represents capital; therefore any one with independent means, no matter how small, runs the danger of being automatically stamped a Fascist. Even the petty bourgeois, the man who owns a tobacco shop or the woman who runs a boarding house, is "suspect." Indeed, it was this class that suffered most at the hands of the mob when Franco led his revolt. Many members of the aristocracy were able to buy their freedom or through their connections to find refuge in various foreign embassies, while Madrid's 40,000 political assassinations took place for the most part among members of the lower and middle classes.

There is a shortage of food all over Government Spain, few of the railroads are running, and petrol is so scarce that all automobiles have been confiscated by the government. From the coast only one road is open to Madrid, and that is under shellfire at a junction forty miles from the city, so that all traffic must use rough, dirt detours.

Most of the proprietors of shops, hotels and restaurants are either dead or in prison, or else they have escaped to Franco territory. The majority of their establishments are run collectively by their employes, all of whom receive an equal wage of 10 pesetas a day, the profits being appropriated by the government for war funds. The hotel at which I stayed in Madrid was in the hands of elevator boys, doormen and clerks, while the restaurant where I ate was managed jointly by a group of waiters. Prices were three or four times their normal level and, although it would have been possible for the restaurant to obtain food from the country sectors near Madrid, the main diet varied between a plate of beans and a plate of rice. Thus, with inexperienced people running trade and administrative departments, much of Republican Spain's privations is obviously due to mismanagement rather than to a shortage of supplies.

In making comparisons between the two sides, however, it is well to remember that Nationalist Spain has experienced little of the war terror to which the republic has been subjected. Madrid is shelled daily, while Valencia and Barcelona have been the targets of dozens of air raids.

Although the civilians in the large cities accept bombardments with amazing fortitude, the terror in villages is great. A distant speck in the sky is sufficient to throw the entire population into pandemonium. I have seen old men and women burst into tears while mothers ran breathlessly through the streets, rounding up their children and hustling them into caves. Most of the village people have dug their own bombproof shelters, sometimes working feverishly all night to complete cellars as deep as forty feet below the ground.

Owing in some cases to war propaganda, in others to bitter experience, Italians, Germans, Moors and Foreign Legionnaires have swollen into such a legend of brutality that often entire populations flee before the Franco advance. There was evidence of the fear in which they are held during the Asturian campaign when, upon entering villages with the Nationalist troops, I could often see not a sign of life stirring; even the children and the old people had left with the retreating army.

When Franco organized his revolt, it is doubtful if he ever envisaged the numbers that would rise against him. The majority of these people are not fighting for communism but for the 10 pesetas a day which they receive under the republic, as compared to the old regime wage of 1 peseta. Considering, however, that the Communists control the most powerful political force in the army, and that nothing but a strong and ruthless dictatorship could hold post-war Spain together, a Loyalist victory would undoubtedly result in their domination.

It seems to this writer that there is little likelihood of such an outcome. Although the republican army today numbers nearly 600,000 men, it is a poor match for Franco's trained forces. It is composed almost entirely of peasants, laborers and factory workers, and there is a dearth of officers to plan out the strategy of the campaigns and to instruct the men in the mechanics of warfare. Many men have found themselves in trenches who could not even load their own rifles, while one trainload of soldiers was given exactly eight hours, en route to the front, to master the intricacies of the highly complicated Spanish hand grenade.

The 20,000 members of the International Brigade have given little assistance in this respect, being composed for the most part of émigrés and proletarian workers rounded up by the Communist parties of the world. And although the Soviet Union sent some 2,000 General Staff officers, technicians and air pilots to organize the army, these numbers have hardly proved equal to the task.

Illiteracy among 40 per cent of the proletariat has also proved an enormous obstacle in the relay of routine orders. Most of the trench schools have found it necessary to organize classrooms, where the men may receive a brief primary-school education. When I visited one of these schools, on the Madrid front, I saw the strange sight of grown men bent laboriously over their copy books, while on the wall there was a huge sign which said: "Beat fascism by learning to read and write."

The heroism has been great. I have seen men with open wounds fighting on the Madrid front, and in the Asturian mountains watched the republican forces holding almost untenable positions against a barrage of high explosive and shrapnel, until they were completely cut off.

The same spirit of dogged determination exists in Madrid. With every street barricaded by a stone parapet, the city stands as a fortress the capture of which can be accomplished only by starvation. Food is so scarce, however, that there are long queues all over the city, women and children sometimes standing from midnight until noon the next day to buy a kilo of fish or half a loaf of bread.

Although the city is bombarded daily, shops, movie houses and tram cars continue to run, while the squares are thronged with people strolling along arm in arm. I was in a cafe once when a shell crashed through the steel awning over the doorway; the waiters offered their clients a drink on the house.

In spite of such courage and stoicism, thousands would crowd the streets of Madrid and dance with joy if the city were to fall today. They are the small shopowners, the hairdressers, the hotel porters, and even the bootblacks who make their living from the rich; they are housewives and half-starved children, tired of endless waits in the queues, and old people who would welcome peace at any price.

To this correspondent there appears little doubt that a victorious Franco could hold these war-weary populations in submission. His task would lie in consolidating the factions on his own side. As the Requetes demand a king, to which the Phalangists offer no objection so long as he plays the role of figurehead, it is almost certain that Franco would seize on the monarchy as one of the few points of cohesion by placing Alfonso's son, Don Juan, on the throne.

The tragedy of Spain lies in 300 years of bad government. If the Right Wing groups had thrown their support to the republic which first came in 1931, the present war might have been averted. But as an aristocrat in Salamanca informed me: "In Spain no gentleman would ever dream of supporting a republic."

Germany and Japan: Striking Parallels

by Miriam Beard

CASUAL OBSERVERS have applied the term "Fascist" to the nationalist movements in Germany and Japan, as though these were made after the Italian pattern. But this is misleading. The two countries, in social structure, historical development and present policies, should be compared with each other rather than with Italy.

All three, to be sure, are "new" nations; the oldest is just sixty-seven years of age. Germany was forcibly unified in 1866; Japan in 1868; Italy in 1870. For all their ancient culture, they have made but a brief trial of the democratic institutions which are now pronounced failures inside their borders; none has had even one-half of the American experience with modern liberal government on a national scale.

All three seem to have reached together the end of the cycle of "progress." Italy, the youngest, returned to autocratic methods a decade before the others; now, however, her older sisters find their national spirits incompletely formed; they would weld the masses of their peoples by the pressure of a strong State applied at the white heat of patriotism.

There, however, fundamental resemblances cease and diver-

From the *New York Times Magazine,* December 17, 1933, copyright ©
1933, 1961 by The New York Times Company.

gences appear. Italy has completed her consolidation of the autocratic State. Germany is now in the throes of transition. In Japan
reaction is still a program only partly fulfilled; the liberal elements there are not yet dispersed and subjected. Moreover, the
methods and aims, as well as the achievements, of nationalists are
different in the three countries.

Italy has by far the simplest social organism and the least
complex problem. Her aim is essentially the preservation of the
status quo. She strives to uphold the present scheme of things by
employing the power of a "totalitarian" State.

German and Japanese conservatives, on the other hand, are
not trying to maintain the present order; they are struggling to
restore an old order. They seek to reestablish in a position of influence, comparable to that of pre-war times, the military-aristocratic classes typified so often in the figures of the Prussian
Junker and the Japanese Samurai. They would bring back to
power these semifeudal forces and achieve a compromise between
them and modern high capitalism. It is not capitalism alone that
they defend, but a peculiar blend of feudalism and capitalism, of
the old and the new; they employ strong-arm methods to protect
against popular unrest this strange union of opposites.

Because German and Japanese reactionaries wish to restore
and not merely to maintain, they are forced into more extreme
positions than the Italian Fascists. They cannot be content with
the suppression of criticism; they must cut away modern culture,
root and branch. It does not satisfy them to silence women,
regiment youth and control public opinion through press and
schools; they must demolish all modernism in art, letters, music,
stage and film, as incompatible with the resurgence of feudal
forces. That is why apparently irrelevant cultural issues claim so
large a measure of their attention.

Hence, too, the militarism of the Germans and the Japanese is
peculiar. The army is to be not merely the defense of the State
but the State itself. The martial caste which seeks restoration
demands the removal of every trace of pacifism from pedagogy
and the diversion of youthful energies from sport to drill. It
wishes to revive the Spartan clan-ideal and hold it before the

folk. That is why the Germans and the Japanese turn with different desire to history: Italy refurbishes the grandeur of Imperial Rome as a support to national pride; whereas Germany and Japan recall the primitive and tribal past of their peoples as the support for caste pride. They seek justification for the habits and ideals of the Prussian Junker or the Japanese Samurai, and they must go back to civilized epochs to do this.

The nationalist movements among the three peoples arise out of very dissimilar social situations. In Germany and Japan they are the product of long-continued combat between old and new, feudalism and capitalism, militarism and liberalism, aristocracy and democracy. Both nations have carried over into modern times a stronger element of the feudal past than Italy has; yet, in both, the tempo of capitalistic progress has been more furious than in the southern land.

In recent years, Japan amazed Asia and Germany astonished Europe by their seemingly insatiable thirst for change. Both appeared leaders of industry. They set baseball stadia beside medieval castles and illuminated the Ginsa and Kurfürstendamm till they almost outshone Broadway. They exhibited every outward sign of "progress" from blast furnaces to soda fountains, golf, pep, suffrage and saxophones. Their intellectuals were alive to every experiment in art, music and letters and made Tokyo and Berlin two of the most fascinating capitals of the world. Their women, unlike the Italian, took a vital part in social transformation. Change was admired and striven for by an ambitious, urbanized and industrialized population which could and did read widely.

This bourgeoning of the new was in striking contrast to the survival of the old. For the old was alive: it clung to existence tenaciously. It was embodied in the military-aristocratic caste and in the class of artisans, both hangovers from the precapitalist age, and both, today, aligned behind, if not always within, the nationalist movement.

The highly developed handicrafts of Germany and Japan were carried over into modern times; for this reason both could jealously compete in the world markets with toys, pottery and sundries. But the small masters and artisans formed a rebellious group, ever ready to revolt against capitalist competition. The reactionaries have mobilized them—Hitler even went so far as to order all cement for his newly enlarged villa and garages to be mixed by hand. But neither in East nor in West can statesmen seriously hope to cut capitalism from the social tissue; they can only hope to divert the wrath of the craftsmen from machines to intangible issues.

In this endeavor the Japanese can appeal to the prejudices of their laborers against Korean immigrants, but they have no such racebogy to raise as the Nazis possess; in Germany the phobia against foreigners and especially usurers, of course, as old as the artisan class itself. Even in medieval days rulers diverted the popular unrest in the same manner from themselves.

The military-aristocracies are, like the craftsmen, survivals of the old order. These are types peculiar to Germany and Japan; in those countries alone was developed such a martial-bureaucratic tradition; only there did the petty nobility so monopolize administrative offices. In England and France, by contrast, where modern commerce came earlier, the bourgeois acquired a greater share in government.

The frugal, disciplined, swordbearing officialdom of Germany and Japan governed up to two generations ago; between this and the humble and laborious common people stood too few wealthy bourgeois to form a mediating class. As a result, the two nations were used to dictatorial methods; neither acquired the bourgeoise art of compromise—politics.

Up to this very hour, the bourgeoisie of Japan and Germany has never been victorious. When both countries became "unified" in the Eighteen Sixties, their governments represented only a coalition of feudalism with capitalism; the merchants had to accept the strong monarch and the strong noble statesman—Prince Saionji in the one land and Prince Bismarck in the other—who could steer the ship. The old Junker and Samurai castes were never demolished; they retained, as generals and officers, as diplomats and statesmen, and as landlords, immense powers over State and army. Indeed, they even grew in power and influence, since they alone could win foreign admiration; it was necessary for Germany to defeat France in 1871 and for Japan to stretch China on the mat to demonstrate their fitness to join the "family of nations."

The aristocracies held aloof from the people, whereas in France and England they had been humbled by sweeping revolutions. Though it was possible for the Mitsubishis in Japan and the Krupps in Germany to rise to the highest circles, the line between noble and bourgeois remained well defined. The German Junkers were never despoiled of their vast estates, not even by the so-called revolution of 1919; indeed they very recently got millions of marks from the government to help in running their farms.

Only for a very few years since the World War has it seemed as though the bourgeois of either land were coming out on top. As democracy spread in both, the civilian governments did succeed in pushing the military elements to the wall. The Japanese Army suffered the stigma of the Siberian blunder and the German Army was discredited by the loss of the war; both temporarily had a setback. Even the German aristocracy got a jolt: Chancellor Bruening threatened to cut down their subsidies; then Chancellor von Schleicher threatened to investigate the subject and a report was actually in process of preparation when the alarmed Junkers went into action. They persuaded Hindenburg, who is of their class, to take in Hitler; the report on the "Osthilfe scandal" was immediately suspended.

The army, in both countries, has been the centre of reaction. It has replied to the charge of inefficiency leveled at it by raising the countercharge of corruption against civilian governments. It has called up the bogies of foreign enemies, America or France. Both Japanese and German Army circles have raised the Red menace of Russia, whom Japan on the east faces across Manchuria and Germany on the west confronts across Poland.

In both countries military men could point to injuries inflicted upon national honor, whether by the American immigration policy or the Versailles treaty. In either, it seems possible to persuade the people that their present woes are due to the flabbiness and degeneracy of liberal civilians, and that hope of happiness lies in the feudal virtues of probity, discipline, unity, to be reestablished by the army. Japanese as well as German leaders assure the people that they are unfitted for democracy, but that they need more room for expansion. The leaders demand, in other words, a greater share of the world in which to grow populations admittedly incapable of self-government.

Against the demands and strengthening forces of the reaction, the liberal-bourgeois elements could make but a feeble counter-exertion; the middle class was ruined by the inflation in Germany, and in Japan, where it has never been so extensive, it is now suffering from economic crisis. In neither country had the bourgeoisie produced a leadership strong enough to sweep the people along with it; the liberals obtained the instruments of democracy, a free press and suffrage, but they could not learn overnight how to use them.

Youth, weary of liberal debates, wanted action. As the high suicide rates in both Germany and Japan have long indicated, it was emotionally overwrought. Impatient with the political action in which even its elders had so little experience, it went marching as Black Dragons or Brown Shirts. It removed its opponents in feudal vendetta style: the "Feme" murderers of Rathenau, now canonized by Nazis as national heroes, were recently paralleled by the three young naval officers of Japan who, after assassinating Premier Inukai, were greeted by thousands as saviors of the land. Youth, looking ahead, is now practicing with gas-masks and dummy hand-grenades for a future of heroic effort on a still larger scale.

Though so many elements in the situation of the one land may be paralleled in the other, reaction has not reached the same stage of acuteness in both. Liberal democracy has met a violent end in Germany; in Japan, though shaken, it still stands. Germany is isolated by an iron barrier of censorship; suppression in Japan is rigorous but not complete. In Japan, men talk aloud; in Germany, voices have sunk to a whisper.

In cultural fields, reaction has taken a far more stormy course in Germany than in Japan. This is partly, of course, because the return to the old order is naturally more difficult in modern Europe than in Asia. To refresh the memory of the Teutons in Germany, the erudition of bespectacled pedants is required, coupled with the brash enthusiasm of youth, horned and hairy, parading with tin swords and runic signs.

No such effort is required in Japan, where the prayers muttered in any Shinto shrine have been handed down from remote antiquity; some of them may be as old as those the Druids chanted at Stonehenge. Nor do the Japanese rend their souls with religious agony; they are not confronted with the necessity of reforming the Bible or inventing some new form of Wotan-worship as a substitute; they have never neglected the old gods, who still sit in mantles of moss by every roadside, receiving the homage of the people.

Ecstasies of nationalism are required to stamp the diverse Germans into one pattern. The Japanese, however, need no such symbol of unity as the Fascist bundle of sticks; they already believe themselves children of one national family under the paternal rule of a direct lineal descendant of the Sun-Goddess.

The feudal palace of the Shoguns survives in the heart of Tokyo, ringed about by office buildings. The Samurai have kept not only their political power, but their costumes and ancient style of homes. Great numbers of the most refined and intelligent men and women have never accepted Western ways. Devoting their lives to fostering the arts and philosophies of ancient Asia, they have always opposed modern civilization and have, moreover, had a splendid, if inadequate, substitute for it. Old Japan survives among the finest people and in the greatest cities.

The most extreme nationalists in both lands, however, scorn all the treasures of the historic past. Nothing contents them but the primeval. Medieval culture, they say, was too universal; and it has been the mission of Germany and Japan to destroy universalism. As each today resigns from the League of Nations so in the Middle Ages each broke away from the fellowship of religion. So Luther shattered the unity of Christian nations under Catholicism; so 250 years before Nichiren sundered the universal bonds of Buddhism and called upon Japan to produce her own version.

Upon all culture, indeed, the most advanced nationalists look with disfavor as a borrowed garment. After all, they say, it was a foreign importation. In early times both Germans and Japanese were described by chroniclers of Rome and China as wild forest-dwelling tribes on the peripheries of the older southern culture lands. Germans and Japanese are now urged to return to the dawn of history in their search for a pure Aryan or Asian spiritual essence.

In the depths of primeval forests, then, we meet the blond Siegfried and the black-haired Susanoo, muscular heroes of the Nibelungen and Nihongi verses, celebrated in mythology as dragon slayers. It is puzzling to find them so alike. True, the Nihongi was composed 720 A.D., whereas the Nibelungen was not transcribed until about 1200 A.D., indicating that the Japanese were writing fluently about five centuries before the Teutons. True, also, Susanoo is no mere figure re-created by a nineteenth century romanticist like Wagner—his sword is preserved to this very hour in the nation's holiest shrine as one of the three Imperial Treasures. But, making allowances for these differences, one must be struck by the fact that the essential Aryan curiously resembles the pure Asian. It seems ironical that Germany and Japan, searching so far for racial uniqueness, should each but uncover one more parallel with the other.

Social and economic causes have produced remarkably similar results on the Aryan and Asiatic races. Both peoples have been governed under similar institutions—Japan copied her schools and her Constitution largely from Germany—and have known similar class conflicts. In both, the professors, responsible for the propagation of nationalist superiority teachings, come from almost exactly parallel social castes: in Germany and Japan they formed aloof groups, apart from democratic contact with the people, tending to live in a dream world, and defending the military-aristocratic castes with which they feel closely associated.

But German and Japanese nationalist leaders would explain this apparent resemblance otherwise: the two peoples behave alike because they are of the same blood. Thus Mazuso Nagai, Ambassador to Berlin, compared their temperaments and characters on April 7 of this year and said: "The nationalist movement * * * in Germany is hardly anywhere on earth so well understood as in Japan."

In return the Foreign Minister, Herr von Neurath, paid the highest compliment within the power of a Nazi spokesman. He assured Mr. Nagai on Oct. 21 that the ban on marriages of Germans to non-Aryans would not apply to those contracted with Japanese. This appears to have been based on serious scientific study, for the Race Investigation Bureau of Berlin has just announced that Japanese blood contains so large an admixture of Caucasian as to make it suitable for alliance with that of the purest Nordic. Hence the brotherhood of Siegfried and Susanoo is officially recognized by Nagai and Neurath.

It is natural to wonder whether two nations so akin in past and present may not face a similar future. In each, the liberal-bourgeois stratum, the product of sixty years of evolution, is very weak; yet only this stands between the opposing forces of feudalism and communism. If it fails in its mediating mission, then the strife between nationalist and radical elements will be fought to the bitter end, or, more unhappily.still, all the passions of the people may be diverted to external enemies.

In any case, the hope of liberals in other lands that the elements of Old and New in Japan and Germany might be fused together painlessly and gradually, yielding beautiful amalgams of ancient culture and modern civilization, must be abandoned. The clash of feudalism and modernism, which formerly delighted tourists, may easily become a combat which will shake the world.

Portrait of Czechoslovakia's "Little Hitler"

by G. E. R. Gedye

PRAGUE

RECENTLY I STOOD on a public platform facing 43,000 disciplined yet fanatical men and women tense with awaiting the deliberately delayed thrill of Konrad Henlein's arrival. Exactly two years before I had lunched with Herr Henlein in a little inn in his home township of Asch and discussed his political problem. The interview had enabled me to form my own conception of the man's personality. Now I was to stand on the platform beside him and see him in his self-chosen role—that of "Fuehrer" of his people.

If not tense with excitement like the 43,000 I was facing, I was agog with curiosity, for at our previous meeting I had encountered a calm, reasonable young man of 38 who looked like nothing more nor less than an athletic bank official. I knew that at 17 he had volunteered for service with the Austrians in the World War and had been wounded and taken prisoner by the Italians in 1918, that he had refused to sit in Parliament, that after a few years as a bank clerk he had become a gymnastic instructor and built up a following among the youth in the German clubs of the

From the *New York Times Magazine,* May 29, 1938, copyright © 1938, 1966 by The New York Times Company.

country which were the nucleus of the Sudeten German party which he formed in 1933.

Had I not known all this about Herr Henlein before we met two years ago I should have said to myself, "Here is an intelligent young man who seems to take quite an interest in politics. He has some rather fantastic ideas about the mission of 'his race,' although he is the son of a German, Konrad Henlein, and a Czech, Hewica Dvorackova. He talks a language of political mysticism which he seems not altogether to comprehend. It is a dangerous language but it can hardly become so in his mouth.

"He is extremely earnest about it all," I should have said, "but he could surely never go to extremes. He seems to be a man of compromise. I like the way his calm gray eyes look straight into yours. He seems too honest for the tortuous paths of politics. Nor has he those striking characteristics essential to political leaders. He has another failing: he seems unable to give a clear answer to any question put to him—there is nothing much to lay hold of except his marked hostility to what he calls 'Marxism.' "

That, of course, was not exactly the impression he produced, because I knew quite a lot about Herr Henlein beforehand. But it was certainly the superficial impression he would have left on a complete stranger. It was therefore fascinating to see how Konrad Henlein's platform manner would correct it.

The scene was set with all the skill of Nazi stagecraft. At an early hour Herr Henlein's followers had been on the march. The songs they sang and the slogans they roared at their leader's instigation I knew from Vienna—that new, brutalized Vienna I had just left behind: "Today Germany belongs to us; tomorrow we shall rule the world"; "one people, one will, one victory"; "we want our Fuehrer"; "Sieg heil, Sieg heil, Sieg heil!" They rang out with the same note of self-assertion, arrogance and menace.

There were no brown shirts. Instead there were white shirts, jack boots and peaked caps. There were no swastika banners— but ranged around the field on tall poles were scarlet Henlein banners with white shields in the center and the monogram, "SDP" (Sudeten Deutsche Partei).

While the leader's appearance was delayed, minor leaders arrived and with each arrival the excitement was whipped up afresh. A well-drilled claque on our right led the chorused slogans and militant anthems, and one felt the emotion rising minute by minute as it does at a revivalist meeting.

Suddenly there was a roar of motorcycles tearing onto the field with open exhausts—Herr Henlein's motorized bodyguard, his own car in their midst. A stentorian voice from the loudspeaker proclaimed, "Der Fuehrer kommt."

A tall, thick-set man of 40, by no means so athletic as I had him in my mind—for something with Goeringesque forebodings in it had happened to his figure during the two intervening years —strode down the center aisle kept open by Storm Troopers amid the cheering thousands, while every right hand shot out in a Hitler salute and a great roar of "heils" went up.

This was not the Henlein who had talked sweet reason to an American newspaper man two years previously, this man in the dark gray uniform and Prussian jack boots who strode down the field with shoulders squared, head thrown back and hand outstretched. And yet it was the same Henlein, this time playing a very different role—not quite convincingly. The leader pose seemed to fit ill on his shoulders. One felt he had been well drilled for the part and knew his "book" perfectly. But his eyes which tried to produce an authentic dictatorial glare from behind gold-rimmed spectacles, his upraised hand which had the true authoritarian rigidity, had something of mechanical perfection.

Not so with the audience. Theirs was a true fanaticism, the herd instinct which is to be found in any Hitlerite gathering, the militarization of mass emotion, the ecstatic surrender of individuality to the absolute will of one man—43,000 Germans in search of a leader. As such they now acclaimed Konrad Henlein. No doubt he would reward this mass abnegation with fiery oratory which would make every one of these 43,000 feel the great leader had stooped to raise him to a level with himself, to the comradeship of triumph over all lesser breeds without the law—which is the fascist compensation for the surrender of individual liberty.

For five minutes Herr Henlein stood silent, awaiting the signal for the delirious applause to die in a fraction of a second—an athletic bank clerk in the pose of a Napoleon.

The thing which strikes me most about Herr Henlein is that here the Germans may have a disciple but not a messiah. Premier Mussolini in the sudden intoxication of awakening the responses of his audience certainly lives his role like any other great actor facing the footlights with a great part to play. Chancellor Hitler works himself up to a fanatical frenzy which they say is followed frequently by a reaction of complete psychic collapse. It is safe to say none of this ever happens to Herr Henlein. He may be a brilliant chief of staff but he is no commander in chief. He is certainly a loyal servant of his master but he himself is no master. He has a likable personality and a telling manner of putting across his sincerity in talk.

The secret of Herr Henlein's leadership lies not in Asch but in Berchtesgaden, of which he is merely the well-trained exponent. The delirious enthusiasm his appearance evokes is for the masses, not for the man. In effect Herr Henlein points to the triumphs up to date of the Hitlerite policy of bluff and covert threats over pacific and hesitant democracies, and says, "See! That God-given chieftain is leading the Teutonic tribes toward the domination of the globe. Follow me and I will bring you to his standards and you will share the spoils his cohorts are about to win. 'Today Germany, tomorrow the world.' "

Herr Henlein is a reliable second in the dueling field—rather a trustworthy exponent of parallelism for Hitler. In 1936 as Nazism's great diplomatic offensive was in full swing (the occupation of the Rhineland and the denunciation of Locarno) Chancellor Hitler spoke in a Munich Braeuhaus on the new German culture. The very same day in Prague Herr Henlein made a big speech on how German culture was to capture Prague. As the Nazis struck out in Danzig and Dr. Arthur Karl Greiser defied the League of Nations and former Chancellor Kurt Schuschnigg was blackmailed into his first disastrous agreement of July 11, 1936, with Germany, Herr Henlein declared in Eger, "We would rather be hated together with Germany than receive benefits because of that hate."

As the Goebbels propaganda machine launched the "nest of bolshevism" campaign against Herr Henlein's native country the Henlein party started its crusade of anti-Marxism. When German

Nazis ran their "true German" and "degenerate art" exhibitions in Munich in 1937, Herr Henlein's party started a "racially pure" art exhibition in Karlsbad while some of his adherents went to Aussig and slashed the modern pictures exhibited there in an "unpurged" exhibition.

When Adolf Hitler speaks to the women of Germany, Konrad Henlein addressès the Sudeten German women at Neudek. Hardly have Hitler and Mussolini cemented the Anti-Communist International on Berlin Maifeld when Herr Henlein in Franzensbad proclaims his movement to be a third anti-Communist factor. Just as big business and capital in the Ruhr diverted toward the Jews the rising wrath of the hungry and distressed workers of Germany by financing and pushing the then obscure minor prophet Hitler, so did their colleagues of the Sudeten industrial areas perform the same sleight-of-hand trick with the unknown Henlein.

It is a great task that Chancellor Hitler has entrusted to his adequate lieutenant in Czechoslovakia—not merely that of arousing revolt in and splitting off the German-speaking areas of this country in order to unite them with the Reich but the far greater one of involving the Czechoslovak State in some way in the German drive to world domination, of harnessing its great armament-production plants to the German war chariot. There are Hitlers and Mussolinis enough to spare in the Sudeten party, but on this occasion the forces behind international fascism selected no master spellbinder or wild fanatic as a leader, but Herr Henlein, with his gift of impressing people with the conviction of his sincerity, moderation and sweet reasonableness.

Why? Because here it was a case of a minority in a State strong in defense of its own national ideal. It was less necessary to arouse this minority to a sudden frenzy than to hoodwink democracies into believing nothing of the sort was in progress and to disguise the arousing of fanaticism as a moderate presentation of real grievances. Brilliantly did Herr Henlein perform his allotted task until the spectacular triumph of Hitler in Austria made the Chancellor feel that the time had come for Herr Henlein to drop his mask. It was dropped in Henlein's programmatic speech in Karlsbad last month.

Part 4

WAR AND THE PREPARATION FOR WAR UNDER FASCISM

THE FOLLOWING ARTICLES tell us something about the preparations for World War II in fascist nations. As we now know, most observers in the thirties exaggerated the amount of direct economic preparation for war in Germany. Paradoxically, very few understood (until *after* Munich) the fascist need for war. And until recently, too much blame for Nazi aggression has been directed at Hitler's violent personality. It was not Hitler's personal love for violence that brought on World War II, nor was it traditional German aggression. It was the Nazi need to resolve German social and economic problems without recourse to "leftist" welfare policies which motivated the drive to the East. War and violence, as I have indicated in the introduction, were fascist social policies, not the reflex actions of gangsters and villains in power.

In this there is a terrible lesson for our time and the younger generation today. The destruction of World War II was immense. Today the presence of nuclear arms systems means that more than ever before we cannot stand idly by should fascism threaten to gain power in any industrializing nation anywhere. The international system for settling disputes by war or threats of war is dangerous enough as it is. It may in fact be suicidal even without the addition of fascism's need for violence. After all, just as in 1914, powerful nations still assume that they have vital interests beyond their own borders; that self-defined national interests cannot be limited by international agencies; that bluff, brinkmanship, and violence are legitimate ways of behaving during international disputes; and, finally, that the popular emotions of aggressive and mindless patriotism are acceptable and even laudatory. Again, as in 1914, we can have total war without fascism. For in this, as in other things, Mussolini and Hitler were but extremists, not revolutionaries.

Hitler Tightens His Control

by Otto D. Tolischus

BERLIN

ADOLF HITLER, CHANCELLOR of the Third Reich and Fuehrer of the German people, served notice on the world last Sunday that Germany was again a great power which demands her place in the sun and that if this place was denied to her she had the military and economic means to obtain it by her own will and strength.

On that day the system of the Versailles treaty tumbled into dust and Woodrow Wilson's dream of a disarmed world governed by law, reason and a league of nations dedicated to the status quo was finally torn to shreds. In their place there reappeared a world still familiar to those who remember prewar days—a fluid and dynamic world of power politics in which might creates its own right and "blood and iron" enforce the vital interests of the strong against the weak. Woodrow Wilson's dream world had been badly battered before, but it was Hitler who on that day gave it the coup de grace; for when he spoke before the Reichstag and the world with a symbolic sun surmounted by a German Eagle shining down on him he spoke as the absolute and unchallenged master of a "nation of a hundred million" who only a fortnight

From the *New York Times Magazine,* February 27, 1938, copyright © 1938, 1966 by The New York Times Company.

previously had concentrated all political, military and economic powers in his own hands.

This concentration of power, accomplished through a "second revolution" against recalcitrant army generals, was in itself the triumph of a master politician. But it was also only a means to an end, and that end is a greater and stronger Germany.

Particularly, however, the "second revolution" was a final step toward that totalitarian mobilization of the nation which General Erich Ludendorff, "Field Lord" of the German Armies during the World War and actual dictator of the Central Powers during the latter half of it, demanded in his political testament, as laid down shortly before his death in his book entitled "The Totalitarian War."

In this book the military master mind of Germany expounded the doctrine that modern war is no longer a conflict between rulers or governments, or even armies and navies, fought frequently for immoral buccaneering purposes. He saw war as an inevitable and highly moral struggle for survival between nations, which draws within its orbit every man, woman and child and, therefore, calls on the last moral, physical and material resources of all of them. Such a totalitarian war, he argued, demands totalitarian policies which in peace must prepare the nation for war; and his specific proposal toward that end was the immediate appointment of a new "Field Lord," who, in view of the totalitarian responsibility he will have to assume for the conduct of the war, should supervise the moral, military and economic mobilization of the nation for that war.

Despite characteristic eccentricities in its exposition, Ludendorff's fundamental thesis of the totalitarian war is official doctrine in Germany today. It is the apotheosis of the heroic National Socialist ideology which holds that continuous struggle is not only inevitable for the "have-nots" among the nations but is also healthy national discipline, the cessation of which means national stagnation and degeneration. In this ideology peace, therefore, becomes a continuation of the war with other means, and in such a peace a high war potential often permits a dynamic nation to attain its aim even without resort to war.

But totalitarian war and dynamic peace both demand the totalitarian mobilization, and that is now in full swing in Germany. In many respects it is a product of the lessons of the last war. In some respects it is being carried out in most countries today, but nowhere with such thoroughness as in Germany.

As a matter of fact, this totalitarian mobilization of Germany began the moment Hitler came to power on Jan. 30, 1933. In it is encompassed the whole significance of the "national uprising," and also the secret of its success. But heretofore it has been proceeding under a technically divided supervision.

Hitler himself, and his National Socialist party, attended to the moral mobilization of the German people by attempting to weld all Germans all over the world into one "solidary national," or racial, community which would blindly obey one central will; some of the party radicals followed Ludendorff's mystic nationalism to the point of repudiating Christianity in favor of a new and more heroic national religion, analogous to the Shintoism of Japan.

The German general staff, that most efficient collectivist organization in the world, under the titular leadership of Field Marshal Werner von Blomberg, attended to the military mobilization and created one of the most powerful military machines in the world, which is rapidly shifting the military and political center of gravity for Central Europe from Paris to Berlin.

But the most important and most complicated mobilization of all proved to be the economic mobilization—important because on it depends the effectiveness of the army and the morale of the nation; complicated because it involves mastering capital, labor and economic law. For the lack of it, Germans feel, they lost the World War, and their present rulers are determined that history shall not repeat itself.

The economic mobilization really began under the magic wand of Dr. Horace Greeley Hjalmar Schacht, who conjured billions out of a country bled white of all capital. But from the very beginning it also developed into a struggle between the nationalistic and capitalistic forces led by Schacht and the equally nationalistic but socialistic forces within the party who still cling to the "Marxist" ideas of their party platform. In this struggle victory went not to the combatants but to Wehrwirtschaft, or military economy, which turned into a Frankenstein monster that eliminated both Schacht and the Nazi radicals.

As its name implies, the principal functions of Wehrwirtschaft are military. It is, therefore, not so much concerned with living standards, profits and finances, but with the strategy of raw materials. Its impetus comes from the virtual conscription of capital, labor and the farmer. Its method is planned economy that is planned, not to balance supply and demand in a land of plenty, but to raise production to the maximum in a land of scarcity. Its goal is the greatest possible self-sufficiency, not in consumption goods as such, but in all essential war materials, in order to enable Germany in time of peace to withstand economic pressure and in wartime to defy another "hunger blockade" or "sanctions."

Since Feb. 4 all strings of the totalitarian mobilization have become concentrated in Hitler's hand; he has therewith become his own "Field Lord" in the sense of Ludendorff's book. The full significance of this development became evident when, on Feb. 20, Hitler revealed that this mobilization had been greatly intensified, and the nature of it is simply documented by the decree of Feb. 4, charging the new "Supreme Command of the Armed Forces," headed by General Wilhelm Keitel, the technical if not titular successor of Blomberg, with "the unitary preparation of the Reich's defense in all fields."

The moral and propagandistic mobilization of the nation for war will, of course, remain with the National Socialist party. That the new developments mean further expansion of Germany's armed forces was proudly announced by Hitler in his Reichstag speech, although he revealed no details. In the economic field they have placed German economy completely under military command, vested not only in General Keitel by the above order, but most especially in Hermann Goering, the "Field Marshal of German Business." Goering, as commissioner for the so-called Four-year plan, superseded Schacht as economic dictator and, in turn, placed active army officers in the Economic Ministry to issue orders that are finally carried out by the "Wehrwirtschaftsfuehrer," or military economic leader, appointed in the various industries and sworn in on Hitler in much the same way as the military.

This set-up is part of the fundamental forces which dominate Germany today. But the brain that, more than any other, determined the present development of economic mobilization is that of a youthful and retiring soldier whom Blomberg once called "the ablest man in the German Army," but who is still little known outside of the German business world, where he is well known indeed. His name is Fritz Loeb, his rank is major general and he bears the modest title of "Chief of Division No. 1" in the Economic Ministry, which is charged with the production of German raw materials and with planning.

In point of fact, however, he is the principal planner of military economy and the father of the Four-year plan, who through many changes has been Goering's economic chief of staff. As such he is, if not the most powerful, certainly the most influential man in German economy today.

Like all army officers, Loeb shuns publicity, and to the German public he is little more than a rank and a name. But he is known by his accomplishments and these speak for themselves.

Fritz Loeb was born in Berlin in 1895 and entered the army as ensign in a pioneer battalion in 1913. During the World War he became first lieutenant and company commander. Afterward he served as first lieutenant in the Sixth Cavalry Regiment in Pasewalk, and in 1926 became captain in the Ninth Cavalry Regiment in Fuerstenwalde, where he stayed for about two years. So far, his record was merely that of normal military promotion; but then his real career began.

It was still the time of German disarmament under the Treaty of Versailles, but the German Army command was already preparing Germany's rearmament—had been doing so, in fact, before the ink on that treaty had dried. The full story of these preparations, which also furnishes the answer to many riddles of German post-war politics, will probably not be told until the army archives reveal their secrets, but it is as fascinating as the history of Prussia outwitting Napoleon after her defeat early in the last century; and Loeb played an important part in it.

Sometime around the turn of the year 1928–29 Loeb was transferred to the then mysterious Truppenamt in the Reichswehr Ministry, which, "it can now be told," was merely the disguise adopted for the German General Staff during the time when its existence was forbidden by the Versailles treaty. The brief official record of his career now available states that he was assigned to the Trup-penamt "temporarily," but the Reichswehr's rank lists reveal that he was in the Truppenamt for several years and that he was assigned to the department for "army organization." It was his special task during that time to study economic mobilization, and it was here that he first displayed his talents. Between times he performed his compulsory field duty as company commander in the Sixth Pioneer Battalion in Minden.

Then, on Jan. 30, 1933, came Hitler, and the veils that had shrouded German rearmament began to fall. Within three months —on May 1, 1933, to be exact—Loeb was transferred as major to the general staff, which had immediately been reconstituted, although no public mention of that fact was made for more than two years afterward. Here he helped to mobilize German industry for military purposes.

Loeb's great chance came a year later, when Goering, then in the midst of his race to build up a German air fleet before any outside power could intervene, "borrowed" Loeb for the Air Ministry to speed up the expansion of Germany's aviation industry and to commandeer supplies for it. In that capacity Loeb did what is generally admitted to be a "magnificent job," and thereby became perhaps Germany's greatest practical expert on industrial mobilization.

By the end of 1935 the mobilization of the aviation industry had been so well organized that it ran of its own momentum. But Germany's rearmament was exhausting her raw-material supplies. Thereupon Goering took Loeb out of the Air Ministry, gave him a special office and told him to study the raw-material situation and to find ways and means for coping with the shortages. In April, 1936, Goering became special commissar for all questions concerning raw materials and foreign exchange and immediately appointed Loeb as his chief of staff for these questions. But inasmuch as the practical work was still being done by Schacht and the other Ministries, with Goering as supreme arbiter, Loeb was at leisure to continue his studies. He studied for nine months and then he drew up his plan. The result was that on Sept. 9, 1936, Hitler announced before the Nuremberg Party Congress the second Four-year plan, designed "in four years to make Germany wholly independent of other countries in all those materials which German capacity, our chemistry, our machine industry and our mining industry, can produce at home." It came as a surprise to the world, which at first did not see its significance; but it also surprised Schacht, and in the end hoisted him out of the Economic Ministry.

Loeb, who had become colonel in the meantime, took personal charge of mobilizing German capacity, science and industry for the production of the needed raw materials. German raw-material production, especially in oil and iron, had already been speeded up by the demands of rearmament, but nowhere near enough to satisfy the army. In fact, it soon became apparent that the demands of military economy were wholly beyond the capacity of private enterprise, which still had to keep an eye on costs and the balance sheet, and that only far-reaching economic planning, controlled and financed by the State, could cope with the situation. That is the function of the Four-year plan.

In the execution of this plan Loeb, now major general, works in close cooperation with Major Gen. Georg Thomas, head of the economic section of the Reich War Ministry, and with Major Gen. Hermann von Hanneken, head of the division for iron, mining and power in the Economic Ministry, which has given rise to the quip about the "triumvirate of generals" running German economy. But the production end of the Four-year plan, which is its heavy end, rests on the shoulders of Loeb.

According to insistent National Socialist protestations, the Four-year plan is not designed to isolate Germany economically nor to hamper her foreign trade. On the contrary, Germany is constantly stressing her desire for economic cooperation, and is at present engaged in an export drive which scored a bigger success last year than that of any other major industrial country except the United States. Goering, like Schacht and Walther Funk, the new Economic Minister, is particularly anxious to expand trade with America, and the interest of military economy in foreign trade is documented by the fact that another officer, Major Eberhard von Jagwitz, has been put in charge of foreign-trade promotion.

But even the limited aim of wartime autarchy is rapidly forcing such readjustments in German economy as to precipitate a new industrial and agricultural revolution. It is introducing new materials, new methods, new processes, new plants, a whole new way of living, in fact; and in that readjustment foreign trade likewise assumes a new position and a new function.

The principles underlying the Four-year plan, as seen by Loeb himself, have often been explained by him in speeches before German business men, and these principles may be paraphrased as follows:

> The aim of the Four-year plan is to end Germany's dependence on foreign countries for any vital necessities in war or peace. Such dependence is dangerous in war, and unworthy of a free people in peace. To end it Germany must utilize her own resources to the extent commanded by Hitler in the Four-year plan announcement.
>
> This aim can be accomplished because Germany has the scientists, the technicians, a hard-working population which no longer wastes its energies in class warfare, and a government able to enforce all measures necessary in the interest of the State.
>
> The scope and speed of this effort is determined solely by the number of workers available and by nothing else. Inasmuch as a labor shortage has replaced unemployment, more workers must be found, because already feasible projects, such as the mining of sufficient copper from (poor) native ores, must be postponed for lack of labor.
>
> The Four-year plan is not hostile to exports, but is a sworn enemy of imports. Imports must be curtailed wherever requirements can be met from domestic resources, and the foreign exchange thus freed must be used for the importation of materials that cannot be produced at home.
>
> Hitler has set Germany greater tasks than ever before, but these tasks are designed to make Germany safe from the outside and more beautiful inside. With the cooperation of indus-

try, which the State guarantees against recessions, and of labor, whom the State safeguards in its right to work, these tasks will be accomplished.

The magnitude of these tasks may be gauged, however, by the fact that of the nineteen basic materials necessary for the conduct of war Germany is self-sufficient by nature in only two, coal and zinc, while the United States, for instance, is self-sufficient in seventeen. But this situation is rapidly being remedied. Under Goering's driving power and Loeb's direction, new industries and new industrial areas are being forged out of the ground throughout Germany, especially in the well-protected interior—all designed to correct nature's niggardliness, either by increased exploitation of Germany's natural resources, even those unprofitable by purely commerical standards, or by the creation of synthetic Ersatz.

This revolution affects, directly or indirectly, all industries, but the main efforts are concentrated on iron, oil, rubber, textiles, food and Ersatz products in light metals and plastic masses.

No war can be conducted without iron, and since the loss of the Lorraine iron mines Germany has had to import no less than 84 per cent of her iron ore. The Four-year plan provides for a fourfold expansion of production from the poor domestic ores, until by the end of the four years at least half of Germany's iron needs are to be supplied from domestic sources. And as proof of his confidence Goering gave his own name to the combined State and private corporation charged with this task.

As regards oil, Hitler announced in September, 1936, that in eighteen months from that date Germany would no longer be under the "compulsion" of importing foreign oil. The eighteen months are virtually at an end and the task is still far from accomplished. But Germany already meets more than 50 per cent of her liquid fuel demands from domestic sources, and additional synthetic oil plants, distilling oil from coal, are to be opened up this Spring.

The production of synthetic rubber, made from coal and lime and called Buna in Germany, is already supposed to be adequate to supply the tire needs of the army, and it is being expanded rapidly. The program calls for a supply of one-third of Germany's total needs by the end of 1938.

In textiles, the production of domestic and synthetic fibers from lumber, straw and other plants, as well as from coal, lime, glass and fish, has increased from 17 per cent of demand in 1932 to around 35 per cent in 1937, and plant capacity already enables production of 50 per cent.

In the metal industry magnesium and aluminum, both of which are found in Germany in great quantities, have become the great Ersatz products, and the plastic masses, numbering now more than 200 different trade names, are completely changing German articles of daily use.

Only in food production has progress been meager, first because of less than middling harvests, second because of the withdrawal of arable land for military purposes. As a result, in spite of all efforts to cut down consumption through managed shortages in various foods and "directed" consumption of what is plentiful, foreign food must still be imported in increasing quantities. And a really bad harvest could mean catastrophe.

It is Loeb's proud boast that the first year of the Four-year plan has been a "100 per cent success." Everything has been accomplished "according to plan" and he is particularly proud of the fact that the larger part of it has been financed from private rather than government sources.

Yet large sections of the German people continue to regard this development with profound skepticism. They are aghast at the growing public indebtedness which threatens to leave them some day holding a bag filled with government paper; they chafe under the growing restrictions and control; they doubt the economic soundness of the Four-year-plan enterprises which, however financed, must still be guaranteed and "protected" by the government; and they fear that rising costs of production and a deteriorating quality of goods will increasingly handicap Germany's export chances and reduce the standard of living.

But these are objections based on a capitalistic ideology which military economy does not recognize, and Loeb and his staff have already given the answer to them. Their argument is that costs are determined by the necessities of State; German economy must be able to produce; production depends on the enterprises of the Four-year plan; ergo, these enterprises are economic.

Germany Is Forging a "Nation in Arms"

by Otto D. Tolischus

BERLIN

IN 1807 PRUSSIA signed the peace of Tilsit, which dismembered
her and reduced her army to 40,000 men. Six years later she
put in the field her biggest army and helped defeat Napoleon
at Leipzig and Waterloo.

In 1919 Germany signed the peace of Versailles, which also
dismembered her and reduced her army to 100,000 men. This
month she began to call to the colors the first drafts under her
new conscription laws. When the process is completed she will
have under her swastika banners a force approaching 1,000,000
men, of whom some 650,000 will actually bear arms in the
various military services. Between 250,000 and 300,000 will be
in pre-military training in the Labor Service camps. It will be
the biggest organized force in Europe.

There is obviously a moral to this parallel which illustrates how
history, even if it does not exactly repeat itself, nevertheless
moves according to certain laws. And one of these laws would
seem to be that there is no way of keeping a vigorous, military-
minded nation like Germany powerless forever.

Today the world faces not only "German militarism" in a far

more "totalitarian" form than ever but also the impact of national socialism, which has abolished the civilian and has introduced the military manner into the shop, the office and the university— yes, even into the family.

There are many today, both in and out of Germany, who prefer German militarism to national socialism and hope that the former will swallow the latter in order to restore a kind of pre-war balance between the civilian and the military spheres of influence. Some such process is, in fact, under way.

But the clock of history cannot simply be turned back again. Every deep experience marks the individual and the nation, and the marks of the National Socialist revolution cannot be deleted from the German scene. They will remain even if national socialism should disappear as an organized force. And any speculations on a conflict between the army and the Nazis that would weaken both are, for the moment at least, premature.

Despite deep-seated differences in world outlook, manners and traditions, national socialism and the German military are natural allies, because each needs the other for two fundamental aims on which they are agreed. These are, *first,* a nation in arms, and, *second,* a greater Germany.

These aims do not necessarily mean war. Adolf Hitler and his paladins have proclaimed often enough their desire for a "peaceful readjustment" that would "free" all Germans and especially those in countries adjacent to the Reich. There are also Germans who believe that a mighty concentration of power is in itself strong enough both to attract the Germans still outside of the Reich and to repel alien powers that would interfere with their "self-determination," which, in turn, is directed into the right channels by Nazi propaganda and organized by National Socialist disciples.

This, then, is the deeper meaning of the alliance between the German military and national socialism, which was formed even before the "national uprising," and whose first aim had to be the destruction of the Treaty of Versailles. The military helped national socialism to power and immediately after attaining power national socialism opened up the way for German rearmament.

It was a compact among "oathbound" men which explains many things otherwise inexplicable in the Third Reich.

Overzealous Nazis, fired by fanaticism or ambition, have at times endangered the alliance. But for practical purposes the two allies have found a mode of cooperation and a division of labor which individual clashes and occasional "purges" cannot seriously disturb. For a nation in arms means more than a strong army or the military training of the population. Germany is committed to the idea of the "totalitarian war," which assumes that modern arms and modern war methods have extended the "front" to the entire nation. The new conscription law specifically provides: "In war, beyond the conscription duty, every German man and every German woman is obliged to service for the Fatherland."

This means that the entire country must be organized with that end in view—politically, socially, financially and economically— and in such a fashion that it will function as one machine, operating on its own power and supplying its own fuel. It means above all the creation of those political and psychological conditions that will enlist the whole nation in this task and make it accept more or less cheerfully the discomforts of regimentation and, if necessary, the hardships of privation.

This, the German military realizes, is beyond its ken. That task can be mastered only by a political organization, and in mastering it the National Socialist régime has been from the military point of view more successful—so far—than any other régime in Germany. As long as national socialism continues to master this task without arousing such antagonisms as to endanger the task itself, the army will support it. But no longer.

According to official theory, the National Socialist party and the armed forces (the Wehrmacht, which includes the army, the navy and the air corps) are equally ranking pillars of the Third Reich which find their common head in Adolf Hitler. The party is the "bearer of the political will of the people"; the army the "sole arms bearer of the nation." They are "comrades"; they wear the same swastika emblems; they salute one another; and for the rest, they are supposed to attend each to his own business.

The business of the army is the training of the country's manhood. That is the purpose of the general conscription law with which Germany stunned the world on March 16. This law was followed up, moreover, with a Labor Service conscription law, which in the excitement almost passed unnoticed.

Conscription, in the proud official language announcing it, is to 'give the German people the conviction, and to other nations notice, that from now on the protection of the honor and the safety of the German Reich is again entrusted to the power of the German nation." The switch from the collective policy of the League of Nations to a policy of power had been completed and the sword which Hitler had declared in his book written a dozen years ago to be the first prerequisite of German world power had been forged.

The army, consisting of twelve army corps and thirty-six divisions, will be at least 550,000 men strong. To it must be added the air fleet and the air defense corps, estimated at 50,000 men. Furthermore, there are the navy, the coast guard, and various police formations, especially in the demilitarized zone and in Danzig, which can be converted into line troops at a moment's notice. Their respective man power is unknown and is in fact changing constantly, but to put it for all of them at 50,000 is more than conservative. This makes a minimum of 650,000 men under arms, which approximates the armed strength of France, but is less than the 800,000 men of pre-war Germany.

The Labor Service, heretofore "voluntary," will depend for its strength on the size of the annual class going through it, and though its weapon is the spade, nevertheless its discipline, drill and "manual of arms" are the same as in the army, making it in effect a preparatory army school.

Under the two conscription laws every German male between the ages of 18 and 45 is liable to military and Labor Service duty. During that period he must serve at least six months in the Labor Service and one year in active military service, or eighteen months in all. In addition, he is liable for "refreshment training" later for periods still to be announced.

In accordance with these conscription laws there are being called this year the classes of 1914 for the army and 1915 for the Labor Service. (In East Prussia, German bulwark toward the east, the class of 1910 has been called as well.) Each class approximates 400,000 fit men and both begin service as of Oct. 1. But on that date only 120,000 of the class of 1915 actually reported for duty, because the class was divided into two instalments which serve six months each. Many of the class had already volunteered.

Though based on conscription, both the Wehrmacht and the Labor Service will also have large numbers of volunteers, long-service men and professionals. Both conscripts and others may volunteer to serve two years in the army and four years in the Flying Corps and the sea-going naval personnel.

The latter two bodies will, in fact, consist of volunteers only, and the number of volunteers for the army is so large that conscripts have been warned publicly not to give up their jobs till called. One reason is that so far only the formation of ten army corps has actually been completed. The other two will take a few more months to complete. The first contingent of army conscripts is expected therefore to be somewhere below 300,000.

The professional element consists, first of all, of the officers and the non-commissioned officers. A magnificent body of the latter was provided by the Reichswehr, every man of which was fit to be at least a corporal. But there is a dearth of officers, and without officers an army is only half an army. The German Army command has refused to create "emergency officers," as so many Storm Troop leaders hoped. It has reduced the officers' training period from four to two and one-half years; meanwhile vacancies are filled by reserve officers surviving from the war.

There are also being created various "specialized troops" for the modern mechanical weapons. Their total number is a military secret, but if the maximum of conscripts is put at 350,000, there are left at least 300,000 longer-term volunteers and professionals, which compares with 290,000 in the French armed forces.

The material rearmament has likewise been under way at a forced pace ever since Hitler came to power. It is, in fact, mainly responsible for the second "miracle" which has tightened the National Socialist hold on the German people, namely, the reduction of German unemployment. For rearmament brought to Germany that "new" industry for which economists in other countries pray to pull them out of the depression.

In this respect the actual equipment of the army with modern weapons denied Germany by the Versailles treaty was, of course, the most urgent task. Today Germany has all the arms that any other country has. She has tanks, heavy artillery and an air fleet, and she has several sorts of equipment still rudimentary in other armies. Among them are an efficient radio telephone and even television for the intelligence service, on which the German Army seems to lay special emphasis.

For the moment, however, this material equipment is not overwhelming. The German tanks are small and apparently intended for other purposes than frontal attack. The German air fleet is estimated at 3,000 planes, but those so far displayed, especially those of the much-advertised Richthofen squadron, are judged by experts to be several years behind modern plane development. The Fall manoeuvres likewise revealed a dearth of heavy artillery.

The actual strength of the German Army is, therefore, still an unknown quantity. The one thing, however, on which all military men agree is that the spirit and morale of the new troops are superb.

Greater even than the mere military equipment, for which a vast and efficient industrial apparatus was available, has been the sweeping economic reorganization still going on. Ever present in the German mind is the "hunger blockade" of the last war, and all efforts finally centre on averting one in a future war.

Agriculture has been organized in both production and distribution to feed the German people as much as possible from their own soil. Official statistics already make the claim that Germany produces 90 per cent of her own food.

A vast "Ersatz" industry is being created to supply as many of the necessary raw materials as possible and to substitute others for those that cannot be produced at home.

An industrial migration has been initiated to transfer "war-essential" industries from endangered border regions to the heart of Germany, the large brown coal deposits in Central Germany forming the basis for a new industrial region.

The entire population has been organized for air defense.

The financial structure of the country has been regimented for the main purpose of financing rearmament.

Finally, rigid government control has been imposed on both imports and exports to make sure that raw materials vital for rearmament remain available and to swing national trade to countries where it will do most good politically.

In other words, every day and in every way Germany is turning more and more into a fortress as impregnable as human ingenuity can make it.

To make sure that this is done in the most scientific manner possible, the Armament College (Wehrmachtsakademie, which is distinct from the War Academy for staff officers) has been created under the command of General Wilhelm Adam to train both soldiers and civilians in the requirements of a "totalitarian war."

Given such a vast concentration of power, the question arises as to just who controls it. Who will make the final decision whether and when this military machine is to be put to use and to what ends?

The answer to that question is not easy. Under the Conscription Law—and military constitution of the Third Reich—Hitler is the supreme commander of the Wehrmacht and the troops have sworn to render him "unconditional obedience." But Hitler was "promoted" to that title because the new Conscription Law transferred the title of commander-in-chief, formerly held by him, to the newly appointed War Minister, General Werner von Blomberg. Even the form of the oath had to be changed to conform, which may or may not be significant.

Under von Blomberg are Werner von Fritsch as commander-in-chief of the army; Admiral Raeder, commander-in-chief of the navy; and Hermann Goering, commander-in-chief of the air force. Finally, there is the great general staff under General Ludwig Beck, who, contrary to the situation existing during the war, when the chief-of-general-staff was the actual commander-in-chief, is now without any titular command. But Beck's word regarding the employment of armed forces is likely to count more than any other man's.

From the whole nature of the alliance between the National Socialist party and the army it is obvious that neither partner will break his alliance lightly. It is, however, interesting to observe that the army is beginning to put distance between itself and the party and that this distance increases the bigger the army grows and the more unrest is carried into the population by various violent party methods and the strain of rearmament itself.

In one respect, the party army has the advantage in inculcating its doctrine into the rank and file, for it trains the nation's youth, through the Hitler Youth Organization, through the Storm Troops and similar formations, and through the Labor Service, all of which are party bodies. As a result, it is said that a large part of the troops and many officers below the rank of captain are Nazi sympathizers.

But the army, as represented by its higher command, has always been both a State within the State and the highest estate in the land. It is not backward in making first claim on each German's loyalty.

In name, of course, the army is National Socialist, and that is also the burden of the educational courses instituted in the army despite opposition of party circles claiming a monopoly on all educational work. But national socialism is a chameleon—it is able to change to many colors according to the surroundings; and the color of the national socialism of the army is distinctly a field-gray rather than a brown.

The army, through which passes the nation's manhood, is rapidly erecting a new framework for the State, both materially and ideologically, and by doing so it automatically decreases the importance of the party. Already party leaders find it necessary to answer in public those who ask why the party is not being dissolved, now that it has fulfilled its mission. The time for dissolution has not yet come, but the questions are among the straws that show which way the wind is blowing.

Fascism's Army
Put to the Test

by Arnaldo Cortesi

ROME

THE NEW ITALIAN ARMY, on which the Fascist régime has lavished
its most assiduous care for the last thirteen years, has received its
baptism of fire. The road to Addis Ababa has provided a test
for the efficiency of the whole Italian military machine.

To fit the army to meet this test or any other it might be called
upon to face in a Europe that is sitting on the traditional barrel of
gunpowder has been a task ever present in the minds of the
Fascist leaders. Fascism does not believe in perpetual peace. It
looks on war not as a thing to be desired for its own sake but
to be considered without abhorrence as the necessary means
whereby the nations with an abundance of vitality and a deficiency
of worldly goods may conquer their place in the sun.

Fascism believes that nations, like individuals, must constantly
fight for life. Imperialism it regards as an expression of the natural wish of all human beings to progress and improve themselves; imperialism is not to be condemned but admitted, respected
and even stimulated.

This is the philosophy on which Fascist youth has been and
is being brought up; it finds hospitality in the public utterances

of all the leaders of fascism. Mussolini once wrote: "Whether war is the generator of all things, as Heraclitus thought, whether it is of divine origin, as Proudhon declared twenty-five centuries later, whether we agree with Renan in considering it the element in which are the roots of all human progress, the fact is that the war we have just fought, and in which I have the pride of having participated, is not the last one."

"Peace and war," says Renato Ricci, head of the Fascist youth organizations, "are two phases of the life of nations equally necessary for their development, their greatness and their future." Giovanni Giuriati, a former secretary of the Fascist party, expresses the opinion that "peace is not justice, but violence that prevails. Peace is the more or less lengthy pause necessary to prepare a new war."

In the article written for the Italian Encyclopedia laying down the Fascist tenets of faith, Mussolini affirms that he believes in neither the possibility nor the utility of perpetual peace, which is, in his eyes, a confession of cowardice and ineptitude. "War," he says, "sublimates all the human energies and places the seal of nobility on the peoples that have the courage to face it. It is for this reason that the doctrine that leads to the postulate of perpetual peace is a stranger to fascism."

It is not to be wondered at that people holding such views should have given their closest attention to developing the strength and efficiency of the armed forces of the State when the responsibility of government fell on their shoulders. They have worked a radical transformation of the fighting services, the true extent and importance of which are still a matter of speculation in more than one European capital.

To many the Italian Army is still a great unknown quantity. Has fascism succeeded in making a military and militarist nation (to quote another of Mussolini's phrases) of the naturally easygoing and rather slovenly Italian people? Has it succeeded in developing the country's resources and equipment for war to a point where Italy may look all the other European powers fearlessly in the eye?

No Italian has any hesitation in replying to these questions, but on the answers that are given to them abroad depend to a large extent the friendships and hates with which Italy will meet from now onward.

When fascism set about remodeling the armed forces of the State it paid particular attention to the spiritual preparation of Italian youth to bear arms. All the modern machinery for dealing out death has not altered the fact that it is the man behind the gun who wins wars. Armies are good or bad according as the human element of which they are composed is good or bad, and fascism has set itself the task of insuring that Italy's shall be of the very highest quality.

Fascism has placed self-sacrifice, courage, heroism, discipline at the summit of the civic virtues. "Is it not better," asks Mussolini in his preface to a book, "Heroic Patrols," written for Italian boys, "is it not better to die on the battlefield in an attack than to succumb to some stupid illness?"

There is no other country in the world, with the possible exception of Germany, which dedicates so much time, money and effort as Italy does to the creation of suitable human material for the army. Boys step out of the cradle into the Balilla organization, which teaches them to march almost before they can walk. From that moment, up to the age of 55, every able-bodied Italian male is virtually a soldier, in accordance with the Fascist maxim that soldier and citizen are synonymous terms.

A vast and complex organization has been created to render the various stages of military instruction—preparatory, pre-military, military and post-military—available to all Italians. At the age of 8 the Italian boy is incorporated in the Balilla organization, which has him in its care till he is 18. He receives moral and physical instruction designed to mold him for his future duties as a soldier.

At 18 he becomes a "Giovane Fascista" and for three years receives military instruction of a more specialized nature. This instruction consists of two annual courses of the duration of six and four months respectively. Up to a short time ago the courses were held on Sundays, but the church complained that the young men of Italy were being taken from their religious duties and the government accordingly decreed the institution of a "Fascist Saturday."

This is in reality nothing but a weekend on the English pattern, except that the Saturday afternoon off is given to Italians not that they may enjoy a well-earned rest from their daily toil but that they may be at the disposal of the Fascist machine for military instruction.

The program of the military instruction imparted to young men between the ages of 18 and 21 includes physical culture and theoretical and practical military courses. According as the young man is later to become an infantryman, or an artilleryman, or an aviator, or a machine-gunner, he receives a thorough grounding in the use of the weapons and machines that he may later be called upon to handle in war. He is taught to march and obey orders. He is taught that to be a soldier is the pride and highest aspiration of any virile people. The number of youths participating in these courses has averaged 1,000,000 in each of the years since 1932.

At the age of 21 all Italians enter the barracks and become soldiers in the true sense of the word. The normal period of service is eighteen months, but in times of stress (as, for instance, at the present moment) this may be extended indefinitely. On his discharge from the army the young reservist must give up his Saturday afternoons to post-military instruction, which has the object of preserving and increasing his military efficiency.

Military instruction complementing that which has just been described is also imparted in all the schools of the kingdom, up to and including the universities. This is one of the novelties introduced this year. These courses of instruction are divided into three phases, to be imparted respectively in the primary and secondary schools and in the universities.

The first-degree courses aim at giving Italian boys an elementary knowledge of how the armed forces of the State are organized. They include a general survey of the army, navy and air force as a whole, a more detailed study of each individual arm, map-reading and the most salient episodes of the World War.

The second-degree courses stretch over a period of two years and are designed especially for the boys who later in life are to become subalterns in the army. The organization of the armed forces is taught in greater detail, together with the Fascist philosophy of the mission of the army in the life of the nation.

The third-degree courses are intended particularly for the men who are later to form part of the directing class of the nation in the political as well as the military field. They deal, therefore, more with intellectual speculation than with material facts. The official program speaks of "the essence of war as a political and social phenomenon," of "the preparation of the nation for war," of "the concept of integral war" and other such subjects.

Courses are compulsory and no scholastic certificate or diploma may be given to any student who has not attended them with profit. They are held by army officers and comprise twenty hours in each scholastic year.

These various forms of military instruction, which are designed to put in practice the ancient Roman aphorism "mens sana in corpore sano," give Italy a vast supply of the raw material from which soldiers are made. The nation could mobilize thirty-seven classes and they would represent a force certainly not inferior to 7,000,000 and perhaps in excess of 8,000,000 men. For the purpose of comparison, it may be mentioned that in the World War Italy mobilized a total of 5,600,000 men.

The mechanization of the Italian Army has not made very great strides, because the mountainous nature of the terrain over which a war in Italy would necessarily be fought renders an excessive use of machinery impractical. The only way to reach the top of an Alpine peak today is, as it has been since the beginning of the world, to climb it on one's feet.

Motorization, on the other hand, has proceeded at a great rate. All the artillery is now motorized except the mountain artillery, which remains faithful to the mule. Alpine tractors have been developed that can negotiate the most difficult routes, and a six-wheel motor truck has been adopted capable of carrying a load of two tons over the roughest ground.

The Italian light tanks, though still comparatively few in number, are considered the best in the world. They carry two machine guns and move at high speed.

The air force has received first preference in the supply of new material. This is quite natural, since the air force was virtually nonexistent thirteen years ago and has been created since then. No recent figures are available of the exact number of machines possessed by the air force, but they are reputed to be about 3,000, counting only the first-line machines of the latest types and in full flying efficiency.

New machines are being turned out as fast as Italian industry can build them. Last year, in fact, Parliament voted the funds necessary for completely renovating the Italian air fleet in five years and bringing it up to its maximum theoretical strength of 4,500 machines. Later events caused this program to be speeded up, with the result that it will be completed before the end of 1936.

When the present government took the military problem in hand it acted on the principle that modern wars can be won only if all the resources of the nation are organized beforehand to contribute their share to victory.

Italy, in some ways, has advanced beyond all other nations in this work of coordination. Credit for this achievement must be given to the Supreme Defense Council, which has been most active in the last ten years in stimulating the production in Italy of essential war materials that were formerly imported from abroad, in finding substitutes for those that cannot be made in the country and in organizing industry and agriculture generally to be ready for the calls that will be made on them in case of war.

The Supreme Defense Council is presided over by the head of the government, and its advisory organs are not merely military, naval and aeronautical, but include a civil mobilization committee. This committee, in its turn, has an offshoot in a service of industrial observers, which reports on the state of industry and its capacity for producing war material.

A proper coordination among the three fighting services is secured by the fact that the three military Ministries are all now in the hands of Mussolini, the intention being later to merge them into a single Ministry of National Defense. Moreover, there is a chief of staff who prepares and coordinates the plans of the army, navy and air force.

Nobody who has watched the recent manoeuvres in the Upper Adige can doubt that the Italian Army is among the most formidable military powers in the world.

With the Empire Builders of Fascist Italy

by Jules Sauerwein

LIBYA

I RECENTLY SPENT fifteen days in Tripolitania and Cyrenaica. I made an airplane flight over the distant oases of the Sahara and I visited, together with Marshal Balbo, the troops stationed behind the Egyptian front. No journey could better reveal the creative and ardently mystical spirit that animates fascism, no trip could be more instructive for one who would know the mentality of the Italians who have in a few months conquered Ethiopia.

Since the amount of man-power and money which Italy is expending in North Africa is entirely out of proportion to the results she has obtained or can hope to obtain, the great effort to improve the country seems to the impartial observer curiously childish. It is only upon reflection that one discovers its hidden springs and the true incentives behind it.

Combined, Tripolitania and Cyrenaica have an area twice as large as France, and the coastline between Tunisia and Egypt measures about 1,300 miles, or almost twice the distance from Paris to Berlin. In this immense territory live 60,000 Italians—not counting the troops—and 750,000 natives. What has been accomplished is amazing, particularly if one considers that, apart

From the *New York Times Magazine,* May 24, 1936, copyright © 1936, 1964 by The New York Times Company.

from some coast garrisons, this territory was completely evacuated during the World War, and reoccupation was not completed until 1931.

Here are the achievements of five years: stately buildings, schools, hospitals, hundreds of dwelling houses under construction, asphalt roads leading in all directions, a modern irrigation system and beautiful promenades bordered with stone balustrades and shaded by palm trees. In the cities of Tripolitania, Bengazi and Derna hotels with every imaginable convenience have been built, but the most astonishing thing of all is to find comparable achievements in humble oases.

I recall my surprise when, after my first air flight, I landed near Nalut, a mountain Berber retreat close to the Tunisian frontier. In this village, hollowed out of the rock, surmounted by an old fifteenth-century fortified castle, peace was not restored until 1929. A famous rebel chieftain who was defeated there at that time by General Graziani was hanged by the Italians without ceremony. But in this little hamlet, hidden among almost inaccessible hills, I found a hotel in which every room was provided with a bath. There was a school, a hospital, a church, a Fascist headquarters, a soldiers' house, an officers' club and heaven knows what else.

I asked the local commandant the reason for this paradoxical luxury. "This is the Fascist method," he told me. "What you see here is l'attrecciatura, the rigging, the framework. These are civic buildings. We do not know whether or not this spot will become important. But the moment that fascism establishes itself in a place it must be represented by a center of urbanization and civilization; no expense is spared.

"You French are excellent colonizers, but your view is too limited. Your great pioneers, with the exception of Marshal Lyautey, have brought such projects to realization but slowly, when the need for them could no longer be ignored. We, on the other hand, feel that we must meet these needs as soon as our occupation begins, that these symbols of civilization must be made to rise from the soil as a mark of our domination. You will see other oases—Ghadames, Ghat, Murzug; and everywhere you will find that in only a few years we have brought there the three symbols of Roman fascism: water, roads and buildings."

As I went on my way I saw how true this was. Unlike the French, the Italians do not enter into the intimacies of native life. They are not even concerned to the same degree as we are about bringing culture and hygiene to the native population. But as builders of roads, canals and houses they have something of the heritage of the ancient Romans.

When you visit the ruins of the largest imperial city of Tripolitania, Leptis Magna, founded by Septimus Severus, you are amazed to find that the civic buildings resemble those in any great capital. The markets were sumptuous, the baths boasted hot and cold water, the theatres and circus were of magnificent proportions. I was dumfounded to see that the court of justice was a huge marble hall, richly adorned with the most beautiful sculpture. Yet Leptis was only a modest commercial city on the shore of the Gulf of Cidra. It is from those ancient Romans that the Fascists derive their inspiration.

I remember also a little bay on the Cyrenaican coast where there was some arable land on which a few hundreds of colonists might settle some time. How would the French have gone about it? They would have brought settlers there by sea, and at the beginning would have placed at their disposal only the most unpretentious barracks. A path would have served to connect the coast with the highway that runs through the elevated plateau of Djebbel, about twenty miles inland. A real road would have come in its own good time.

The Italians, on the other hand, had laboriously built that road during the past few months. At the moment it led to no settlement, but it was there, ready for the day when settlers should come.

Cyrenaica and Tripolitania, to be sure, have always had governors who were able statesmen or great soldiers and who felt that they should demonstrate their ability to perform miracles. The first of these was Count Volpi, one of Italy's wealthiest noblemen, who today has an incomparable palace at Venice, owns the seven-terraced mansion that stands near the Royal Palace at Rome and, in the oasis of Tripolitania, the magnificent villa built long ago by the Karamanli Princes when they were lords of that land. He was followed by Marshal Badoglio who, while less quick to make expenditures, also was eager to leave his mark on this African soil. Today there is Marshal Balbo.

It is surely unnecessary to remind American readers that Balbo is a personality in whom the most romantic youthful boldness is combined with a rare gift for prudently weighing the risks of an enterprise. As we were dining together in his mansion at Tripolitania one day he said to me with utmost frankness:

"Do you know why I succeeded in my great air expedition to Chicago? People will tell you that it was because I am a good aviator and because I was wise enough to entrust the machines in my squadron to first-class pilots. Actually, however, the reason is quite different. I had concluded that the fundamental difficulty of the flight was to avoid alighting off the Labrador coast in a fog. Fog would have meant death for us. Once we had left Iceland, however, we should have had to alight off Labrador if we had encountered fog. I found a German meteorologist, Baumann by name, in whom I had so much confidence that we did not start on that lap of our flight until the day when he telegraphed me that we could safely go."

Once or twice a month Balbo takes his hydroplane, a great three-motored Savoia Marcchetti, 2,200 horsepower, and goes off to lunch in Rome, returning to Tripolitania in the evening. He covers the distance in four hours, but he does not undertake this aerial excursion unless impelled by the imperious invitation of Mussolini. At other times he flies off to Bengazi in his ship. There he takes a small plane and surveys the troops ranged along the entire Egyptian frontier.

Sometimes he even alights in the open desert, without knowing exactly where he is landing; but his eye is so practiced that he can see from a great distance just where a slightly darker area indicates that the earth is solid enough for landing. Once on the ground he hunts gazelle or wild sheep, and in the evening he flies back to Tripolitania or to one of those oases which the Italians have established as military and tourist centers.

Marshal Balbo regards the colony of Libya not as territory for expansion, but as a sort of experimental field where Fascist

Rome must demonstrate that it really is the heir of ancient Rome. Not more than 3,000 families, about 25,000 individuals altogether, have been sent to Libya as colonists, at what must have been high cost to the government. I visited half a dozen villages in Tripolitania and Cyrenaica where these colonists are living.

Here was nothing reminiscent of those American clearings where, after felling the trees of the forest, the settlers found a rich soil ready for the plow. In Tripolitania there is nothing but sand, so that they must either dig very deep or bring arable soil from some other place, while at the same time they must undertake extremely laborious irrigation. In the oasis of Ghadames, for example, the Italians had to drive more than 1,500 feet for an artesian well.

The people of Cyrenaica cherish the illusion that their land is more fertile. The earth is reddish, and olive trees grow there without difficulty, but the soil is so full of rocks that the planting of a wheatfield or an orchard must be preceded by the dynamiting of huge stones. Settlers have told me that the planting of a single olive tree costs about 50 lire.

What does Tripolitania mean for Italy? First of all, it has strategic value. On the Sicilian coast, on the south side of the island, are great aviation bases such as the fortified camp Augusta. I have seen naval guns transported in this station, and numerous airplanes drilling over the aviation camp.

About half way between Sicily and the African coast is the island of Pantelleria, a base for submarines, airplanes and provisions. If Italy were the mistress of the Tunisian coast she would cut the Mediterranean in half, and actually could prevent the passing of any ship from Gibraltar to Suez. She would need nothing more than the establishment of such a barrier to be able to give the name Mare Nostrum to a sea in the centre of which her geographic position gives her incontestable supremacy.

But Tunisia is held by France, not Italy. Tripolitania is almost a hundred miles further to the southeast. That is why the entente with France is indispensable. Allied with France, Italy can do what she likes with England; but England, with the French base of Bizerta at her disposal, an excellent substitute for exposed Malta, has the power to dominate Italy.

But to return to Tripoli. To its naval advantages it adds a first-class land base. My own observations have enabled me to compare the Italian Tripolitan front to the British front which I had seen some weeks before in the Western Desert. The question is not which of these two armies would be greater in combat. The British officers and troops stationed around Mersa Matrouh were splendid professional army men, and the Italian officers to whom Marshal Balbo introduced me were true soldiers both in their technical knowledge and in their profound sense of duty. But there was a difference.

For the British this Libyan front was a place of tiresome exile. They had been taken from their cool English garrisons to live in a land of thirst, under the tyranny of sand that penetrates even their luggage. They were not very sure that the Italians really were their enemies.

The Italian officers and men, on the other hand, belong to that generation which for fifteen years has been subjected to a course of vigorous spiritual training. Over and over again they have been told that Italy is suffocating within her frontiers, that 44,000,000 men cannot, in the long run, live in a peninsula with only about 38,600 square miles of cultivable land. They have been imbued with the spirit of ardent pioneers whose duty it is to find land, a territory where the excess of their population can live.

What does land as such mean to an Englishman? Very little, for he does not live from the soil. In his own country it is used for the pleasures of the rich; it is left wooded, or used as lawns for strollers or golfers, or kept as moorland for hunters and gunners. For the Italian, however, every scrap of land has an element of divinity; even in the ancient Latin poets we can find this reverence for agricultural labor, which immediately provides an industrious family with a livelihood.

The Italian soldier in Africa has the impression—or perhaps it is an illusion—that he is the predecessor of the worker, or that he will himself become a worker there. With what loving care he works on this land! Though he cannot cultivate it, he digs in it, and it is with admiration that one sees those splendid roads running through waterless deserts.

The dream which spurs on the Italian in Tripolitania is the

revival of the ancient riches of the Roman provinces on this un-grateful soil. The ruins of Cyrene, Leptis and other cities convince him that at one time there lived here men who grew rich by exploiting the resources of the country or receiving the products of the interior. He tells himself that such a restoration would be difficult, but not impossible with plenty of men and work. And he goes much further: He is shown the map of the ancient Roman Empire, and he imagines that, as master of Tripolitania and Ethiopia, he is closing in on Egypt from two sides and that some day, if the British Empire should be in danger and unable to fight on all its fronts throughout the world, the descendants of ancient Rome will recover their Mediterranean legacy.

The armies and colonists of Ethiopia will then invade the Sudan and march down the Nile Valley. Others, from Tripolitania, will march on Alexandria and Cairo. Thus Italy will become mistress of rich and vast territories and, like France, will have a productive African empire which, in alliance with France, she will be able to defend against the attacks of other powers. Italy's actual dream of her political future must inevitably include the appropriation of part of the British territories, which means that in the next world war she will surely oppose England. For Italy the ideal state of affairs would be an estrangement between France and England, for then she could choose another alternative—that of taking over the French colonies.

As for an alliance with Germany—even though at times it seems to be approaching realization—it can be only a tactical device to cause trouble. In case of a world war one of two things must happen: Either the European coalition would defeat Germany, so that a German alliance would do Italy no good but rather force her to share the fate of Germany; or Germany would emerge victorious. In the latter event none who know her could imagine that she would give Italy an equitable share of the spoils. Rather than embark on the doubtful project of conquering Russian territory, victorious Germany would seize North Africa—and Italy's hopes of glory and profit would be reduced to nothing.

These hypotheses about the future are not mere theory or based only on imagination. Six months ago they would have appeared fantastic. But none can call them that today, when Italy has reached Addis Ababa and has established herself on the shores of Lake Tana where, it was said, England would never permit her to gain a foothold. Italy has won the military campaign, but she has not yet won the political, economic and financial campaigns. At Geneva, it must be said, she is less skillful than in Africa. She has not succeeded in dividing France and England. Her diplomats are not as good as her roadbuilders and her soldiers; yet, after all, she has conquered positions of importance.

These are things of which intelligent and courageous Italian officers spoke to me in the pleasant twilight of Barca. In the evening, when once again in Derna, I turned these audacious plans over in my head—plans which, let it be understood, are still in the domain of hypothesis. Yet audacity of any sort must appear entirely natural when one dines facing a man who has achieved feats of aviation that no one could have believed possible a few years ago. I remember that Balbo had returned from the front and that he was very nervous.

Some unpleasant incidents had taken place, such as the capture of an officer of the carabinieri by the British. He complained about their Intelligence Service, and especially about a certain Kent who encouraged the natives enlisted in the Italian Army to desert their posts. He had caused representations to be made to the Governor of the Western Desert.

"Yet you would not want war with England?" I asked.

"No," he replied. "But if they go too far we will know what to do. Perhaps we will perish in such a conflict, but I can swear to you that not much will be left of the famous British Mediterranean fleet." And his small blue eyes grew bright with a light that was slightly mad, but disturbing.

The next day, after piloting his great hydroplane from Bengazi to Tripoli, with me as a passenger, he said as we were climbing into the boat which had come up to the machine: "You see what the Mediterranean is. Too big for a battleship, and therefore all the smaller for a hydroplane."

Suggested Reading

William Sheriden Allen, *The Nazi Seizure of Power: The Experience of a Single German Town, 1930–1935,* Chicago, Quadrangle, 1965 (Quadrangle paperback).

Alan Bullock, *Hitler: A Study in Tyranny,* New York, Harper and Row, 1964 (Harper Torchbook paperback).

John M. Cammett, *Italian Fascism: Its Origins and Nature,* Holt, Rinehart, and Winston, New York, 1969.

Alan Cassels, *Fascist Italy,* New York, Crowell, 1968.

Frederico Chabod, *A History of Italian Fascism,* London, Weidenfeld and Nicholson, 1963.

Istvan Déak, "Hungary," in Hans Rogger and Eugen Weber, eds., *The European Right,* Berkeley, University of California Press, 1965.

S. William Halperin, *Mussolini and Italian Fascism,* Princeton, Van Nostrand, 1964 (Anvil paperback).

Christopher Hibbert, *Benito Mussolini,* London, Penguin, 1962 (paperback).

Eugen Kogon, *The Theory and Practice of Hell: The German Concentration Camps,* New York, Berkley, 1958 (paperback).

George L. Mosse, *The Crisis of German Ideology: Intellectual Origins of the Third Reich,* New York, Universal Library, 1964 (paperback).

Franz Neumann, *Behemoth: The Structure and Practice of National Socialism, 1933–1944,* New York, Harper and Row, 1966 (Harper Torchbook paperback).

Peter G. Pulzer, *The Rise of Political Anti-Semitism in Germany and Austria,* New York, Wiley, 1964 (Wiley paperback).

William L. Shirer, *The Rise and Fall of the Third Reich,* New York, Simon and Schuster, 1960 (Crest paperback).

Robert Soucy, "The Nature of Fascism in France," in Nathanael Greene, ed., *Fascism: An Anthology,* New York, Crowell, 1968.

A. J. P. Taylor, *The Course of German History,* New York, Putnam, 1962 (Capricorn paperback).

John Weiss, *The Fascist Tradition: Radical Right Wing Extremism in Modern Europe,* New York, Harper and Row, 1967 (Harper paperback).

Index

A Note on the Editor

John Weiss was born in Detroit, Michigan, and studied at Wayne State University and Columbia University. The author of *The Fascist Tradition: Radical Right Wing Extremism in Modern Europe,* he is now Associate Professor of History at Herbert H. Lehman College of the City University of New York.